CANADIAN PACIFIC SHIPS

THE HISTORY OF A COMPANY AND ITS SHIPS

IAN COLLARD

The
History
Press

First published 2022
Reprinted with corrections 2024

The History Press
97 St George's Place, Cheltenham,
Gloucestershire, GL50 3QB
www.thehistorypress.co.uk

British Library Cataloguing in Publication Data.
A catalogue record for this book is available from the British Library.

ISBN 978 0 7509 9875 8

Typesetting and origination by The History Press
Printed in Turkey by IMAK

Cover illustrations: Front: *Empress of Canada* (3); back: *Empress of France* (2).
Below: *Princess Maquinna*.

CONTENTS

FOREWORD BY SENIOR MERSEY PILOT, STUART WOOD

IT IS A GREAT PRIVILEGE to have been asked to put a few words together as a foreword for this remarkable book by my good friend Ian Collard.

We first met many years ago at opposite ends of one of his many cameras. My profession of pilot on the Mersey took me past his doorstep on countless occasions. The ships under my charge were often the subject of photographic attention from his very high balcony overlooking one of the most iconic rivers in the world. Whilst my ships were, of course, some distance away from the Collard balcony, as our relationship grew I soon learned to ensure that my tie was properly tied. Ian's attention to detail is totally clinical. The results of this care can be seen in the many books Ian has published, all containing examples of his craft supported by the necessary written detail from his own archives and elsewhere.

With this latest and grandest offering, Ian has broadened his approach and stepped further back in time than perhaps he has done in the past. The history of the operation carrying a number of labels, the principal one being Canadian Pacific, reads more like that of a major, powerful, global state. As Ian's story unfolds it becomes clearer that without the wide variety of interlinked companies and families operating all forms of transport from Canada westwards across the Pacific into and beyond Asia, eastwards across the Atlantic into the United Kingdom and Europe, and within the country itself, which together made up Canadian Pacific, it is certain that Canada would not be the Canada we know and love today.

I have greatly enjoyed reading this amazing story and am confident that you will too.

Stuart Wood MNI
Licensed Liverpool Pilot, 1968–2009

INTRODUCTION AND ACKNOWLEDGEMENTS

THIS BOOK IS A COMPLETE history of one of Britain and Canada's main shipping companies and contains a detailed fleet list of all ships owned and chartered by Canadian Pacific. It is also a story about the history of Canada and shows how the company contributed to the development of the transport and economy of the country. Steamships and railways played an important part in the progression of Canada from the earliest days. Both modes of transport were responsible for bringing supplies to the construction sites and isolated areas. Ships were used to bring materials to be utilised by men and machines building the new country. The ports of Liverpool, Greenock and London contributed greatly to the growth of the Dominion, being the ports of departure for so many of the emigrants whose subsequent efforts in the new country resulted in Canada becoming a powerful and successful nation. The story of the ships employed between England, Scotland and New York has often been told, but the Canadian services have usually been overlooked, despite the fact that many interesting vessels of the smaller type have been engaged in the North Atlantic routes. In earlier years, the competition for passengers was intensely keen and companies competed for the available traffic. Although the ships bear Canadian names, the majority were designed and built in Britain, and helped to maintain the very close political and economic ties between both nations.

All images are from the author's collection. I am most grateful to many people for the valuable help and assistance in preparing and researching this piece of work, including *The Journal of Commerce*, the World Ship Society, George Musk, Duncan Haws, Frank C. Bowen, Alan L. Cary, Robert D. Turner and Peel Ports.

Princess Victoria arriving at Victoria, BC.

1

THE DEVELOPMENT OF SHIPPING LINKS BETWEEN EUROPE AND CANADA ACROSS THE NORTH ATLANTIC

CANADA SHARES A LAND BORDER with the United States of America to the south and the US state of Alaska to the north-west. The country stretches from the Atlantic Ocean in the east to the Pacific Ocean in the west, and the Arctic Ocean lies to the north. It is the second largest country in the world, after Russia, and by land area it stands fourth, due to it having the world's largest proportion of freshwater lakes. Only Alberta and Saskatchewan of the country's thirteen provinces and territories are landlocked as the others border one of the oceans. The country covers 9.98 million square kilometres (3.85 million square miles). The southern border with the United States is 8,891 kilometres (5,525 miles) and is the world's longest land border.

The Confederation Act proclaimed Canadian Confederation on 1 July 1867, creating Ontario, Quebec, Nova Scotia and New Brunswick, and Yukon joined a year later. British Columbia and Vancouver Island joined in 1871, and Prince Edward Island two years later. Alberta and Saskatchewan became provinces in 1905, and Newfoundland in 1949.

Because of the increase in European immigration, it was decided to construct transcontinental railways to open the west to development by families making a new life in Canada. The creation of the Canadian Pacific Railway was discussed by the prime minister, Sir John A. Macdonald, and Sir Alexander Tilloch Galt, the owner of the North Western Coal and Navigation Company. British Columbia had insisted upon a land transport link to the east as a condition for joining the Confederation and in 1871 the government agreed to build a railway linking the Pacific to the eastern provinces within ten years.

Although the pioneer ships of the Cunard Line – then known as the British and North American Royal Mail Steam Packet Company – called at Halifax on passage to Boston and New York, they did not operate to Montreal until the early years of the twentieth century. The Montreal Ocean Steamship Company was formed in 1854 by Hugh Allan, a native of Saltcoats, Ayrshire, where he was born in 1810. At the age of 16 he arrived in Montreal and found employment in a shipping office. His obvious flair for the business of shipping enabled him to progress sufficiently to establish, with the help of members of his family in Glasgow and Liverpool, the first viable steamship link with the St Lawrence River. However, the Crimean War caused the suspension of the service after only two voyages, as the pioneer steamer, the *Canadian*, was requisitioned by the government as a troopship. In 1856, the service resumed, but the hazards of navigation in the St Lawrence were great, and in its first nine years the company lost eight ships – all in the St Lawrence. The *North American*, *Nova Scotian*, *Hibernian*, *Saint Andrew*, *Saint George* and *Peruvian* were all involved in the trade, with the *Austrian* and *Nestorian* being added in 1867. At this time the Inman Line and the Anchor Line were interested in these services but did not enter into the St Lawrence shipping routes.

The Canada Shipping Company was founded in 1867 by a number of wealthy Montreal merchants to run a line of fast iron sailing ships between Liverpool and Montreal, but it only enters the story proper in 1875, when it ordered steamers. William Murray, Alexander Buntin, Alexander Urquhart, and John and Hugh McLennan were all involved in this new venture. Five iron ships were built on the Clyde, and all these had the prefix 'Lake' before their name. *Lake Erie* and *Lake Ontario* were built by Barclay Curle, and Robert Steele of Glasgow built *Lake Superior*. *Lake Huron* was the fourth vessel, and *Lake Michigan* completed the first fleet.

Lake Nipigon, *Lake Champlain* and *Lake Megantic* introduced steam into the fleet, and were all built by the London and Glasgow Shipbuilding Company. In 1895, the English debenture holders accepted 7s 6d in the pound, handing everything over to the Canadians, for whom D. & C. MacIver continued as managers for the Beaver Line. Competition to the line appeared when British shipping company Elder Dempster and Company took over the Dominion Line's Bristol Channel service. D. & C. MacIver floated the Beaver Line Associated Steamers Limited, and chartered tonnage. In 1898, the Beaver Line was transferred to Elder Dempster, who set about building up the fleet with new vessels. D. & C. MacIver then chartered the Pacific Steam Navigation Company's (PSNC) *Lusitania* and *Tongariro*, and the Cunarder *Gallia*. Beaver Line Associated Steamers went into voluntary liquidation in 1900, leaving Elder Dempster with no competition in the Atlantic. However, in 1903 it was announced that Elder Dempster had sold its Canadian interests to the Canadian Pacific Railway for just under £1.5 million. *Lake Manitoba* took the last Beaver Line sailing on 31 March 1903, and the Beaver Line flag was replaced by the chequered flag of Canadian Pacific.

In 1870, the Liverpool and Mississippi Steamship Company was formed to trade between the Mersey and the southern states of America. In 1872, this company decided to break the monopoly of the Allan Line and become the Mississippi and Dominion Steamship Company Limited, popularly known as the Dominion Line. The Allan Line commissioned some new tonnage, which included the *Polynesian*, *Samaritan* and *Circassian*, all of which were in service by 1873. They were followed in 1875 by the *Sardinian*. In 1874, the Allan Line *Caspian* brought the first consignment of frozen meat from Canada to Liverpool. In 1880, the Dundee firm of William Thomson began carrying store cattle from Canada to Britain, and Birkenhead developed as a terminal for this traffic.

The Canadian Pacific Railway (CPR) was created on 1 February 1881 and construction began on 2 May at Montreal. However, financial problems caused some delays, which were resolved by Donald A. Smith (later Lord Strathcona) and George Stephen (later Lord Mount Stephen). George Stephen became the first president of the CPR, Sandford Fleming was appointed as chief engineer and surveyor, and William Van Horne was in charge of construction. In 1884, the company agreed to:

> have the power and authority to erect and maintain docks, shipyards, wharves, slips and piers at any point on or in connection with the said Canadian Pacific Railway and at the termini thereof on navigable water, for the convenience and accommodation of vessels and elevators, and also to acquire and work elevators and to acquire, own, hold, charter and run steam and other vessels for cargo and passengers upon any navigable water which the Canadian Pacific Railway may reach or connect with.

Grain storage elevators were built along the north shore of Lake Superior and other elevators were provided to receive prairie grain for onward shipment. *Algoma*, *Alberta* and *Athabasca* were introduced to the fleet and were able to be divided in half at Montreal to fit through the canal and towed to Buffalo. The new vessels also carried construction workers and material along the lake while the railway was being constructed. A service from Vancouver to Hong Kong was

Donald Smith, later Lord Strathcona, drives the last spike on 7 November 1875.

advertised, with two sailings a month, and on 7 November 1885, the last spike of the CPR line was driven in at Craigellachie, British Columbia. However, on the same day, the *Algoma* sank in a storm off Isle Royale. Four days earlier, the last spike of the Lake Superior section had been driven in west of Jackfish, Ontario. The Lake section alone had taken 12,000 men and 5,000 horses to construct.

By 1885, a network of lines was created from Quebec City to St Thomas, Ontario, following the acquisition of the Quebec, Montreal, Ottawa and Occidental Railway from the Quebec Government. A fleet of Great Lakes ships linked the terminals and the leases of a number of railways were purchased, including the Ontario and Quebec Railway. A 999-year lease had been acquired on the Ontario and Quebec Railway on 4 January 1884, and the following year a minority interest was obtained in the Toronto, Hamilton and Buffalo Railway. This gave the company a link to New York and the north-east United States. On 28 June 1886, passenger services were inaugurated between Montreal and Port Moody, with a journey time of five and a half days. The train consisted of two baggage cars, a mail car, one second-class coach, two immigrant sleepers, two first-class coaches, two sleeping cars and a diner. A service by ship was introduced between Montreal and Port Moody, and several sailing ships were chartered, including the *W.B. Flint*, which arrived at Port Moody on 26 July 1886 with its cargo of tea. The western terminus was moved from Port Moody to Granville, which was renamed Vancouver on 23 May 1886. *Bylgia*, *Carrie Delap*, *Eudora*, *Flora P. Frieda*, *Gramph*, *Stafford* and *Zoroya* were chartered, and the steamship *Skuzzy* was used by the construction engineer Andrew Onderdonk for work on the Fraser River. Adamson, Bell and Company were appointed as agents in Hong Kong, and *Port Fairy*, *Straits of Belle Isle*, *Sussex* and *Zambesi* were chartered for single voyages on the Hong Kong–Japan–Vancouver route. Adamson Bell had also signed an agreement with Canadian Pacific, on 11 February 1887, for the *Abyssinia*, *Batavia* and *Parthia* to operate on Pacific routes. A Vancouver–United States service was introduced to cater for the increase in Chinese workers crossing the Pacific, and another from Vancouver to Hong Kong via Shanghai was offered in 1889.

In 1886, Canadian Pacific built several small hotels to accommodate travellers. Glacier House was built in Glacier National Park at Rogers Pass, and Mount Stephen House in Field, British Columbia, along with hotels at Kicking Horse Pass, North Bend in Fraser Canyon, Sicamous on Shuswap Lake, and Revelstoke. Some of the original

The Royal York Hotel, Toronto.

The Empress Hotel, Victoria.

Windsor Street Station, Montreal headquarters of CPR.

smaller hotels were designed to provide meals for passengers in the Rocky Mountains, where railway grades were too severe to justify the operation of dining cars. However, Glacier House and Sicamous were destination hotels. Most operated for several years before dining-car service made them unprofitable. Glacier House was very popular until the diversion of the main passenger service to the Southern Mainline disconnected it from the main track. Small hotels were built in the Kootenays region at Balfour, where Balfour House provided accommodation for ferry passengers travelling across Kootenay Lake, which was part of the service on the Southern Mainline.

Van Horne built Fraser Canyon House in North Bend in 1886. It was originally referred to as the CPR Hotel, and later became the North Bend Hotel. The original building burned down in 1927 and a new hotel opened two years later. CPR's Hotel Department was established when the Hotel Vancouver opened on 16 May 1888, followed by the Banff Springs Hotel on 1 June. The Château Lake Louise opened in 1890, as a single-storey building of log construction, and several additions were made over the following years. The Banff Springs Hotel was extended during the first two decades of the twentieth century. The company also owned five bungalow camps across the country and leased a number of camps, tea houses and chalets in the Rockies, which were all served by Canadian Pacific lines. Château Frontenac was opened at Quebec City on 11 December 1893, with additions to the building made in 1904, 1906, 1916 and 1923, which included the great central tower. It was improved in 1926 and in 1992–93, with the addition of the Claude-Pratte Wing.

The Place Viger Hotel in Montreal was built in 1898 and closed in 1935. The Hotel Sicamous, overlooking Shuswap Lake, British Columbia, was opened in 1900 and later operated under lease; it was demolished in 1964. One of the smaller hotels, the McAdam, was opened at McAdam, New Brunswick, in 1901, and this was followed a year later by the Emerald Lake Chalet, near Field, British Columbia. In 1903, the Algonquin Hotel at St Andrews, New Brunswick, was taken over by CPR. The Royal Alexandra Hotel in Winnipeg was completed in 1906, with substantial alterations made in 1914. However, with the dominance of the airlines, the hotel closed in December 1967, and was demolished in 1971. The Empress Hotel at Victoria, British Columbia, was opened in January 1908 and renovated and refurbished in the 1960s and 1970s. The Palliser Hotel at Calgary was enlarged in 1929, and the Hotel Saskatchewan at Regina was a favourite for visitors to the Queen City of the West. Once advertised as the largest hotel in the British Empire, the Royal York hotel opened in June 1929 in Toronto. In Nova Scotia, the CPR was the lead investor in the Lord Nelson Hotel in Halifax, which was opened in 1927 to rival Canadian National Railway's Hotel Nova Scotia. Originally built in 1892, the Aberdeen Hotel at Kentville in the Annapolis Valley was renamed the Cornwallis Inn in 1919 after it was purchased by DAR and later reopened in the much grander CPR Baronial style in 1930, and the Château Montebello was opened in 1930, with 211 guest rooms and suites. The Digby Pines Hotel was rebuilt and the new rustic Lakeside Inn resort at Yarmouth was completed in June 1931.

In the 1890s, Canadian Pacific were building a rail line through the Kootenays and acquired the Columbia & Kootenay Steam Navigation Company for $200,000. The steamboat *Rossland* was built by David Bulger of Nakusp, and she operated at a speed of 20 knots. She was followed by *Kootenay* and *Minto*, all three constructed for service on the Arrow Lakes. The company intended to send *Minto* to the Stikine River for the gold rush of 1898, but she was diverted to the Columbia route. *Bonnington* was introduced in 1911 and operated until 1929, when business started to fall off due to increasing road traffic. In 1904, *Minto* was tied up at Arrowhead when around 600,000 tons of rock broke away from a mountain and slipped into the lake. This created a 6ft-high wave, which reportedly lifted her out of the water and set her down on the dock; the after wave heaved her clear of the dock and back into the water again.

Manitoba replaced *Algoma* in 1889 and she was fitted with *Algoma*'s machinery. A ten-year Canadian Mail contract was signed with the British Government for the Pacific service from Vancouver to Yokohama, Shanghai and Hong Kong, which was to be accomplished in 684 hours from Hong Kong to Quebec between April and November, and 732 hours from Hong Kong to Halifax between December and March. On 12 October 1889, three ships were ordered for the route; they were named *Empress of India*, *Empress of Japan* and *Empress of China*. A transatlantic service was suggested by the government but it was felt that this would not be viable because of the competition from New York.

As traffic on the railway increased, the company became profitable and loans from the federal government were repaid. A branch line was opened between Sudbury and Sault Ste Marie, which connected with the United States railroad system and its own steamships. A line was constructed between London, Ontario and the American border at Windsor, Ontario, and this was opened on 12 June 1890. The following year, the New Brunswick Railway was leased for 991 years and a connection was made from Montreal to Saint John, New Brunswick. This allowed transatlantic cargo and passenger services to continue year-round when ice in the Gulf of St Lawrence closed the port of Montreal during the winter months.

A branch line was constructed from London, Ontario, to Detroit, and the ferries *Michigan* and *Ontario* were introduced for the crossing of the Detroit River. *Alberta* and *Athabasca* were introduced on the Toronto–Chicago and Montreal–Chicago routes and three delivery around-the-world cruises were announced for the new Empress liners. The itinerary was Liverpool–Gibraltar–Naples–Port Said–Suez–Colombo–Penang–Singapore–Hong Kong–Woosung–Nagasaki–Kobe–Yokohama–Vancouver, with a rail connection to Montreal and an Atlantic sailing back to Britain.

Canadian Pacific Facts and Figures (revised edition, 1946) states that Sir William C. Van Horne (1843–1915), the second president of the CPR, 'even took time out to design the red and white checkered house flag of the company steamships'. In the chapter 'Ocean Steamships' by Pat Donovan, assistant press relations officer at Vancouver, it states:

> To many people the steamships service is symbolized by the Canadian Pacific house flag, the six squares, red and white, checker-board style, which proudly enters ports all over the world and adorns the uniform caps of all captains, officers and warrant officers of the company's fleets. It was designed by Van Horne, which was particularly appropriate since it was he who was at the helm for the first maritime development.

Mr D. Duff, assistant manager, who later became assistant to the chairman, said that he wrote to Van Horne asking if it was true that he had designed the flag. The letter came back with Sir William's answer written in the left-hand margin: 'Yes, I designed the house flag, partly to differ from any in use and partly that it might be easily recognized hanging loose. It has no historical or heraldic significance.'

The three new Empress liners were introduced in 1891, with the *Empress of Japan* taking the transpacific record on her second voyage. The Yokohama mail reached London in less than three weeks, which was ten days less than the contract time. *Abyssinia*, *Batavia* and *Parthia* were released from passenger services. A railway was constructed through Crowsnest Pass to the south shore of Kootenay

Clockwise from right:
Empress of Japan.
Empress of India.
Sir William Van Horne.

Lake in exchange for the company agreeing to reduce freight rates in perpetuity for key commodities shipped in western Canada. In 1897, Canadian Pacific Railway purchased the Columbia & Kootenay Steam Navigation Company, entering into the sternwheeler traffic of the lakes and rivers of the Canadian Rockies. *Athenian* and *Tartar* were purchased from the Union Steamship Company and were loaded with cargo for their delivery voyage across the Atlantic. The *Hongkong Maru* and *America Maru* were introduced by the Japanese in 1898, but were never as popular as the Canadian Pacific Empress ships, although serious competition arrived in 1910 in the form of *Korea* and *Siberia*, which were built for the Pacific Mail Company. They were larger and faster than the Canadian Pacific vessels.

When the branch railway line from Sicamous to Okanagan Landing was built, the Canadian Pacific Railway opened a shipyard near the railhead in 1893. On 22 May, they launched the sternwheeler *Aberdeen*, which was designed to provide a connection to Penticton. *York* was added in January 1902, and the *Okanagan* in April 1907. They were followed by the *Bonnington*, *Nasookin* and *Sicamous*. The *Sicamous* would leave Penticton at 5.30 a.m. each day, returning at 8 p.m. after calling at fourteen places. Following the completion of the Canadian Pacific branch into Kelowna, the number of passengers travelling on the lake began to decline. *Sicamous* was laid up at Okanagan Landing in 1931, but the service was reinstated for a short period until it finished in 1935. It was planned to operate *Sicamous* as a freight-only vessel but this proved unsuccessful; she was taken out of service in October 1936. In June 1949, she was sold to the city of Penticton for $1, moved to a permanent berth and operated by the Gyro Club. Following extensive work, she was finally opened to the public on 24 May 1952. Canada West Inspection Services were contracted to test the hull in 1987, and they concluded that it was in a fair condition. The SS Sicamous Restoration Society was formed to undertake work on the ship and she was leased by the city to the society on 1 June 1988. She reopened in 1993, allowing visitors to tour her decks and view her boiler and engine rooms. More than 30,000 people visited her in 1996–97. The steam tug *Naramata* remained in service until 1965, when she was laid up, and she is also preserved at

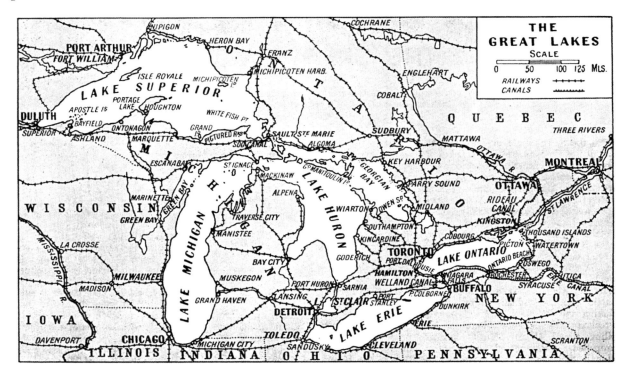

The Great Lakes.

Okanagan Landing. Both vessels are part of the SS Sicamous Inland Marine Museum at Penticton.

The ships and coastal services of the Canadian Pacific Navigation Company were purchased in 1901. However, the largest vessel, the *Islander*, was lost before entering Canadian Pacific service and was replaced by *Ningchow*, which was renamed *Princess May*. In 1903, a deal was announced with the Canadian Government when the CPR purchased the interests and fleet of fifteen vessels of the North Atlantic routes of Elder Dempster and Company Limited, including the Beaver Line. The ships were *Lake Manitoba*, *Lake Michigan*, *Lake Champlain* and *Lake Erie* from the Beaver Line, and *Milwaukee*, *Montreal*, *Montcalm*, *Montfort*, *Monterey*, *Monteagle*, *Montrose*, *Monmouth*, *Montezuma*, *Mount Royal* and *Mount Temple* from Elder Dempster. Canadian Pacific services were then introduced from Liverpool, London and Avonmouth. The deal was heavily oversubscribed and shares exchanged hands at a premium.

On 20 January 1904, the *Princess Beatrice* started a new year-round service between Seattle and the British Columbian capital of Victoria. Vancouver was later added to the schedule and *Princess Victoria* was also placed on this service. She was able to maintain 20 knots and was popular with regular passengers. The Canadian Pacific service competed with the American Puget Sound Navigation Company, who operated *Chippewa* and *Iroquois*. *Montrose*, *Montreal*, *Mount Temple* and *Montfort* were placed on the London service, and Antwerp was added as an additional port of call. On 11 June 1905, *Princess Victoria* established a record for the Seattle–Victoria route and carried a broom on her foremast to signify her conquering speed.

Empress of Britain entered service between Liverpool and Quebec and was joined by the *Empress of Ireland*. The CPR was awarded the half mail contract with Allan Line's *Victorian* and *Virginian*. The two companies later amalgamated and the Beaver Line vessels were transferred to the second service. *St George* was introduced on the Bay of Fundy service between Saint John, New Brunswick and Digby. *Tartar* and *Athenian* were sold for demolition and were replaced by *Monteagle*. *Princess Ena* and *Princess Royal* were delivered for the Alaska service and *Assiniboia* and *Keewatin* were allocated to the Great Lakes route, replacing the *Athabasca* and *Alberta*.

Keewatin left Greenock on 14 September 1907, arriving at Montreal on 23 September. The following month she was cut in half at the Lévis Dry Dock to allow her to sail through the Welland Canal, and she was

rejoined at Buffalo. She was fitted with quadruple expansion machinery, which gave her a speed of 14 knots, and she was able to cover the 600 miles between ports in two days, with a round trip taking five days. Her hull colour was changed from black to white and green in 1919, and a ballroom was added in the 1920s. Her wheelhouse was enclosed in 1946, and the funnel given the CPR chequerboard flag. Her wooden masts were later replaced by steel masts. She continued to operate on the Great Lakes service until 1965, when new regulations were introduced regarding her wooden superstructure, which could be regarded as a fire risk. It was decided that it would be too costly to rebuild her cabin and passenger accommodation in steel so the company withdrew the

Keewatin advertisement.

Keewatin.

vessel from service. She was sold to Marine Salvage of Port Colborne in November 1966, and it was expected that she would be dismantled. However, she was resold the following year and left Port McNicoll on 24 June 1967 in tow of the tug *Amherstburg* for her new home at Douglas. She was later opened to the public, visitors being allowed to tour the ship and view the lobby, purser's office, barber's shop, boiler room and engine room. Her sister ship, *Assiniboia*, was converted to burn oil fuel in the 1950s and was sold in 1967 to be used as a floating restaurant, but caught fire and was destroyed during the conversion.

In 1908, the *Princess Charlotte* operated on the Seattle–Victoria–Vancouver service and the North Atlantic Conference was formed. An anonymous offer was made for the Allan Line by the Royal Trust Company of Montreal and a Canadian Pacific appointee joined the Allan Board. The Detroit River Tunnel was opened in 1910, which reduced the number of cars travelling on the trans-service river ferries. Following the opening of the electric railway, the sternwheeler services on the Vancouver–Chilliwack route ceased. *Montrose* became the first vessel to use wireless in assisting the police when Dr Crippen and his mistress were discovered to be aboard. This was radioed to England and two detectives later arrested Crippen.

On 26 July 1911, *Empress of China* was wrecked near Yokohama and the Japanese Toyo Kisen Kaisha Line introduced three new express steamers on the transpacific services. The following year, the Dominion Atlantic Railway Company was leased to Canadian Pacific for 999 years, with its six ships. However, all but the *Prince Rupert* were sold. The control of the Allan Line moved to Montreal, and a Canadian Pacific director was appointed as chairman. In 1913, the Allan Line and Canadian Pacific collaborated by setting up joint victualling and stores depots at Liverpool, England. Allan's general manager retired and was replaced by a Canadian Pacific appointee. Following competition from the Japanese company, Canadian Pacific introduced the *Empress of Russia* and *Empress of Asia*.

A passenger and freight service was introduced between Trieste, Italy, and Canada. *Lake Erie* was renamed *Tyrolia*, and *Lake Champlain* became *Ruthenia* for the route, which only operated until the outbreak of the First World War the following year. Allan Line's *Alsatian* and *Calgarian* came into service in 1914 and were regarded as being superior to other vessels employed on Atlantic routes.

On 29 May 1914, the *Empress of Ireland* sank near the mouth of the St Lawrence River following a collision in fog with the Norwegian

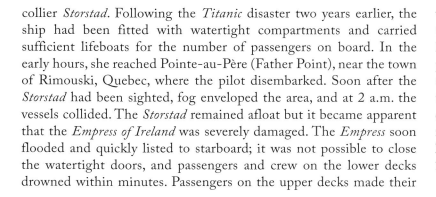

Empress of Ireland ship's officers.

Empress of Ireland.

collier *Storstad*. Following the *Titanic* disaster two years earlier, the ship had been fitted with watertight compartments and carried sufficient lifeboats for the number of passengers on board. In the early hours, she reached Pointe-au-Père (Father Point), near the town of Rimouski, Quebec, where the pilot disembarked. Soon after the *Storstad* had been sighted, fog enveloped the area, and at 2 a.m. the vessels collided. The *Storstad* remained afloat but it became apparent that the *Empress of Ireland* was severely damaged. The *Empress* soon flooded and quickly listed to starboard; it was not possible to close the watertight doors, and passengers and crew on the lower decks drowned within minutes. Passengers on the upper decks made their

way to the lifeboats, but the list was so severe that the boats on the port side could not be launched. When attempts were made to launch them, they crashed into the side of the ship and spilled their passengers into the cold water. Five lifeboats were finally launched successfully and, ten minutes after the collision, the *Empress of Ireland* turned onto her starboard side, which allowed many passengers and crew to crawl out of the portholes. She lay on her side for several minutes, having run aground, and fifteen minutes after the collision, her stern rose out of the water and she sank. It was reported that over 1,000 people lost their lives in the tragedy.

2

THE FIRST WORLD WAR AND THE FORMATION
OF CANADIAN PACIFIC STEAMSHIPS LIMITED

FOLLOWING THE OUTBREAK OF THE First World War, the *Princess Irene* and *Princess Margaret* were converted into naval minelayers, and the British Admiralty requisitioned *Montezuma*, *Montcalm*, *Mount Royal*, *Tyrolia*, *Ruthenia* and *Montrose*. *Missanabie* and *Metagama* entered service in 1915. The new ships were the first to introduce the Atlantic cabin class, which accommodated 520 passengers, with 1,100 in third class. On 16 March 1915, the government in Ottawa granted Canadian Pacific the right to operate ships independently from any railway undertaking. Canadian Pacific Steamships Limited was established as a subsidiary, with separate accounts. The *Princess Irene* suffered an internal explosion on 27 May 1915 at Sheerness and was destroyed.

Canadian Pacific Ocean Services Limited was formed on 1 October 1915 to manage the North Atlantic fleet. The following year, the Allan Line and Canadian Pacific fleets were merged. The Allan Line ships comprised *Alsatian*, *Calgarian*, *Corinthian*, *Corsican*, *Grampian*, *Ionian*, *Mongolian*, *Pomeranian*, *Pretorian*, *Sardinian*, *Scandinavian*, *Scotian*, *Sicilian*, *Tunisian*, *Victorian* and *Virginian*. The tonnage of the combined fleet constituted 239,000 Canadian Pacific and 155,000 Allan. The staff and assets of the Allan Line were incorporated into Canadian Pacific and the head office was located at 8 Waterloo Place, London. All of the Allan Line vessels retained their names.

The Cunard Steamship Company took over the Canadian Shipping interests of the Canadian Northern Railway in 1916, which gave them an entry into the St Lawrence trade from Avonmouth, Bristol, on the resumption of peacetime trading. The formation of the Anchor-Donaldson Line, within the orbit of the Cunard group, was an assurance that the company intended to participate fully in the Canadian trade. Donaldson's had employed vessels to the St Lawrence from Glasgow for many years, and from 1904 had engaged in passenger traffic with the *Athenia*, *Letitia*, *Saturnia* and *Cassandra*. The first two were lost during the war.

Canadian Pacific carried over 1 million troops and passengers during the First World War, as well as 4 million tons of cargo and munitions. The company took over two cabin-class ships, the *Melita* and *Minnedosa*, from the Liner Requisition Scheme in 1918. The ships were ordered before the war for a British subsidiary of the Hamburg America Line, and it was planned to operate them on the Liverpool–Canada route. After having served as troopships, in 1925 *Melita* was sent to Palmers Shipbuilding & Iron Company at Jarrow, and *Minnedosa* to Hawthorn Leslie at Hebburn. They emerged from their refit with accommodation for 480 cabin-class and 1,250 third-class passengers. *Melita* and *Minnedosa* were based at Liverpool in 1927, and also operated comprehensive cruise programmes from Greenock and Belfast in the early 1930s. Both vessels were laid up in 1934 and were sold to Ricuperi Metallici the following year with the expectation that they would be broken up. However, they were purchased by the Italia Line to operate as troopships, with *Melita* becoming *Liguria* and *Minnedosa* renamed *Piemonte*. Both ships were eventually scuttled – the *Liguria* on 22 January 1941 and the *Piemonte* at Messina on 15 August 1943.

Empress of Britain in 1917.

Canadian Pacific lost nine vessels during 1918 and efforts were made to replace them with available tonnage. In January, *Montreal* was rammed by White Star Line's *Cedric* and sank. *Calgarian, Pomeranian, Medora, Milwaukee, Missanabie* and *Montfort* were torpedoed. *Princess Sophia* was lost in the Pacific when she was swept off a reef by high seas, with the loss of all 345 people on board. The final loss was the *Corinthian. Batsford, Dundrige, Holbrook* and *Mottisfont* were acquired from Harris & Dixon. *Lake Manitoba* was severely damaged by fire at Montreal in 1919, and she later left the fleet.

In August 1920, *Empress of France* made a new record when she crossed between Liverpool and Quebec in five days, twenty hours and six minutes, with an average speed of 18.8 knots. Because of the fluctuating price of coal, Canadian Pacific converted its Pacific ships back to coal. When the mail contract came up for revision, the Dominion government transferred some mail from *Empress of Asia* to a Nippon Yusen sailing but the United States authorities used Canadian Pacific and diverted their mail via Vancouver. Following a press campaign, the Canadian Pacific contract was renewed.

On 8 September 1921, the operating company became Canadian Pacific Steamships Limited. The ships' funnels were painted buff, and a white band was added to the hulls. The Canadian Pacific Railway vessels on the Pacific and Bay of Fundy were not affected by this change. The passage time of five days, nine hours and thirty minutes was attained by the *Empress of Britain* in 1921. *Empress of India, Empress of Australia* and *Empress of Scotland* were added to the fleet. The United Kingdom base was transferred from Liverpool to Southampton in 1922 and *Metagama* joined *Tunisian, Corsican* and *Scotian* on the joint Canadian Pacific–Anchor service from the Clyde to Canada. *Montcalm, Montrose* and *Montclare* were introduced to replace a number of older vessels. These three ships increased the cabin-class capacity on the routes.

CANADIAN PACIFIC
TO
THE ORIENT

EMPRESS OF RUSSIA and EMPRESS OF ASIA

SPECIAL FEATURES

Gross register, 16,850 tons.   Quadruple screws.   Turbine engines.
Sea speed, 20 knots. Length, 590 feet; width, 68 feet.
Smoking rooms unparalleled on any ocean.   Attractive drawing rooms
and writing rooms.   Magnificent main saloon, 74 feet long, 65 feet wide.
Luxurious suites : Parlor, bedroom and bath room. Electric fans and berth
lights. Electric Heaters.

ENCLOSED PROMENADE, 240 FEET LONG
LIBRARY   LAUNDRY
DARK ROOM FOR AMATEUR PHOTOGRAPHERS
MUSIC : FILIPINO BAND

For further particulars apply to—
CANADIAN PACIFIC RAILWAY
European Head Office :
62/65, CHARING CROSS, TRAFALGAR SQUARE, LONDON, S.W. 1.

LONDON	103, Leadenhall St., E.C.3	PARIS	1, Rue Scribe
LIVERPOOL	Pier Head	ANTWERP	25, Quai Jordaens
GLASGOW	25, Bothwell Street	ROTTERDAM	42, Coolsingel.
BRISTOL	18, St. Augustine's Parade	CHRISTIANIA	Jernbanetorvet, 4
BELFAST	41, Victoria Street	BRUSSELS	98, Boulevard Adolphe Max
BIRMINGHAM	4, Victoria Square	HAMBURG	Alsterdamm, 24
MANCHESTER	1, Mount Street		

SIR GEO. McLAREN BROWN
European General Manager, London.

H. G. DRING
European Passenger Manager, London

T. J SMITH
European Freight Manager, London

JAPAN CHINA MANILA

Via Vancouver

EMPRESS OF CHINA
EMPRESS OF CANADA
EMPRESS OF ASIA
EMPRESS OF RUSSIA

Sailings   Fares
T. P. 4,   JUNE   1921
CANADIAN   PACIFIC
RAILWAY

Japan, China, Manila
via Vancouver sailing list for 1921.

1922 advertisement.

Atlantic and Pacific routes.

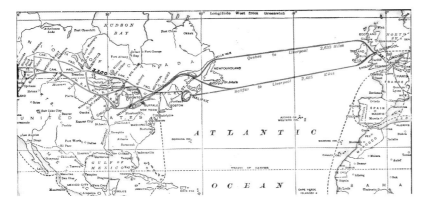

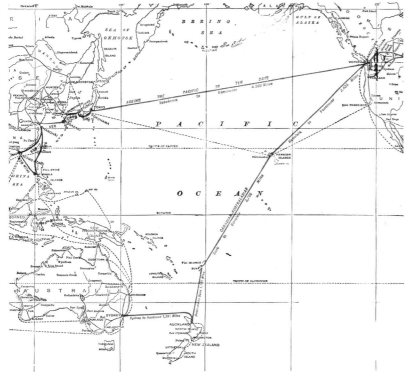

STEAMERS.—Providing regular Passenger and Freight
Services to Canada and U.S.A., and from
Vancouver to the Orient and Australasia.

TRAINS.—Operating over 19,600 miles of railway in Canada
and United States.

HOTELS.—Ensuring excellent accommodation at all important
Tourist and Commercial Centres.

Money Orders issued and Parcels forwarded
by the Dominion Express Co. to all parts
of Canada and U.S.A.   :   :   :

For Fares, Sailings, &c., apply :—

CANADIAN PACIFIC RAILWAY,

62-65, Charing Cross, London, S.W.1 ; or Local Agents everywhere.

Empress of Canada was delivered for Pacific services, which brought
the Pacific fleet up to four vessels. *Empress of Scotland* made her first
post-war cruise of seventy-nine days to the Mediterranean during the
winter of 1922 for the Frank C. Clarke Travel Agency of New York.
In no other year had the company seen so much activity as in 1922.
Between January and August there were eighteen notable sailings – not
all from Liverpool – of new ships or newly acquired ships of which all
had some association with Canada.

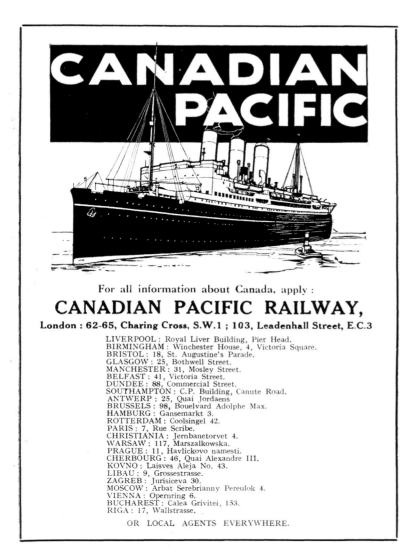

CANADIAN PACIFIC

For all information about Canada, apply :
CANADIAN PACIFIC RAILWAY,
London : 62-65, Charing Cross, S.W.1 ; 103, Leadenhall Street, E.C.3

LIVERPOOL : Royal Liver Building, Pier Head.
BIRMINGHAM : Winchester House, 4, Victoria Square.
BRISTOL : 18, St. Augustine's Parade.
GLASGOW : 25, Bothwell Street.
MANCHESTER : 31, Mosley Street.
BELFAST : 41, Victoria Street.
DUNDEE : 88, Commercial Street.
SOUTHAMPTON : C.P. Building, Canute Road.
ANTWERP : 25, Quai Jordaens.
BRUSSELS : 98, Bouelvard Adolphe Max.
HAMBURG : Gansemarkt 3.
ROTTERDAM : Coolsingel 42.
PARIS : 7, Rue Scribe.
CHRISTIANIA : Jernbanetorvet 4.
WARSAW : 117, Marszalkowska.
PRAGUE : 11, Havlickovo namesti.
CHERBOURG : 46, Quai Alexandre III.
KOVNO : Laisves Aleja No. 43.
LIBAU : 9, Grossestrasse.
ZAGREB : Jurisiceva 30.
MOSCOW : Arbat Serebrianny Pereulok 4.
VIENNA : Opernring 6.
BUCHAREST : Calea Grivitei, 153.
RIGA : 17, Wallstrasse.

OR LOCAL AGENTS EVERYWHERE.

1922 advertisement.

Settling in Western Canada

A New and Splendid Opportunity for Farmers,

THE CANADIAN PACIFIC RAILWAY
ANNOUNCE
AN ENTIRELY NEW SCHEME
OF
LAND PURCHASE

Improved and Semi-improved farms in Canada ready for immediate occupation can now be acquired under the following conditions :—
(1) One year's free use of the land.
(2) A payment of one-fifth of the crop during the 2nd year.
(3) A payment of one-third of the crop during the 3rd year.
(4) A payment of one-third of the crop during the 4th year.
(5) Future payment to be on a rental-purchase plan over 34 years.
(6) Rates and taxes during the first four years to be paid by the C.P.R

Farms can be selected in the best agricultural districts close to markets, railways, schools and towns. Farm telephone system available.
CONDUCTED PARTIES to view the Farm at frequent intervals

SEND the Coupon TO-DAY
for booklet about
How to own a Farm in anada
and information about
How to obtain Farm Work in Canada.

A. EWAN MOORE,
Colonization Manager,
Canadian Pacific Railway,
62-65, Charing Cross, London,
S.W.1.

To A. EWAN MOORE, Colonization Manager, Dept. 33, Canadian Pacific Railway, 62-65, Charing Cross, London S.W.1.

Please send me information as to How to own a Farm in Canada. How to obtain Farm Work in Canada.

Name...

Address...

....

1925 advertisement for farmers.

Scandinavian was sold for scrap and *Montcalm* was sold to Norwegian interests for conversion into a whale factory ship in 1923. On 1 September that year, when *Empress of Australia* was leaving her berth at Yokohama an earthquake struck and she returned to berth to give assistance. The British Columbian sternwheeler fleet was reduced to five vessels – *Nasookin*, *Kuskanook*, *Moyie*, *Bonnington* and *Minto* – and twelve cargo ships were given names commencing with 'B'. In 1924, Belfast was added to the Clyde–Canada route.

The increase in tonnage built during the First World War and the lower number of immigrants crossing the Atlantic meant that there were too many vessels trading in 1925. Restrictions were placed on immigrants to the United States, and the Canadian Government brought in a scheme for two years where immigrants to Canada paid £2 and they made up the balance. *Pretorian*, *Scotian* and *Grampian* were sold to ship-breakers and the Clyde–Canada service was reduced to *Metagama* and *Montnairn* in 1926.

Beaverburn, Beaverford, Beaverdale, Beaverhill and *Beaverbrae* were introduced, and *Bawtry* (ex-*Mottisfont*) was sold in 1927. The following year it was decided to land registered mail at Father Point, near the mouth of the St Lawrence, and fly it to Quebec and Montreal. The 'Beaver' boats were easily distinguishable by their four sets of 'goal post' masts and a single tall funnel. They all entered service in 1927 and were normally based at the Surrey Commercial Docks, London, and regularly called at Hamburg and Antwerp, with occasional calls at Le Havre, before sailing to Montreal or Saint John in the winter. The *Duchess of Bedford* entered service on 1 June 1928, and *Balfour, Berwyn, Brecon* and *Brandon* were sold. The following year, *Metagama* was transferred to the Antwerp–Quebec–Montreal service via Southampton and Cherbourg, and Canadian Pacific made a record of 127 Atlantic crossings.

Duchess of Bedford was the first of four twin-funnelled vessels with cruiser sterns; they were fitted with geared turbines driving twin screws, which gave a maximum speed of 19 knots in service. They operated from Liverpool to Quebec and Montreal in the summer, and to Saint John, New Brunswick, in the winter months. The *Duchess of Bedford* was followed by the *Duchess of Atholl, Duchess of Richmond* and *Duchess of York*.

On 27 April 1928, the first air–sea mail service took place when deliveries for Canada, carried by the *Empress of Scotland* to Quebec, were flown on from Rimouski, at the mouth of the St Lawrence, to Montreal and Toronto without any extra charge. On the return flight to connect with the *Empress of Scotland*, mail for England was also carried. This service was repeated in 1931 when mail from the *Duchess of Richmond*, which had left Glasgow on 9 May for Quebec, was flown on the 600 miles to Toronto from Rimouski. These air–sea services operated during the summer season only and were repeated in 1932, starting again with the *Duchess of Richmond*'s sailing from Glasgow on 9 May. In both years, the inclusive charge for each letter was 2½d.

In 1932, the Imperial Economics Conference was held in Ottawa and a special combined air–sea service was laid on to meet the needs of the event. Mail was flown from Croydon Airport by a three-engined Westland Wessex aircraft to Cherbourg to connect with the *Empress of Britain*, which carried it to Canada. The mail was landed from the ship in the Strait of Belle Isle, between the northern tip of Newfoundland and the southern shore of Labrador, and was flown by a Bellanca

STEAMSHIPS
RAILWAYS
HOTELS
EXPRESS
TELEGRAPHS
CRUISES
LANDS

THE SHORT SEA ROUTE TO CANADA *and* UNITED STATES

FREQUENT SAILINGS BY FAMOUS CANADIAN PACIFIC STEAMSHIPS *from* LIVERPOOL · GLASGOW SOUTHAMPTON · CHERBOURG ANTWERP · BELFAST & COBH

THE COMPLETE TRAVEL SERVICE TO CANADA—Empress, Duchess, and Cabin Class Steamships. ◀ ACROSS CANADA— 20,400 miles of railway line, serving all the important cities, industrial sections, agricultural regions and holiday resorts, reaching also many points in the United States. Main Line, Montreal to Vancouver, 2,886 miles. ◀ ACROSS THE PACIFIC— Empress Steamships from Vancouver for Japan, China and Manila. Canadian-Australasian Line to Australia and New Zealand. ◀ HOTELS—fourteen, including the largest in the British Empire—and nine Bungalow Camps. ◀ TELEGRAPHS operated by Canadian Pacific. ◀ Canadian Pacific EXPRESS, for Travellers' Cheques and package merchandise. ◀ WINTER CRUISES—Round the World, West Indies, West Africa, etc. ◀ FARM LANDS for sale, Industrial and Development Branches.

CANADIAN PACIFIC
World's Greatest Travel System

62-65, Charing Cross (Trafalgar Square), S.W. 1	4, Victoria Square	- BIRMINGHAM
103, Leadenhall Street, E.C. 3 - LONDON	31, Mosley Street	- MANCHESTER
Royal Liver Building - LIVERPOOL	14, Donegall Place	- BELFAST
18, St. Augustine's Parade - BRISTOL	Canute Road	- SOUTHAMPTON
25, Bothwell Street - GLASGOW, C. 2	10, Westbourne Place	- COBH
88, Commercial Street - DUNDEE	or local agents everywhere.	

1930 advertisement.

Canadian Pacific offices in London.

seaplane the 300 miles from Red Bay to Harve-Saint-Pierre, in the Gulf of St Lawrence. Then it was flown by a Vickers Vancouver flying boat to Rimouski, from where it was transported to Montreal and Ottawa by a Fairchild landplane. The first of these flights left for Cherbourg on 13 July and was followed by another on 30 July and a third on 13 August. There was one flight eastbound from Ottawa to Bradore Bay on 12 July, the mail being transferred to the *Empress of Britain*. However, on the last of the three westbound services, the mail had to be sent on from Rimouski by train because bad weather stopped flying.

The *Empress of Japan* was introduced in June 1930, when she left Liverpool for Quebec before sailing to Vancouver. She was the largest and fastest ship on the route. *Empress of Australia* was brought back to the United Kingdom for a refit and was then placed on the Atlantic service. The opening of the Kettle Valley Railway in British Columbia reduced traffic on the Upper and Lower Arrow Lake service operated by Canadian Pacific's sternwheeler vessels. The service via Trail to Washington State was terminated, and *Montroyal* was broken up.

Empress of Australia (2) in No. 6 dry dock at Southampton, with *Megantic* and *Homeric*, on 4 November 1931.

1930 advertisement.

Fairfield Shipbuilding & Engineering Company Limited 1930 advertisement.

Empress of Britain (2).

First-class entrance hall on *Empress of Britain* (2).

Repairs on *Empress of Britain* (2) in the floating dry dock at Southampton.

Empress of Britain (2) in the floating dry dock at Southampton.

Duchess of Bedford at Liverpool landing stage.

Dominion Express Company of Canada deliver good to a 'Duchess' at Liverpool.

On 28 January 1931, a notice of dissolution of the Allan Line was lodged in Edinburgh and it was disclosed that reserves of $8.4 million were transferred to the Canadian Pacific Replacement Fund. The Canadian-Australian Line Limited was formed with the Union Steam Ship Company of New Zealand, and *Empress of Britain* was delivered to Canadian Pacific. In April 1931, all sternwheeler services, except for *Sicamous*, were withdrawn. *Empress of Britain* made her fastest crossing from Father Point to Cherbourg in four days, six hours and fifty-six minutes. *Metagama* and *Empress of France* (ex-*Alsatian*) were broken up in 1934. *Empress of Australia* carried King George VI and Queen Elizabeth to Canada for their royal tour in 1939, and they returned on the *Empress of Britain*. The King and Queen should have travelled in HMS *Repulse*, but the international scene was so unsettled that it was decided to use the *Empress of Australia* and *Empress of Britain*. It was the last royal occasion on the North Atlantic, because within three months, the world was at war.

1936 advertisement for service to Japan and China.

Duchess of Richmond 1932 cruise advertisement.

Gay Holiday Cruises by Famous Atlantic Liners equipped for your personal comfort. Glorious Sunshine, Healthy Sea Air, Fun and Good Companionship.

Itineraries planned to interest, instruct and amuse. Cruises for everybody, five days to four and a half months duration. Prices to suit all purses.

Mediterranean   Atlantic Isles
Norwegian Fjords   West Indies
Round the World

WORLD'S GREATEST TRAVEL SYSTEM

**31 Mosley Street, MANCHESTER,
Royal Liver Building, Pier Head, LIVERPOOL**
Or LOCAL AGENTS EVERYWHERE.

Canadian Pacific Cruises advertisement.

FARES FOR SERVANTS ACCOMPANYING CABIN CLASS PASSENGERS

To and from Quebec or Montreal—Summer Halifax or Saint John—Winter or New York	Empress of Britain			Empress of Australia Duchess of Bedford Duchess of York Duchess of Richmond Duchess of Atholl			Montclare Montrose Montcalm		
	Off Season		Summer Season	Off Season		Summer Season	Off Season		Summer Season
	One Way	Round Trip	One Way	One Way	Round Trip	One Way	One Way	Round Trip	One Way
	$	$	$	$	$	$	$	$	$
British Ports	146	284	161	133	259	146	128	249	141
	—	—	—	*128	*250	—	*123	*240	—
Cherbourg Havre Antwerp	151	294	166	138	269	151	133	259	146
Ostend Rotterdam Hamburg	—	—	—	143	278	156	138	269	151
Bremen	—	—	—	151	294	164	146	284	159
Scandinavian Ports	—	—	—	151	294	164	146	284	159

*THESE FARES APPLY ONLY FOR BOOKINGS EFFECTED IN THE BRITISH ISLES TO CANADIAN DESTINATIONS DURING THE PERIOD WHEN THE RIVER ST. LAWRENCE IS CLOSED

OFF SEASON FARES apply all the year round except during the Summer Season. SUMMER SEASON FARES apply as follows :—

	WESTBOUND	EASTBOUND
Empress of Britain	July 24 to September 24	May 29 to July 23
Other Ships	July 24 to September 17	May 29 to July 16

CHILDREN'S AND INFANTS' FARES

Under one year—$10.00 Cabin Class, $4.00 Tourist and Third Class.
One year and under ten, half fare—The age of children should be authenticated before tickets are issued at half fare. Half fare applies only to children aged under ten years at date of outward or homeward sailing. A child within the age limit outward but beyond the age limit homeward, must be charged adult fare for the homeward sailing.
Two half-fare children will be charged one adult fare. For exclusive use of one room for one child charge the one-in-room fare.
Ten years and over, full adult berth fare in room occupied.
The Company reserves the right to decline the sale of rooms for adults and children at less than full adult fares for the children.
Suites For a half-fare child with one or more adults in a suite charge the mean between the rates with and without an additional adult :
e.g. To arrive at rate for 2½ in suite—

Take 2 in suite		$687.00
3 in suite		$843.00
Charge mean Fare		$765.00

CHERBOURG AND HAVRE PORT TAXES

French State and Port Taxes must be collected at time of booking on all Cabin and Tourist Westbound and Eastbound cash and prepaid business, as follows :—

Cabin Class	Frs. 75.00	or equivalent in other currencies
Tourist Class	Frs. 30.00	at current rate of exchange.
Third Class	Nil.	

These taxes are to be collected as a separate charge for all bookings.
Taxes for both outward and homeward journey must be collected at time of booking on round trip business.
Children between one and ten years will pay half the above amount. Infants nil.
All Contract Tickets and Prepaid Certificates on which tax is collected must be endorsed as follows :—
"French State and Port Taxes $............collected."
N.B.—French Port Taxes are applicable to all passengers booked at French Port Rates embarking or disembarking from Atlantic steamer directly at a French Port.

Details of 1938–39 fares.

CABIN CLASS MINIMUM FARES

OFF SEASON FARES apply all the year round except during the SUMMER SEASON :—

	WESTBOUND	EASTBOUND
Empress of Britain	July 24 to Sept 24	May 29 to July 23
Other ships...	... July 24 to Sept 17	May 29 to July 16

To or from Quebec or New York	EMPRESS OF BRITAIN Off Season One Way	Off Season Round Trip	Summer Season One Way
	$	$	$
SOUTHAMPTON—QUEBEC	228.00	445.00	251.00
CHERBOURG—QUEBEC	233.00	455.00	256.00
SOUTHAMPTON—NEW YORK	244.00	476.00	—
CHERBOURG—NEW YORK	249.00	486.00	—

To or from Quebec or Montreal—Summer Halifax or Saint John—Winter or New York		EMPRESS OF AUSTRALIA			Duchess of Atholl, Duchess of Bedford, Duchess of Richmond, Duchess of York			Montcalm, Montclare, Montrose		
		Off Season		Summer Season	Off Season		Summer Season	Off Season		Summer Season
		One Way	Round Trip	One Way	One Way	Round Trip	One Way	One Way	Round Trip	One Way
		$	$	$	$	$	$	$	$	$
BRITISH PORTS	via direct steamship	170.00	332.00	185.00	165.00	322.00	182.00	137.50	269.00	152.00
	via direct steamship to Saint John* or Halifax*	—	—	—	*160.00	*312.00	—	*132.50	*259.00	—
CHERBOURG, HAVRE	via direct steamship or British Ports	175.00	342.00	190.00	170.00	332.00	187.00	142.50	278.00	157.00
ANTWERP, OSTEND	via direct steamship, French or British Ports	180.00	351.00	195.00	175.00	342.00	192.00	147.50	288.00	162.00
HAMBURG	via direct steamship, British or French Ports	188.00	367.00	203.00	183.00	357.00	200.00	155.50	304.00	170.00
DANZIG	Danzig via British or French Ports	193.00	377.00	208.00	188.00	367.00	205.00	160.50	313.00	175.00
ESTHONIA	Tallinn(Reval) via British or French Ports	201.00	392.00	216.00	196.00	383.00	213.00	168.50	329.00	183.00
FRANCE	Boulogne via British Ports	175.00	342.00	190.00	170.00	332.00	187.00	142.50	278.00	157.00
GERMANY	Bremen via British or French Ports	188.00	367.00	203.00	183.00	357.00	200.00	155.50	304.00	170.00
	Pillau via British or French Ports	193.00	377.00	208.00	188.00	367.00	205.00	160.50	313.00	175.00
GREECE	Patras, Piraeus, Salonika via British or French Ports — WEST	235.00	444.00	‡256.00	230.00	434.00	‡253.00	195.50	371.00	‡216.00
	EAST	244.00	444.00	‡266.00	239.00	434.00	‡263.00	205.50	371.00	‡227.00
HOLLAND	Rotterdam via British or French Ports	180.00	351.00	195.00	175.00	342.00	192.00	147.50	288.00	162.00
LATVIA	Libau, Riga via British or French Ports	196.50	384.00	211.50	191.50	374.00	208.50	164.00	320.00	178.50
LITHUANIA	Memel, Kaunas via British or French Ports	195.00	381.00	210.00	190.00	371.00	207.00	162.50	317.00	177.00
POLAND	Gdynia via British or French Ports	193.00	377.00	208.00	188.00	367.00	205.00	160.50	313.00	175.00
U.S.S.R.	Leningrad via British Ports	208.00	406.00	223.00	203.00	396.00	220.00	175.50	343.00	190.00
DENMARK										
Aalborg, Aarhus, Copenhagen, Esbjerg, Frederickshavn, Odense, Sonderborg	via British or French Ports	188.00	367.00	203.00	183.00	357.00	200.00	155.50	304.00	170.00
FINLAND										
Abo, Hango, Helsingfors, Mariehamn	via British Ports	202.00	394.00	217.00	197.00	385.00	214.00	169.50	331.00	184.00
NORWAY										
Bergen, Haugesund, Kristiansand S, Oslo, Stavanger	via British or French Ports	188.00	367.00	203.00	183.00	357.00	200.00	155.50	304.00	170.00
Aalesund	via British or French Ports	195.00	381.00	210.00	190.00	371.00	207.00	162.50	318.00	177.00
Kristiansund N.	via British or French Ports	196.50	384.00	211.50	191.50	374.00	208.50	164.00	321.00	178.50
Molde	via British or French Ports	196.00	383.00	211.00	191.00	373.00	208.00	163.50	320.00	178.00
Trondheim	via British or French Ports	198.00	387.00	213.00	193.00	377.00	210.00	165.50	324.00	180.00
Arendal	via British or French Ports	190.00	371.00	205.00	185.00	361.00	202.00	157.50	308.00	172.00
Larvik	via British or French Ports	191.00	373.00	206.00	186.00	363.00	203.00	158.50	310.00	173.00
SWEDEN										
Arvika	via British or French Ports	191.75	374.50	206.75	186.75	364.50	203.75	159.25	311.50	173.75
Helsingborg	via British or French Ports	189.25	369.50	204.25	184.25	359.50	201.25	156.75	306.50	171.25
Gothenburg, Malmo	via British or French Ports	188.00	367.00	203.00	183.00	357.00	200.00	155.50	304.00	170.00
Stockholm	via British or French Ports	195.50	382.00	210.50	190.50	372.00	207.50	163.00	319.00	177.50
ICELAND										
Reykjavik	via British Ports	205.00	400.00	220.00	200.00	390.00	217.00	172.50	337.00	187.00
FAROE ISLANDS										
Thorshavn	via British Ports	200.00	393.00	215.00	195.00	381.00	212.00	167.50	327.00	182.00

**THESE FARES APPLY ONLY FOR BOOKINGS EFFECTED IN THE BRITISH ISLES TO CANADIAN DESTINATIONS DURING THE PERIOD WHEN THE RIVER ST. LAWRENCE IS CLOSED.*

‡ **Round Trip Summer Season fare, Empress of Australia $496, Duchesses $491, Monts $422.**

The above are minimum fares only. Passengers occupying berths which take higher than minimum fares will pay the difference between the minimum berth fare and the fare for the accommodation occupied, according to to the ship on which it is secured.

Fares quoted via British Ports include Third Class rail in England, First Class on North Sea steamers and Second Class rail on Continent ; also board and lodging in England waiting first available connections. Fares to and from Patras, Piræus and Salonika include Second Class accommodation and meals on Steamer between Marseilles or Trieste and Greece and 50 kilos free baggage allowance. If no convenient connecting steamer all rail forwarding may be provided. **SEE PAGE 16 FOR FRENCH STATE AND PORT TAXES.**

3

FARES FROM EUROPE TO THE FAR EAST

The examples of through fares quoted below cover minimum rate accommodation

CLASS OF TRAVEL	EUROPE TO Yokohama One Way	Yokohama Round Trip	Kobe One Way	Kobe Round Trip	Nagasaki One Way	Nagasaki Round Trip	Shanghai One Way	Shanghai Round Trip	Hong Kong One Way	Hong Kong Round Trip	Manila One Way	Manila Round Trip
	£ s.	£ s.	£ s.	£ s.	£ s.	£ s.	£ s.	£ s.	£ s.	£ s.	£ s.	£ s.
CABIN CLASS ATLANTIC, FIRST CLASS BEYOND												
By Empress of Britain and Empress of Japan ...	107 16	199 11	109 9	202 11	—	—	115 4	212 11	120 3	221 5	124 5	228 7
By Duchess type and Empress of Russia or Empress of Asia ...	90 11	167 11	92 4	170 7	95 9	176 2	97 19	180 11	102 17	189 2	107 0	196 7
By Duchess type and Empress of Japan ...	98 15	181 18	100 8	184 17	—	—	106 3	194 17	111 2	203 12	115 4	210 13
By Mont type and Empress of Russia or Empress of Asia	86 12	159 19	88 5	162 15	91 10	168 10	94 0	172 19	98 18	181 10	103 0	188 14
CABIN CLASS ATLANTIC, FIRST RAIL, TOURIST PACIFIC												
By Mont type and Empress of Asia or Empress of Russia ...	66 1	123 19	66 17	125 9	68 10	128 4	70 3	131 4	72 12	135 9	75 2	139 15
By Duchess type and Empress of Russia or Empress of Asia	70 0	131 12	70 16	133 1	72 9	135 17	74 2	138 16	76 11	143 2	79 1	147 7
By Duchess type and Empress of Japan ...	76 11	143 2	77 8	144 11	—	—	80 13	150 6	83 3	154 12	85 12	158 17
By Empress of Britain and Empress of Japan ...	85 12	160 16	86 9	162 5	—	—	89 15	168 0	92 4	172 6	94 13	176 11
TOURIST ATLANTIC, FIRST RAIL, TOURIST PACIFIC												
By Duchess type and Empress of Russia or Empress of Asia	63 18	118 15	64 14	120 5	66 7	123 1	68 0	126 0	70 9	130 6	72 18	134 11
By Empress of Britain and Empress of Japan ...	72 7	133 18	73 3	135 7	—	—	76 9	141 2	78 18	145 8	81 7	149 13

The above fares are based on Off Season Atlantic Fares. An extra charge is payable by Passengers travelling on Atlantic steamers during the Summer Season. The approximate additional charge can be seen from the list of minimum fares on page 3. For bookings in the British Isles from British Ports to or from Saint John or Halifax, when the River St. Lawrence is closed, the Atlantic fares are slightly less than during the off season.

Fares to Honolulu quoted on application.

The above Fares include—First Class rail transportation from Landing Port to Vancouver, with privilege of stopover at all points. Meals and Sleeping Berth to be paid for extra.

Baggage—Free baggage allowance of 350 lbs.—steamship and rail—per adult passenger, is granted to holders of through tickets to the Far East.

FARES FROM EUROPE TO FIJI, AUCKLAND, N.Z., AND AUSTRALIA

The examples of through fares quoted below cover minimum rate accommodation

CLASS OF TRAVEL	EUROPE TO Suva, Fiji One Way	Suva, Fiji Round Trip	Auckland, N.Z. One Way	Auckland, N.Z. Round Trip	Sydney, N.S.W. One Way	Sydney, N.S.W. Round Trip	Melbourne One Way	Melbourne Round Trip
	£ s.	£ s.	£ s.	£ s.	£ s.	£ s.	£ s.	£ s.
CABIN CLASS ATLANTIC, FIRST CLASS BEYOND								
By Empress of Britain and Aorangi ...	95 0	178 1	102 1	185 5	111 19	205 0	113 11	208 6
By Duchess type and Aorangi ...	85 19	160 7	93 0	167 11	102 17	187 6	104 10	190 12
By Duchess type and Niagara ...	83 9	156 5	90 11	163 9	100 8	183 4	102 1	186 10
By Mont type and Niagara ...	79 10	148 12	86 12	155 17	96 9	175 11	98 2	178 17
CABIN ATLANTIC, FIRST RAIL, CABIN PACIFIC								
By Duchess type and Aorangi or Niagara ...	67 4	128 12	73 9	134 17	81 7	150 13	82 19	153 19
By Mont type and Aorangi or Niagara ...	63 5	121 0	69 10	127 5	77 8	143 0	79 0	146 6
TOURIST ATLANTIC, FIRST RAIL, CABIN PACIFIC								
By Empress of Britain and Aorangi or Niagara ...	62 19	119 8	69 4	125 13	77 2	141 9	78 15	144 15
By Duchess type and Aorangi or Niagara ...	61 2	115 16	67 7	122 1	75 4	137 17	76 17	141 3

The above fares are based on Off Season Atlantic Fares. An extra charge is payable by Passengers travelling on Atlantic steamers during the Summer Season. The approximate additional charge can be seen from the list of minimum fares on page 3. For bookings in the British Isles from British Ports to or from Halifax and Saint John, when the River St. Lawrence is closed, the Atlantic fares are slightly less than during the off season.

Fares to Honolulu quoted on application.

The above Fares include—First Class rail transportation from Landing Port to Vancouver, B.C., with privilege of stopover at all points. Meals and Sleeping Berths to be paid for extra.

Baggage—Free baggage allowance of 350 lbs.—steamship and rail—per adult passenger, is granted to holders of through tickets to New Zealand and Australia.

THROUGH BOOKINGS TO CENTRAL AND SOUTH AMERICA, AND PANAMA

A reduction of 10 per cent. is allowed off Atlantic One-Way Fares in connection with triangular tours Europe/North America/South America/Europe, any class; also off Atlantic one-way or round trip fares for through bookings to the following countries. A similar concession will be allowed by the connecting sea or air Lines.

South America:—Argentine, Brazil, Chile, Columbia, Ecuador, British Guinea, Peru, Uruguay, Venezuela

Central America :—Belize, Cristobal, Balboa, Costa Rica, Guatemala, Spanish Honduras, Nicaragua, Salvador

THROUGH BOOKINGS FROM SOUTH, WEST AND EAST AFRICA TO CANADA AND UNITED STATES VIA EUROPE, AND VICE VERSA.

A reduction of 10 per cent. is allowed off Atlantic One-Way or Round Trip Fares in connection with through bookings provided that a similar reduction is allowed by the connecting Line from Africa to Europe. A reduction of 10 per cent. is also allowed off Triangular Tour bookings Africa/Europe/North America/Africa. Such Tours may commence in Africa, Europe or North America, and the concession applies off the Atlantic Ocean Fare and off the connecting Lines Fares.

THE ABOVE 10 PER CENT. THROUGH BOOKING REDUCTIONS APPLY ONLY WHEN THE ENTIRE THROUGH BOOKING IS EFFECTED AT THE OUTSET.

ROUND THE WORLD — INDEPENDENT TOURS.

A choice of 67 Routes at fares ranging from £93 to £229 according to class and route.
Tickets valid for two years—full particulars on application.

17

Details of 1938–39 fares.

3

THE SECOND WORLD WAR

WAR WAS DECLARED AT 11 a.m. on Sunday, 3 September 1939. Before the day was out, a German submarine sank the *Athenia*, which had left Liverpool the previous day. *Athenia* was the first British ship to be sunk by Germany, and the incident accounted for the Donaldson Line's greatest single loss of life at sea, with 117 civilian passengers and crew killed. The sinking was condemned as a war crime. Among those dead were twenty-eight US citizens, leading Germany to fear that the United States might join the war on the side of the European countries. Wartime German authorities denied that one of their vessels had sunk the ship. An admission of responsibility did not come from the German authorities until 1946.

Following the declaration of war with Germany, *Princess Marguerite* and *Princess Kathleen* were converted to coastal troopships operating in Europe. On 26 October 1940, *Empress of Britain* was carrying troops and was bombed by German Fw Condor aircraft; she was taken in tow by the destroyer *Burza*. Two days later, she was torpedoed by German submarine *U-32* and sank. *Beaverburn* was attacked and sunk by *U-41* in February 1940, and *Beaverford* was part of a convoy that was attacked by the German pocket battleship *Admiral Scheer* on 5 November and sank. *Niagara* was on a voyage from Auckland on 19 June 1940, and sank in the Hauraki Gulf as a result of an explosion. Mines had been laid in the area by, it was later determined, the German auxiliary cruiser *Orion*. In 1941, on a voyage from Liverpool to Canada, *Beaverbrae* was sunk by air attack, and *Beaverdale* was torpedoed and sunk by *U-48* in the North Atlantic.

On 7 December 1941, Pearl Harbor was attacked by Japan and the United States entered the Second World War. *Empress of Asia* was sunk by bombers of the Imperial Japanese Navy Air Service near Singapore in 1942, and *Duchess of Bedford* sank a U-boat with its deck guns two days out of Liverpool that same year. *Princess Marguerite*, with over 1,000 troops on board, was sunk by *U-83*: fifty-five people lost their lives. In October 1942, the *Duchess of Atholl* was sunk by the German submarine *U-178*, 2,000 miles off Ascension Island, with 825 people on board. Four crewmen were lost and the 821 survivors were rescued by HMS *Corinthian*. The *Duchess of York* was lost after being attacked and set on fire by German bombers in July 1943, and *Empress of Canada* was sunk by an Italian submarine off Cape Palmas on 13 March 1943. There were 1,800 people on board; many were Italian prisoners of war. The last 'Beaver' cargo vessel, *Beaverhill*, was wrecked outside Saint John, New Brunswick, on 24 November 1944 and broke in two. While refitting at Barrow-in-Furness, the *Empress of Russia* suffered a serious fire in September 1945 and was later scrapped. Canadian Pacific lost twelve ships due to enemy action.

Awards and honours to Canadian Pacific seagoing personnel during the Second World War numbered eighty-five. Included were two CBEs, one DSO, five DSCs, eight OBEs, eight MBEs, one George Medal, two Lloyd's Medals and twenty-four Mentions in Despatches. Two-thirds of the pre-war fleet were lost. Many seagoing employees, including three masters and several other senior officers, perished, some of them serving on ships allocated by the Ministry of War Transport for operation by the company. Canadian Pacific ships were engaged in all major operations from the commencement of hostilities, including those of Singapore, North Africa, Sicily, the Eastern Mediterranean, the expedition to Spitsbergen, the capture of Madagascar, and the landings on the coast of Normandy. Among the passengers on various occasions were 6,000 British children carried safely out of the war zone to Canada in the summer of 1940, and over 59,000 German and Italian prisoners of war sent to Canada. Newfoundland lumbermen coming to Britain for special work were also carried, as well as 23,000 troops, most of whom were transferred from West Africa to East Africa during the height of the Italian campaign. At the outbreak of hostilities, all Canadian Pacific vessels of British registry were taken over by the British Government under the provisions of the liner requisition scheme. Also taken over under charter arrangements were the *Empress of Asia*, *Empress of Russia*, *Princess Kathleen* and *Princess Marguerite* of Canadian registry. All vessels of both the Atlantic and Pacific fleets of Canadian Pacific and two of the coastal steamships, comprising a gross tonnage of 335,000, were engaged in war service.

The *Duchess of Bedford* became a troopship in August 1939, leaving Liverpool for Bombay with troops and reinforcements. She completed a series of voyages between Liverpool and Saint John, New Brunswick, and was then converted into a troopship. *Duchess of Atholl* remained on the Atlantic service until December 1939, and was then converted into a troopship, sailing to Egypt. She was involved in the British landing on the Vichy French island of Madagascar. These were backed by an assault force of thirty-four vessels and the operation was completed in sixty hours. On a voyage from the Middle East, she was attacked and sunk on 10 October 1942 by the German submarine *U-178*. She was part of a convoy that had left Table Bay for Freetown, with 825 people on board, and 200 miles north-east of Ascension Island she was hit by a torpedo. Four members of the crew lost their lives in the attack.

The *Duchess of Richmond* also maintained the Atlantic service until the end of 1939, and was converted into a troopship.

Duchess of York became a troopship in 1940, sailing from Liverpool to Bombay in June that year. She was attacked and damaged by German aircraft about 300 miles south-west of Cape Finisterre on 14 March 1943. In a convoy sailing from the Clyde to Freetown, she was attacked by three Fw Condor aircraft on 11 July that year. *Duchess of York*, Anchor Line's *California* and the *Port Fairy* were west of Portugal, and *Duchess of York* and *California* were set on fire and abandoned. The survivors were taken on board the destroyers *Douglas* and *Iroquois*, and the frigate *Moyola*; 106 people lost their lives in the attack. The warships then torpedoed the blazing ships and they both sank. *Port Fairy* continued to Casablanca the following day, with the frigate *Swale* as her escort. Both vessels were attacked and *Port Fairy* was hit by a bomb and set on fire. *Swale* assisted in the fire-fighting and after four hours the fire was extinguished. Both ships arrived at Casablanca on 14 July.

The *Duchess of Richmond* completed her trooping duties in May 1946. Following refurbishment she was renamed *Empress of Canada* and entered service with the CPR house flag on her funnels. *Beaverdell*, *Beaverglen* and *Beaverlake* were delivered, and *Beavercove* was launched on 16 July 1946. To supplement the four 'Beavers', the company bought two Empire-type turbine vessels, the *Empire Captain* and the *Empire Kitchener*, which became *Beaverburn* and *Beaverford* respectively, entering the fleet in 1946.

4

THE DEVELOPMENT OF SERVICES IN PEACETIME

IN 1947, THE CUNARD LINER *Ascania* began sailing, in 'austerity condition', from Liverpool to Halifax, and in 1948 was trading to the St Lawrence ports. Berths had been available in troopships for persons with urgent business in Canada. Canadian Pacific announced that its transpacific service would not be restored and that its surviving ship, *Empress of Scotland* (ex-*Empress of Japan*), would be transferred to the Atlantic service on completion of a major refit following the end of her war service. They also announced that the *Duchess of Richmond* and *Duchess of Bedford* would be reconstructed to enable them to carry out a service similar to that given by the war 'Empresses', and that the ships would be named *Empress of Canada* and *Empress of India*, the last named being altered to '*France*' when India had achieved her independence. The company also confirmed that the service would be based in Liverpool, not Southampton, as in pre-war days.

The Cunard Line service to Canada from Liverpool was maintained by the *Ascania* and the *Franconia*, which was a veteran of the New

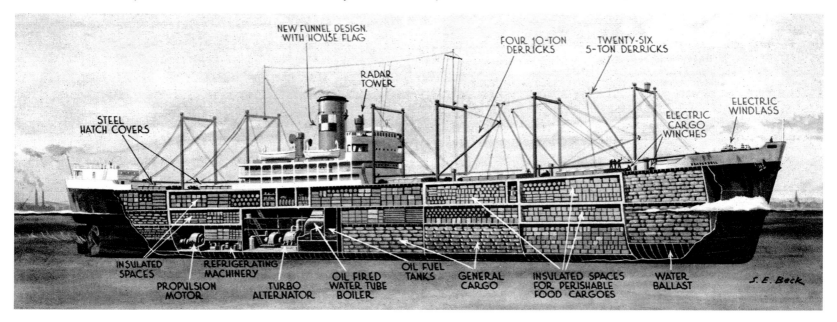

Beaverdell drawing by S.E. Beck.

Canadian Pacific

LIVERPOOL TO MONTREAL

Receiving Dates

S.S. *Beaverford*	May 25th —	June 3rd
▲ S.S. *Empress of Canada*	May 25th —	June 4th
▲ S.S. *Empress of France*	June 6th —	June 11th

▲ Via Quebec.

Loading Berth : North No. 1, Gladstone Dock

THROUGH BILLS OF LADING issued to all the principal points in Canada and Western United States	**Insurance** at low rates.
	Goods are Received for shipment only subject to the terms and conditions of the Company's usual form of Wharfinger's Receipt and/or Bill of Lading.
EXPORT LICENCE (where required) and Exchange Control Form (C.D.3) with shipping instructions should be forwarded, and Customs Entry passed, before goods are tendered for shipment.	
	CANADIAN PACIFIC EXPRESS CO. Merchandise, samples, livestock and valuables sent by Express Service to all parts of Canada and the United States. When travelling, carry Canadian Pacific Express Travellers' Cheques.

For rates and other information, apply :—

CANADIAN PACIFIC RAILWAY COMPANY,
Royal Liver Building, Liverpool.
Telephone : Central 5690

or to any other Canadian Pacific Office, a list of which is overleaf
Subject to change without notice

1949 sailing list.

York trade that dated back to 1923. *Samaria* and *Scythia* were employed from Southampton, but none of the ex-New York ships proceeded to Montreal. The Canadian Pacific service was fully restored when the refitted *Empress of Scotland* began her first voyage from Liverpool on 9 May 1950, almost twenty years after she left the Mersey as the *Empress of Japan* on a voyage to Quebec, on 14 June 1930, from which she returned to Southampton before proceeding to enter the Pacific service.

A double record for the crossing of the Atlantic between the St Lawrence and the Clyde was reported by Captain E.A. Shergold, master of the *Empress of Scotland*, when she arrived at Greenock from Quebec on 6 July 1950. The liner made the outward voyage from Greenock to Father Point in four days, fourteen hours and forty-two minutes, giving an average speed of 21.3 knots, pilot to pilot. The crossing back to Greenock was made in four days, twenty-three hours and thirty minutes. Captain Shergold said that the speed was reduced during the eastward crossing to avoid reaching Greenock before daylight. Otherwise, at least ten hours could have been saved. Conditions on both crossings were almost ideal, with a calm sea. The previous records for both the westward and eastward crossings, from and to the Clyde, had been established by the *Empress of Scotland* earlier in the year, but each was slightly over five days.

In 1952, *Empire Regent* was purchased and renamed *Beaverlodge*. Between 1952 and 1965, *Beaverlake* and *Beavercove* spent four years on the Pacific, when they were given the names *Mapledell* and *Maplecove*. *Huascaran* was acquired to transport immigrants from Europe to Canada and she was renamed *Beaverbrae*. *Princess Patricia*, *Princess Marguerite* and *Princess Nanaimo* were delivered.

In 1949, for the first time since the outbreak of the Second World War, a Canadian Pacific transatlantic liner was wearing the Blue Ensign. The commander, Captain B. Grant, the chief officer and three able seamen on the *Empress of France* comprised the ship's complement of naval reserve members. The *Empress of Australia* had flown the Blue Ensign for a short period since 1939, but she was not engaged on North Atlantic commercial service, having been requisitioned by the Ministry of Transport and employed as a troopship.

Princess Elizabeth and the Duke of Edinburgh travelled from Newfoundland to Britain on *Empress of Scotland* in November 1951. In the same year, *Princess Victoria* was sold and converted into a timber barge. The following year, *Princess Kathleen* grounded on rocks and was

Maplecove.

Tourist lounge on *Empress of Scotland* (2).

Dining saloon on *Empress of Scotland* (2).

Tourist-class cabin on *Empress of Scotland* (2).

lost. The *Empress of Australia* never returned to the fleet as she continued trooping duties after the war. She was sold in 1952 and broken up at Inverkeithing. On 25 January 1953, the *Empress of Canada* caught fire in Gladstone Dock, Liverpool, and capsized against the quayside. Salvage of the vessel took over twelve months to complete and she left Liverpool in September 1954, in tow for Italian ship-breakers. As the ship had been fully booked with visitors planning to come to Britain for the coronation of Queen Elizabeth II in 1953, the company purchased *De Grasse* from the French Line and she was renamed *Empress of Australia*. She was clearly purchased as a stopgap as her speed of 16 knots was hardly enough for her to keep her place on a seventeen-day round-trip schedule. She had been built by Cammell Laird at Birkenhead in 1924, and her career had been a hard one, including a period underwater after German forces had scuttled her at Bordeaux.

Cunard was providing the first new tonnage for the Canada trade since 1931, with *Saxonia* sailing from Liverpool to the St Lawrence, which she entered on 2 September 1954, being later joined by the new *Ivernia*, *Carinthia* and *Sylvania*.

Arthur Patrick Gray, of West Derby, Liverpool, retired in 1953 after forty-five years' service with Canadian Pacific. He served in the *Empress of France* for twenty-five years, and completed his last voyage in the vessel as smoke room steward when she arrived at Liverpool from Canada on 19 June. He had begun his career with the company at the age of 20 as assistant steward in the *Empress of Ireland*, at £3 per month, and he was serving in the ship when she sank in May 1914 after a collision in the St Lawrence with the Danish collier *Storstad*. He later served in the *Missanabie*, the first *Empress of France* and the *Montrose*.

The capsized *Empress of Canada* in Gladstone Dock, Liverpool.

A new Empress takes the water

On May 9th, at Vickers-Armstrongs' Naval Yard, Lady Eden launched the latest Canadian Pacific 'White Empress'— the 26,000-ton 'Empress of England'. Soon this luxury liner will be voyaging regularly across the Atlantic, bringing new comfort and enjoyment to thousands of travellers to and from North America.

Vickers-Armstrongs have over sixty years' association with the famous C.P.R. and take pride in this new vessel. They wish good luck to the ship and to all who sail in her.

VICKERS-ARMSTRONGS

1956 Vickers-Armstrongs advertisement.

Swan, Hunter & Wigham Richardson, Ltd
Shipbuilders · Shiprepairers · Marine Engineers

The 27,000 ton Passenger Liner "Empress of Canada" entering our No. 4 Dry Dock

WALLSEND-ON-TYNE
LONDON OFFICE: ARMADORES HOUSE, BURY STREET, LONDON E.C.3

Swan, Hunter & Wigham Richardson advertisement.

By 1954, the immigrant traffic had declined and the company disposed of *Beaverbrae*. The *Empress of Britain* entered service in 1956, followed by *Empress of England* the following year. In 1958, *Empress of Scotland* was sold to the Hamburg America Line, and *Princess Elizabeth* and *Princess Joan* were sold to Epirotiki in 1959. In April 1959, the St Lawrence Seaway was opened and Canadian Pacific chartered *Elise Schulte* and *Hermann Schulte*.

Liverpool to Toronto, Hamilton and Detroit 1963 sailing list.

Canadian Pacific

LIVERPOOL TO TORONTO, HAMILTON, DETROIT
(AND OTHER LAKES PORTS IF INDUCEMENT)

	Receiving Dates	
RAMORE HEAD (Toronto and Hamilton only) (Via Glasgow)	May 6	- May 10
Loading Berth: N. E. Brocklebank Branch		
HERMANN SCHULTE (also calling Three Rivers)	May 13	- May 17
Loading Berth: No. 1 North Gladstone Dock		

For rates and all information apply to :—

CANADIAN PACIFIC RAILWAY COMPANY
Royal Liver Building, Pier Head, Liverpool 3

Telephone : CENtral 5690   L.145. May 3rd, 1963

Montreal.

5

THE LAST WHITE 'EMPRESS' LINERS

EMPRESS OF CANADA WAS THE final vessel in the trio of new Canadian Pacific liners introduced in the 1950s and 1960s for the Liverpool to Canada service via Greenock. She was the largest ship built for the route and was air-conditioned throughout, even the glass-enclosed promenade decks. The ship was conceived and designed as a modern cargo-passenger liner for the North Atlantic service and for winter cruising in tropical climes.

The fact that the *Empress of Canada* would be engaged in two trades meant that a compromise had to be made with her design, as the first consideration was the provision of a staple, 'bread-and-butter' liner service between Britain and Canada, and during the winter months she would leave the well-travelled Atlantic route and begin her cruising schedule. Special attention was made to converting her from her two-class service to a single class for cruising. Public rooms covered a greater total area than in any other post-war Canadian Pacific liner, and large, unobstructed areas of open deck space were provided.

Accommodation ladders and landing platforms were specially constructed and four launches supplied, adapted for embarking seventy passengers at a time at intermediate ports. When on cruise service, the *Empress of Canada* would carry 750 one-class passengers, and on the North Atlantic run, 1,048 passengers would be carried – 192 first class and 856 tourist. She was designed with 112 first-class staterooms and 293 tourist-class staterooms. Several communication doors were arranged to allow two staterooms to form a single unit and others were equipped with settee-type beds for conversion to sitting rooms during the day.

At the planning stage, various alternatives were considered for the design of *Empress of Canada* as a dual-purpose vessel. The alternatives looked at included having the machinery aft, machinery amidships with centre-line casings, and machinery amidships with split casings. All aspects were carefully considered, including the idea of a funnel-less profile, but the company decided to adhere to the pattern previously established.

The popularity of the seven-day North Atlantic voyage was enhanced by the fact that two days were spent in the sheltered estuary of the St Lawrence. This 1,000-mile-long route, with rocky coasts and hills and towns, cities and forests, made it an unusual setting for an ocean voyage. Six hours out from Montreal, chimneys of the famous paper mills of the Three Rivers could be seen and the ship slid under Quebec Bridge and past Quebec City. The route then took the ship through the narrow Strait of Belle Isle or via Cape Race, Newfoundland. It is easy to see why many passengers regarded the North Atlantic transit as an enjoyable cruise.

Beaverfir was acquired for the Great Lakes service. Later that year, Canadian Pacific Airways were granted a licence to operate across the Atlantic, but British Overseas Airways objected and the company never actually operated any flights. *Beaverpine*, *Beaverelm* and *Beaverash* were delivered in 1962–63 for the Great Lakes service. *Beaverdell*, *Beaverlake* and *Beaverford* were sold in 1962.

The Canadian Pacific's coastal steamship service was resumed between Port Angeles and Victoria, British Columbia, in the summer of 1962. A Canadian Pacific spokesman said in Vancouver that the service was being restored because of heavier traffic expected to develop as a result of the Seattle World's Fair. In addition, Victoria was observing its 100th anniversary. Five round trips daily were provided at the height of the season by the *Princess Marguerite*, beginning on 15 June.

Sports deck on *Empress of Britain* (3).

Empress of Britain (3) and *Empress of Canada* (3) at the CPR berth in Gladstone Dock, Liverpool.

Mr N.R. Crump, chairman and president of the Canadian Pacific Railway Company, said in a speech in Liverpool in 1962 that shippers were not going to go on using one particular port if they could get a better service elsewhere. He gave the sternest warning to seamen and dockers on Merseyside, and intimated without any wavering that Canadian Pacific passenger sailings out of the Port of Liverpool could not stand any more of the losses, which 'the irresponsible behaviour of seamen and dockers alike have inflicted on his company in the past'. The Lord Mayor of Liverpool, Alderman Peter McKernan, said:

> It would be regrettable if a shipping company of the size of Canadian Pacific had to withdraw ships from the Port of Liverpool. Such a drastic development would be bad for the port and would be regretted by every loyal citizen. Liverpool, at the present time, cannot afford to lose the trade of the Canadian Pacific Company.

This followed a number of unofficial strikes and walk-offs, and it was suggested at the time that Canadian Pacific may be driven outside the United Kingdom, which seemed unthinkable, but not impossible. *Empress of Britain* and *Empress of England* were chartered to Max Wilson's Travel Savings Association in 1963, where members paid regular monthly subscriptions to participate in a cruising programme. When the decline in passenger numbers was discussed by the Pacific Steam Navigation Company board in 1963 it was decided to charter the *Reina del Mar* to the Travel Savings Association, in which the company had a 25 per cent share. The other partners were the British & Commonwealth Shipping Company Limited, Canadian Pacific Steamships Limited and Mr Max Wilson. The Union Castle Line took over the management of the *Reina del Mar* for the period of this project and offered cruises from the United Kingdom, and also provided voyages in the South African market to South American ports. Union Castle used *Stirling Castle* and *Capetown Castle* on cruises at the end of their careers.

The Travel Savings Association chartered the *Empress of Britain*, *Empress of England*, *Stratheden* and the *Reina del Mar*. *Stratheden* completed only four cruises, and cruises operated by *Reina del Mar* and *Empress of England* included the New York Trade Fair and the 1964 Tokyo Olympics. The *Empress of Britain* was withdrawn in 1964 and the Travel Savings Association collapsed the following year. *Empress of England* was sold to the Shaw, Savill & Albion Line in 1970 and, renamed *Ocean Monarch*, received a £2 million upgrade and conversion by Cammell Laird at Birkenhead. However, she also

Ocean Monarch in dry dock at Cammell Laird's yard, Birkenhead.

suffered mechanical problems and was withdrawn and sold to be broken up in 1974.

Max Wilson had written about his pioneering ideas of sea travel in 1962, claiming, 'Everyone in this country, and others with long-standing ties with Britain, is a potential sea traveller. If the shipping lines are not getting these travellers it is largely their own fault.' He claimed that the fundamental weakness at the time was the care of the passenger, particularly in the provision of good standards of food and services and a variety of entertainment. He felt that many shipping people regarded a sea voyage as little more than the transport of passengers and this was the wrong attitude as a voyage on a ship should be regarded as:

> a holiday in itself or the beginning of a holiday, even if the primary purpose of a passenger is to travel from one destination to another then the ship-owner must devote his energy and imagination into making it a holiday. There are still those diehards in the industry who regard passengers as a necessary evil.

Wilson felt that entertainment was one of the most important issues on cruise ships. He conducted interviews with 200 people, who told him that they found much of the voyage dull and boring, and at times they did not know what to do with themselves. During his initial charters of passenger ships he had a special cabaret and band flown out from Britain to entertain the passengers. He employed calypso singers during cocktail hour and even arranged to fly out a different cabaret at the last port of call before Southampton so that passengers had a change in entertainment for the last three days of the voyage. He also organised large prizes to encourage passengers to take part in fancy-dress competitions and other activities. He recognised that:

Another vital part of a sea voyage is food. I doubt if it is necessary to give elaborate meals and menus. What the average passenger wants is good food, well cooked and attractively presented. There is room for much thought. Why not a charcoal grill on deck, with steak and salad only. Against tropical skies, and with skilful lighting effects and atmosphere, it could be most attractive and could easily be done.

Wilson thought that the standard of service provided was equally important as 'the airlines go to a great deal of trouble to choose the right stewards and stewardesses, and train them to look after passengers really well'. He thought that the standard of civility, from pursers to cabin boys, 'left a lot to be desired, and that complaints should be taken more seriously and used in a positive way to train future staff'. The shipping lines 'should be prepared to introduce stewards and stewardesses from any part of the world who will give their passengers a better service. If the British seaman does not wish to compete, then he must find other work.'

Wilson also looked at the management and planning aspects of cruising and felt that:

Shipping lines could do very much more in the field of sales and promotion. Ports of call should be as interesting as possible and should be varied from one voyage to another. No shipping company, so far as I am concerned, has really gone out of its way to create new traffic. It is high time they did to regain some of the traffic they have lost to the airlines. However, the price should be right and there is no reason why a fortnight's holiday on a ship should cost more than a good holiday ashore.

The lack of imagination and enterprise was the main reason for the failure to create new traffic, according to Wilson, 'not only in the shipping companies, but in the travel agencies that serve them'. He felt the key was to find out what the public want and:

when a shipping company can get its passengers to their destination feeling that they have had a wonderful time, that it has been just what they wanted, and that they don't want to get off … then passenger ship problems will be largely solved.

The scheme was successful initially but the Association had difficulty in maintaining bookings over a twelve-month period. An attempt was made to operate cruises from South Africa with *Reina del Mar*, but this proved unsuccessful and the organisation failed.

Empress of Britain was sold to Greek interests in 1964 following reduced profits and declining passenger figures. Canadian Pacific (Bermuda) Limited, Hamilton, Bermuda, was formed to operate a fleet of bulk carriers and tankers. *Beaveroak* was delivered for the Great Lakes service in 1965, and the London landing rights of CP Air were transferred to Air Canada. A decision was made by Canadian Pacific in 1966 to build or acquire ships for long-term charter to other companies. *Lord Mount Stephen* and *Lord Strathcona* were built for this purpose. *Trailer Princess* entered service across Schwartz Bay, Vancouver.

Mr Frank E. Wolff, European general manager of Canadian Pacific, said in 1967 that Liverpool would continue to be the prime centre for their passenger liner operations. In terms of passengers and cargo, it was their wish that Liverpool should become increasingly known throughout Europe as the major gateway to Canada. Canadian Pacific, he said, had long historical ties with Liverpool. Although they were a Canadian company, the 'Empress' liners were British registered and had always been operated by British seamen. He knew of no finer personnel to run them.

6

A NEW LIVERY

IN 1968, A NEW CANADIAN Pacific livery was introduced with a circle and incut triangle representing the letter 'C'. The ships were rebranded as CP Ships and this was painted on their hulls. *H.R. MacMillan*, *J.V. Clyne* and *N.R. Crump* were placed on wet charter to MacMillan Bloedel. *Pacific Logger* was placed on a ten-year charter and *T. Akasaka* and *W.C. Van Horne* were delivered. *Port Hawkesbury*, *T.G. Shaughnessy* and *I.D. Sinclair* were built for charter. It was during this period that containerisation was becoming popular and a consortium of major shipping companies joined together to meet the high capital investment required in building and operating an innovative fleet of container vessels. CP *Voyageur* introduced a new weekly container service from Europe to Canada in 1970 and was followed by CP *Trader* and CP *Discoverer*. *Beaveroak* was renamed CP *Ambassador* and *Beaverpine* became CP *Explorer*.

It was announced in 1968 that the familiar red and white chequered flag on the yellow funnel would disappear and would be replaced by a new symbol: a triangle, a segment of a circle and a portion of a square. The new funnel colour would be green, with the remainder of the device in white. The company said that the triangle was intended to suggest motion or direction, the circle represented global activities and the square stability. At the same time, the ship-owning company would cease to be known as Canadian Pacific Steamships and would be known as CP Ships, and each vessel would bear the legend on their sides. The new symbol was to be applied to all the different divisions of the Canadian Pacific organisation, a different colour being used for each division. CP Rail would feature the symbol in red, CP Air in orange, CP Ships in green, CP Transport and CP Express in blue,

CP Hotels in grey, and CP Telecommunications in ochre. In reply to the criticism of the new colours, John D. MacGregor, Canadian Pacific public relations representative, said:

> it would be a pity if people were left with the impression that our company has just slapped a new coat of paint in strange colours over our two ocean liners and left it at that. This has not been just an isolated 'paint job'. The entire Canadian Pacific transportation complex is undergoing a profound change to draw together under a unique symbol all the diverse entities that make up the whole. This major change affects not only our liners, but the cargo fleet, international airline, railway system, hotels, trucking and express operations and telecommunications. The purpose is to bring a clear and identifiable picture for all to see of the scope of the company's worldwide activities. In the context of the company's total operation, both the flagship and the *Empress of England* can now be seen, not in isolation, but as an integral part of the world's most complete transportation system.

Canadian Pacific purchased ten bush airlines in the early 1940s, and acquired Canadian Airways in 1942, to form Canadian Pacific Air Lines. In 1968, the airline was rebranded as CP Air to align the airline's name to that of its other subsidiaries, including CP Hotels, CP Ships and CP Transport. It was denied international and transcontinental routes, which were operated by the government-owned and -financed Trans-Canada Air Lines. However, the 'great circle' or 'polar' route was operated from CP Air's Vancouver base, and this became a cornerstone of the airline. Flights to Amsterdam, Australia, Hong Kong and Shanghai were secured, and the airline's revenue grew from $3 million

Empress of Canada (3) in the River Mersey.

Swedish Lloyd's *Kungsholm* and *Empress of Canada* (3) at Liverpool.

CPR CF-CZE3CP Douglas DC-6 aircraft.

in 1942 to $61 million by 1964. Flights were operated to Sydney via Honolulu, Kanton Island and Fiji, as well as to Hong Kong via Tokyo from 1949, with Canadair North Star aircraft, a version of the DC-4. Flights to Lima, Peru, started in 1953, Amsterdam in 1955, and Buenos Aires in 1956.

Although they were not allowed scheduled routes to certain European countries, they were permitted to fly to countries that Trans-Canada Airlines / Air Canada did not wish to serve, and routes were developed to Amsterdam, Milan, Rome, Athens, and several other international destinations. Charter flights were operated in the mid-1960s, and the 1970s and 1980s to Britain, France, Germany, and some other European countries. In 1979, the federal government eliminated the fixed market share of transcontinental flights for Air Canada, and CP Air was able to upgrade its fleet to enable it to expand its services. The cost of this massive fleet renewal was estimated at around $1 billion, and this debt, along with increased competition and economic downturn in Asia, would later work against the airline's future. In 1986, the airline reverted to its original name, Canadian

Pacific Air Lines, with a new navy-blue colour scheme and logo. Less than a year later, Canadian Pacific Air Lines was sold, along with Quebec's Nordair, to Calgary-based Pacific Western Airlines (PWA) for $300 million. PWA assumed the airline's debt of $600 million and announced that the new merged airline would be named Canadian Airlines International. In 2000, Canadian Airlines was taken over by and merged into Air Canada.

A move to take the company into the container age took a step forward in 1968 with the placing of an order by CP Ships for three specially designed 14,000-ton container ships. The order, worth £8 million, was placed with Cammell Laird & Company, Birkenhead, and was won against strong competition from Scandinavia, Germany, Holland, Japan and two other United Kingdom shipyards. The company issued a statement saying that the new vessels were likely to operate from London and Rotterdam to Quebec. They also stated that there was no intention to relinquish their long-established 'break-bulk' service from Liverpool. The new container ships would have an operational speed of 20 knots, which would cut up to a week off traditional cargo time, and each ship would carry 700 containers. The company would invite tenders for containers worth between £2 million and £3 million for the three ships. The container service would begin in April 1969, with the company chartering two container ships until the new vessels were delivered. The company also announced that CP Rail and CP Express would spend $5 million in purchasing rail container cars and installing handling facilities and tracks at Quebec City. The Canadian land portion of the service provided an integrated resource, with one company handling containers by rail and road from the ship's side to and from points in the Maritime Provinces, Ontario and Quebec, the United States Midwest and Western Canada. The plan was part of the company's land bridge concept, which saw Canada being used as a rail link for containers moving between Europe and the Orient within five to eight years.

The Boeing 747 aircraft's first flight took place on 9 February 1970, and its introduction forever changed the way people travelled around the world. The aircraft was a major factor in the demise of passenger liner services in the 1960s and 1970s. Together with the development of containerisation, the Boeing 747 brought about a dramatic change in the pattern of passenger and cargo services provided by shipping operators. It was two and a half times larger than the Boeing 707 and operated as a passenger or a freight-carrying aircraft. The 747-400 has a range of 7,260 nautical miles and can carry up to 660 passengers.

Air travel became increasingly popular in the 1960s with the introduction of the Boeing 707 and the Douglas DC-8. It was Pan American Airways who envisaged an aircraft twice the size of these and Boeing were asked to come up with a design for this mammoth carrier. It was thought at the time that this design may have a short shelf life as it would soon be superseded by supersonic aircraft. It was important that the new aircraft could be easily adapted to carry freight when required.

The contract for the first 747 was signed by Pan American and Boeing in April 1966, and consequently, Pan Am had a greater influence in the design of the new aircraft. It was fitted with a revolutionary high-bypass turbofan engine, which was developed by Boeing, Pan American and Pratt & Whitney. The aircraft was built at a new plant near Seattle and the first flight took place on 9 February 1969, with test pilots Jack Waddell and Brien Wygle in command. Following a display at the Paris Air Show in 1969, the 747 received its FAA airworthiness certificate in December that year. It entered service on 22 January 1970 on Pan

American's New York–London service. This was followed by orders received from all of the major airlines. However, during the recession of the early 1970s, Boeing sold few of the aircraft, and some airlines converted them to freight carriers and used smaller aircraft for passenger services. As economic conditions improved, orders for the aircraft resumed, and it was further developed and improved by the manufacturer.

As the advantages of air travel became apparent to the traveller it was becoming clear to the shipping lines that the airlines were making considerable inroads into their passenger traffic. The final nail in the coffin for many British passenger ships was the four-fold increase in fuel cost that took place in 1973–74. Many of the ships were relatively old and soon became uneconomic to operate. The results of the National Seamen's Strike of 1966 had burdened the shipping operators with additional crew wages, there was a decline in demand, and other costs were also rising in the early 1970s.

The name of the company was changed to Canadian Pacific Limited on 3 July 1971, and it was decided to end the Atlantic passenger service at the end of the summer season that year. Ted Arison had been involved as operator/manager of the Norwegian Cruise Line (NCL) through Arison Shipping until NCL decided to take over the control. Arison decided to develop the cruising business and formed Carnival Cruise Lines in 1972. He was initially interested in the two laid-up Cunard passenger vessels *Carmania* and *Franconia*. However, he could not agree on terms with Cunard, and visited the *Empress of Canada* at Tilbury. He immediately saw the potential in the ship and purchased her. *Empress of Canada* sailed from Tilbury on 25 February 1972 to Miami, and was renamed *Mardi Gras*. The new company retained most of the funnel detail of the *Empress*, although the green sections of the funnel mark were repainted in red and blue. Canadian Pacific objected to this but following minor adjustments, the issue was resolved. She was billed as 'the largest cruise ship sailing out of Miami' but unfortunately ran aground on a sandbank on her first cruise. After being refloated she continued her maiden voyage from the port. The local press reported that the company took money from her casino to pay a fuel bill early in her career. The former Mayfair Room on the Promenade Deck was renamed the Showboat Club Casino, and the Banff Club on the Empress Deck became the After Discotheque. A temporary pool was fitted in one of her aft cargo hatches and the derricks and booms were removed. A bow thruster was later fitted to increase manoeuvrability when arriving and sailing from ports, following the installation of a

R.A. Emerson.

Fort Assiniboine.

unit on the *Festivale*. In 1975, *Mardi Gras* was joined by her former fleet mate *Empress of Britain*, which was renamed *Carnivale*, and soon became very popular operating cruises in the Caribbean.

The oil product carriers *G.A. Walker*, *W.A. Mather* and *R.A. Emerson* were delivered, and *Carrier Princess* was introduced. Incan Marine Limited was formed by Canadian Pacific and Inchcape (Canada) Limited. This was followed by a joint venture with CP Ships and Incan Marine Limited. The ore-bulk-oil (OBO) vessels *E.W. Beatty*, *D.C. Coleman* and *W.M. Neal* were delivered in 1973. It was announced in 1974 that as a result of an agreement between Manchester Liners Limited and Canadian Pacific, the latter would be basing their transatlantic container service wholly at Tilbury, and the service which operated from Liverpool jointly with the Head and Donaldson lines was to be withdrawn. Manchester Liners would be serving shippers from the north of England with their regular container service to Canadian ports from Manchester. The change was brought about by

the sale of CP *Explorer*. *Fort Macleod* was delivered in 1974, and *Incan Superior* inaugurated a service from McKellar Island, Thunder Bay, Ontario, to Superior, Wisconsin. The main cargo was newsprint and wood pulp from the Great Lakes Paper Company of Thunder Bay. *Fort Nelson* was followed by *Leda*, which was registered as *Fort St John*, and she eventually became *Fort Nanaimo*. *Port Vancouver* and *Port Quebec* were delivered in 1977 and placed on short-term charter. The following year, *Fort Walsh*, *Fort Carleton* and *Fort Hamilton* were delivered to the company. In 1980, three second-hand bulk carriers, *Fort Fraser*, *Fort Douglas* and *Fort Erie*, were purchased, and four chemical tankers were ordered from the Sanoyasu Dockyard. They emerged as *Fort Assiniboine*, *Fort Garry*, *Fort Rouge* and *Fort Toronto*. *E.R. Brussel* was chartered, becoming CP *Hunter*, and the following year, *Dart Atlantic* was chartered and renamed CP *Ambassador*. *Fort Providence*, *Fort Resolution*, *Fort Dufferin* and *Fort Frontenac* were delivered to the company in 1982–83. A loss of £74,293 was reported in 1983.

Canadian Pacific cruises.

Empress of Scotland (2).

Empress of France (2).

Empress of Scotland (2) advertisement.

Empress of France (2).

Empress of France (2).

Passengers relax on an Atlantic passage on *Empress of France* (2).

Empress of France (2) bell.

A crew member at work painting the *Empress of France* (2) on an Atlantic crossing.

Canadian Pacific

MAIDEN VOYAGE
EMPRESS OF CANADA

LIVERPOOL - QUEBEC & MONTREAL · MONDAY, APRIL 24, 1961

Receiving Cargo April 15 - April 20.
Loading Berth—North No. 1 Gladstone Dock, Liverpool.

SUPERB PASSENGER ACCOMMODATION—FULLY AIR-CONDITIONED—
FIRST CLASS AND TOURIST. SHIPPERS' ENQUIRIES DIRECT OR THROUGH
THEIR USUAL AGENTS, WILL RECEIVE IMMEDIATE ATTENTION

FAST SERVICE: This vessel is scheduled to maintain a six days' passage between
Liverpool and Montreal.

THROUGH BILLS OF LADING: Through Bills of Lading are issued to inland
destinations in Canada and U.S.A.

CANADIAN PACIFIC EXPRESS: Merchandise, samples, livestock and valuables sent
by Express Service to all parts of Canada and U.S.A.

Goods are received for shipment only subject to the terms and
conditions of the Company's usual form of Wharfinger's receipt
and/or Bill of Lading.

For rates and information apply:—

CANADIAN PACIFIC RAILWAY CO.
Royal Liver Building, Liverpool, or any other
Canadian Pacific Office, a list of which is overleaf.

Subject to change without notice

Sailing list for the maiden voyage of *Empress of Canada* (3).

Liverpool pier head and landing stage.

Empress of England prepares to sail from Liverpool.

Canadian Pacific

LIVERPOOL TO MONTREAL Via QUEBEC

Through Bills of Lading to inland destinations in Canada and the United States

Receiving Dates

RAMORE HEAD (Montreal only)	Mar. 22 —	Mar. 29
*EMPRESS OF BRITAIN	Apr. 1 —	Apr. 5
RATHLIN HEAD (Montreal only)	Apr. 8 —	Apr. 10
*EMPRESS OF ENGLAND	Apr. 11 —	Apr. 19
*EMPRESS OF BRITAIN	Apr. 22 —	Apr. 26

* Via Greenock

LIVERPOOL TO TORONTO, HAMILTON, DETROIT, (and other Lakes Ports if inducement)

HERMANN SCHULTE	Mar. 22 —	Mar. 28
RATHLIN HEAD (Toronto and Hamilton only)	Apr. 4 —	Apr. 10
MARIA ANNA SCHULTE	Apr. 18 —	Apr. 23

Loading Berth : North No. I Gladstone Dock

TO AVOID DELAY IN LOADING, shippers are advised to deliver their cargo as early as possible within the receiving date period, and to avoid the risk of short shipment, Customs Pre-Entry papers should be lodged either in advance of, or at the latest with, the goods at time of delivery at loading berth.

BILLS OF LADING must be presented by Shippers or agents not later than the day after closing.

INSURANCE at low rates.

GOODS ARE RECEIVED for shipment only subject to the terms and conditions of the Company's usual form of Wharfinger's Receipt and/or Bill of Lading.

CARGO OF HAZARDOUS NATURE can be accepted only by special agreement.

CANADIAN PACIFIC EXPRESS. Merchandise, samples, livestock and valuables sent by Express Service to all parts of Canada and the United States. When travelling, carry Canadian Pacific Express Travellers' Cheques.

Also Regular Service from London, Antwerp, Hamburg, Havre, etc.

For rates and other information apply:—

CANADIAN PACIFIC RAILWAY COMPANY
Royal Liver Building, Liverpool
Telephone: Central 5690
or to any other Canadian Pacific Office, a list of which is overleaf.
Subject to change without notice.

L.142 March 18th, 1963

Empress of Canada (3) in Gladstone Dock, Liverpool.

1963 sailing list.

Empress of Britain (3) in Canada Dry Dock at Liverpool.

Empress of Canada (3) in the same dry dock.

Empress of England at Liverpool.

Empress of England becomes *Ocean Monarch* in Canada Dock, Liverpool.

Queen Anna Maria.

Empress of England in the new livery at Liverpool landing stage, preparing to sail to Canada.

CP *Voyageur.*

Mardi Gras.

Carnivale.

Lake Champlain.

Montcalm.

Hanseatic.

Carnivale.

Olympic.

Topaz.

Topaz as the Peaceboat.

Alexandra tugs assist *Empress of England* to the berth at Liverpool landing stage.

Ocean Monarch.

Mardi Gras.

Apollon.

Beaverpine.

Beaverpine.

Andes Discoverer.

Andes Trader.

Lord Mount Stephen.

H.R. MacMillan.

D.C. Coleman.

Princess Charlotte.

C. P. R. CO. S. S. PRINCESS MAY, WRECKED ON
SENTINEL ISLAND, ALASKA, AUG. 5. 1910.

Princess May.

Princess Louise.

Princess Marguerite (2).

Princess Patricia (2).

Princess Patricia (2).

Sicamous.

Princess of Acadia.

Assiniboia.

Clockwise from top left:

Cast Bear.

Cast Lynx.

Cast Wolf.

ACQUISITIONS AND JOINT VENTURES

IN 1981, CP SHIPS ACQUIRED a one-third share of the Dart Container Line, a consortium formed in 1970 by Bristol City Line, Bibby Brothers, Compagnie Maritime Belge (CMB), and Clarke Traffic Services of Montreal. *Dart Atlantic*, *Dart America* and *Dart Europe* were later joined by *Dart Canada* from C.Y. Tung of Hong Kong. *Dart America* was later renamed *Manchester Challenge*, *Dart Atlantic* became CP *Ambassador* and *Dart Canada* was renamed *Canadian Explorer*.

In 1984, Canadian Pacific managed thirty-two bulk and oil carriers; Canadian Pacific Bulkship Services Limited operated three for Centennial Shipping. They were *Andes Trader* (ex-CP *Trader*), *Andes Voyageur* (ex-CP *Voyageur*) and, for the Dart Consortium, *Dart Atlantica*. Canadian Pacific Limited managed *Carrier Princess*, *Trailer Princess* and *Princess Patricia*. Canadian Pacific Steamships Limited owned five 'Forts' and CP *Ambassador*, *Dart Americana* and *Andes Discoverer* (ex-CP *Discoverer*). The company entered into a joint venture with Compagnie Maritime Belge in 1984, and Canada Maritime was formed to secure the North Atlantic container traffic for the Port of Montreal. *Canmar Ambassador* and *Canmar Europe* operated with *Manchester Challenge* and *Canadian Explorer*, from C.Y. Tung. Canadian Pacific bought out its partner in 1993 and merged it with CP Ships.

Canada Maritime was converted into a clay and paper carrier and was renamed *Repap Enterprise* for the Liberian Ozmillion Shipping Corporation of Monrovia in 1986. In 1988, Canadian Pacific (Bermuda) Limited sold its bulk carrier fleet for US$149.1 million to B&H Bulkships Corporation, who were a subsidiary of Bergvall & Hudner, Bermuda. It was reported that Canadian Pacific (Bermuda) Limited made a profit of over US$100 million on the deal. Canadian

Pacific (Bermuda) retained its six speciality tankers, which carried caustic soda, chemicals and vegetable oils, and one roll-on roll-off (ro-ro) vessel. The tankers were then moved to a new division, Canadian Pacific Tankers Limited. The Belgian-operated container ships *Sea Falcon* and *Sea Pride* were acquired by Canadian Pacific in 1993. They had been operated by CMB Transport SA, of Antwerp, and had both been built in 1979. It was reported that they cost $7.5 million each. The Cast Group entered bankruptcy and were taken over by CP Ships in April 1985, who then bought Lykes Lines out of bankruptcy in 1997.

Canadian National's hotel chain was purchased by the company in 1988, making Canadian Pacific Hotels and Resorts (CP Hotels) the nation's largest hotel owner. The Delta Hotels chain and the international Princess Hotels chain were purchased in 1998, and the following year, the San Francisco-based Fairmont Hotels and Resorts chain was acquired, giving the company control of The Plaza in New York City. In April 1999, Canadian Pacific Hotels & Resorts announced that it was teaming up with Kingdom Hotels (USA) Limited and Maritz Wolff & Company to form Fairmont Hotel Management, with Canadian Pacific having a 67 per cent share in the company. On 30 January 2006, Fairmont agreed to be acquired by a venture of Kingdom Hotels International and Colony Capital, which own the Raffles and Swissôtel chains.

Contship Containerlines was acquired in 1997, and the Australia-New Zealand Direct Line (ANZDL) in December 1998. This line was owned by SCAC-Delmas-Vieijeux of France and Brierley Investments of New Zealand. The deal included ANZDL's container shipping services and brand name in two regional trades – the United States

Château Lake Louise.

West Coast/Australia and New Zealand and Trans-Tasman. Included in the deal were the company's organisation, chartered ships and containers. ANZDL became part of CP Ships and built on the Australian regional platform that was created when the company acquired Contship Containerlines. ANZDL and their predecessors have been serving the Australian/New Zealand trade for many years and became part of Delmas in 1988. They were merged with Brierley's Australian shipping interests in 1997. The ANZDL fleet comprises seven chartered container ships and two chartered ro-ro vessels. The chief executive of CP Ships stated that the company now led the field in three key regional markets: the North Atlantic, Latin America and Australia. Ivaran Lines was acquired in May 1998, 50 per cent of TMM Lines in January 1999, and 50 per cent in January 2000. Americana Ships was formed in 1999 and consisted of Lykes Lines, Ivaran

Lines and Contship Med-Gulf, plus the participation of TMM in Transportation Maritima Grancolombiana, Compañía Transatlántica, Española (Transatlantic Company of Spain, CTE) and the economic interest in TMM's Pacific joint venture with APL. Each separate company operated under their own brand name. They also purchased Christensen Canadian African Lines in August 2000 and the Italia Line in August 2002. In 2001, the company was the seventh largest carrier in the world, and dominated the North Atlantic.

In 2003, the company had revenue of $3.13 billion as one of the world's leading container shipping companies, offering customers door-to-door as well as port-to-port containerised services for the international transportation of a broad range of industrial and consumer goods, including raw materials, semi-manufactured and finished goods. They operated a fleet of eighty vessels (sixty container ships and twenty on charter) in twenty-two trade lanes, focusing on four principal markets. Ships were registered under each individual company until 2005, when they were renamed with CP names. In 2003, the company transported 2.2 million 20ft equivalent units (teu), the standard measure of volume in the industry, on behalf of approximately 23,700 customers. Based on standing capacity, CP Ships ranked as the eleventh largest carrier in the world, giving it the economics of scale available to global carriers. CP Ships was proud of its role as a regional specialist, offering direct services to a wider range of ports within a particular market than is generally offered by global carriers. This allowed the company to provide customers with the local expertise and market presence of a regional specialist combined with many of the operating advantages of a global carrier. Scheduled services were provided in its four principal markets: Transatlantic, Australasia, Latin America and Asia, which it served through seven brands – Canada Maritime, Cast, Contship Containerlines, ANZDL, Lykes Lines, TMM Lines and Italia Line.

CP Ships operated in an industry whose annual volume growth had on average exceeded global gross domestic product growth by two or three times over the previous twenty years. Since its introduction in the 1950s, the container shipping industry facilitated world trade because of its simplicity, efficiency and low cost, and became an integral part of the global sourcing strategies for many of the world's major manufacturers and retailers. CP Ships claimed that it outperformed, on the basis of return on capital employed, in both weak and strong market conditions due to its business model, which was based on its competitive strengths and strategy.

The business model was based on six principles. There was a concentration on container shipping, which allowed the management to focus, plan for and quickly respond to often rapidly changing economic, political and trade conditions in a truly international business. The company built strong positions in a number of regional markets and became the leading carrier in the majority of its core trade lanes, which allowed it to offer the best schedules and services to its customers and maximise trade lane economics of scale. Since 1993, nine acquisitions had been executed and integrated successfully, often involving the turnaround of under-performing businesses. CP Ships' revenue in 2003 was seven times larger than in 1994. The company predicted that in a relatively fragmented and cyclical industry, there would likely be further acquisition opportunities, and expected to continue to pursue a disciplined acquisition strategy, enabling it either to grow in its existing markets or to carefully expand into new markets, thereby helping it to achieve further economies of scale to improve operating performance.

The company intended to selectively and modestly develop logistics services. In April 2004, CP Ships completed the acquisition of Montreal-based ROE Logistics, a family-owned business specialising in providing a range of freight forwarding, customs brokerage, logistics, warehouse and distribution services. CP Ships offered two or more of its well-recognised brands in nearly all of its trade lanes and expected to respond to the evolving needs of its customers by selectively expanding its services, improving service frequencies and transit time as well as the efficiency of its inland transportation networks, and implementing effective training and staff retention programmes. The company also recognised that integrated door-to-door or intermodal container transportation was the largest component in the logistics supply chains of international trade. CP Ships emphasised consistently reliable, tailor-made intermodal supply-chain solutions for its customers to strengthen customer relationships and protect operating margins. Between 1996 and 2003, it reduced its cost per teu by 14 per cent, to help deliver a low-cost, high-quality service in the highly competitive container shipping industry.

On 1 January 2004, CP Ships operated in the following trade lanes of its principal markets under the following brand names:

Principal Market	Services	Trade Lanes	Brands
Transatlantic	12	US/Canada via Montreal–North Europe	Canada Maritime, Cast
		US/Canada via Montreal–Mediterranean	Canada Maritime, Cast
		West Coast North America–Mediterranean	Lykes Lines, TMM Lines, Contship Containerlines, Italia Line
		US East Coast–North Europe	Lykes Lines, TMM Lines
		Gulf–North Europe	Lykes Lines, TMM Lines
		Gulf–Mediterranean	Lykes Lines, TMM Lines, Contship Containerlines, Italia Line
Australasia	6	Europe and US East Coast–Australasia	Contship Containerlines, ANZDL, Lykes Lines
		US West Coast–Australasia	ANZDL, Contship Containerlines
		Trans-Tasman	ANZDL, Contship Containerlines
Latin America	10	North Europe–East Coast South America	Lykes Lines, TMM Lines, Contship Containerlines
		Mediterranean–East Coast South America	Lykes Lines, Contship Containerlines, Italia Line
		US East Coast–East Coast South America	Lykes Lines, TMM Lines
		Gulf–East Coast South America	Lykes Lines, TMM Lines
		Gulf–Caribbean	Lykes Lines, TMM Lines
		Mexico–Central America–West Coast	Lykes Lines, TMM Lines, Italia Line
South America	5	Mediterranean–West Coast South America	Lykes Lines, TMM Lines
		Panama–West Coast South America	Lykes Lines, TMM Lines, Italia Line
Asia	5	Asia–Americas	Lykes Lines, TMM Lines, Canada
		Europe–India/Pakistan	Contship Containerlines
		US East Coast–India	Contship Containerlines, Lykes Lines

In addition to its four principal markets, CP Ships also operated in the North America–West/South Africa trade lane and provided a small break-bulk service for Asia–Latin America–Caribbean, both under the Lykes Lines and TMM Lines brands.

In 2003, 53 per cent of CP Ships' volume was in the Transatlantic market, where it provided services under the Canada Maritime, Cast, Contship Containerlines, Italia Line, Lykes Lines and TMM Lines brands. Through efficient links to an extensive transportation network in North America, Mexico and Europe, the company provided its customers with the choice of seamless door-to-door services as well as port-to-port service options. Within the Transatlantic market, CP Ships was the leader in the United States/Canada via Montreal–North Europe and the United States/Canada via Montreal–Mediterranean trade lanes, with five weekly services, using a fleet of owned ice-strengthened container ships that were designed to operate throughout the year. Two ice-strengthened newbuilds were introduced in the second half of 2003 in the Montreal–North Europe trade lane. The consequent cascading of ships that took place within the services, including the Montreal–Mediterranean trade lanes, served to modernise, upgrade and improve each of the five weekly services.

CP Ships operated six services in the trade lanes in the Australasian market through its Contship Containerlines, ANZDL and Lykes Lines brands. The Australasian market accounted for 14 per cent of CP Ships' volume in 2003 and the company was a leader in the trade lanes. In cooperation with P&O Nedlloyd, CMA-CGM, Hamburg Süd, Hapag-Lloyd and Marfret, the services in the Europe–Australasian and round-the-world trade lanes were restructured. The Latin American market accounted for 11 per cent of volume in 2003, with ten services in eight trade lanes. The North American services were marketed under the Lykes Lines and TMM Lines brands, and the European services under the Lykes Lines, TMM Lines, Italia Line and Contship Containerlines brands. Lykes Lines and TMM Lines also marketed services in the Asia–Americas trade lane as well as the Gulf–North Europe and Gulf–Mediterranean services included in the Transatlantic market, all of which called at Mexican ports.

The Asian market accounted for 21 per cent of CP Ships' volume in 2003, and its presence in Asia was established with the acquisition of Contship Containerlines in 1997, and expanded with the formation of the Americana Ships joint venture in January 1999. Three services were operated in the Asia–Americas trade lanes: one service between Asia and the West Coast North America and Mexico, one between Asia and the West Coast North America, Mexico and West Coast South America, and a fixed-day weekly service between North East Asia, including China, and Vancouver, deploying five ships. In 2004, a new service was announced to complement the existing Asia–Vancouver service to strengthen the market presence in the Asia–Americas trade lane, where trade growth remained strong.

On the Europe–Indian subcontinent trade lane, CP Ships co-operated with P&O Nedlloyd and CMA-CGM, providing two of the seven vessels deployed in a fixed-day weekly service. Hapag-Lloyd and Hamburg Süd also participated in the service through means of slot charter arrangements. Safmarine withdrew from service in July 2003, but sustained growth in the Indian economy allowed the remaining members of the agreement to absorb the capacity vacated by Safmarine. The service scope covered Europe, Red Sea, Arabian Gulf, Pakistan and India. Other markets comprised approximately 1 per cent of CP Ships' 2003/2004 volumes. Lykes Lines operated a roll-on roll-off service between North America and West/South Africa, with vessels designed to handle cargo that is driven on and off the ship, as well as containers.

In nearly all of its trade lanes, CP Ships participated in joint services with other container shipping companies by either contributing ships to a joint service agreement or entering into slot charters. The company preferred to contribute owned or chartered ships into a joint service agreement where the economic benefits justified the capital investment. In the United States/Canada via Montreal–North Europe trade lane, CP Ships operated two services in partnership with Orient Overseas Container Line (OOCL) under the St Lawrence Co-ordinated Service, which was established in 1981. Canada Maritime provided four ships and OOCL provided two ships. In December 2002, CP Ships and OOCL agreed to charter a fixed number of slots to members of the Canex consortium: Maersk Sealand, Mediterranean Shipping Company and P&O Nedlloyd. The two-year agreement took effect from January 2003, and at the same time, Canex moved its existing service to CP Ships Montreal Gateway Terminals. From October 2000, the Lykes Lines and TMM Lines operated two joint weekly services in the United States East Coast–North Europe trade lane and three joint weekly services in the Gulf–North Europe trade lane with the Grand Alliance partners P&O Nedlloyd, Nippon Yusen Kaisha, OOCL and Hapag-Lloyd. CP Ships contributed nine of the thirty-one ships deployed in this agreement.

In 2003–04, CP Ships cooperated with P&O Nedlloyd, CMA-CGM, Hamburg Süd, Hapag-Lloyd and Marfret to restructure the services within the Europe–Australasia and Ocean Star round-the-world trade lanes. The trade lanes between the Indian subcontinent and Europe and the Indian subcontinent and the United States East Coast were governed by Joint Service Agreements. The service to Europe was operated in conjunction with CMA-CGM and P&O Nedlloyd, and slots were also agreed with Hapag-Lloyd and Hamburg Süd. In this period, the company restructured and rationalised its operations in many trade lanes, most frequently by combining with other carriers a larger number of independent services into jointly operated routes. This rationalised operations, and enhanced service on the trade lanes by increasing frequency, expanding port calls, improving reliability and reducing costs.

During 2003–04, CP Ships completed its $800 million ship replacement programme, commenced in 1999, to replace a number of its chartered ships, building ten new ships and entering into long-term charter arrangements on a further six new ships. It followed the integration of various acquisitions during the 1990s and a comprehensive review of its ship fleet requirements, and took into account three key factors. Firstly, CP Ships believed that it could reduce its costs over the medium to long term by owning ships rather than chartering them. Secondly, a higher proportion of owned ships would reduce its exposure to volatility in operating costs from the charter market and therefore improve the stability of CP Ships' expenses. Thirdly, it may be difficult to charter ships with optimum characteristics for certain trade lanes at the time they were needed.

The twenty-three replacement ships were medium sized, from 2,100 to 4,100 teu, which the company believed to be the optimal size range for operations in regional markets. Each of the new ships was specifically designed for the trade in which it was intended to operate. Three, which operated in the Australasian trades, had the capacity to carry a significant number of refrigerated containers for temperature-sensitive cargo, two were ice-strengthened to operate into Montreal, and the remaining five were geared, enabling them to operate in Latin American and other ports without shoreside cranes. The replacement programme resulted in the percentage of CP Ships' owned fleet capacity, including long-term charters, increasing from 28 per cent as of 30 June 2000 to 68 per cent at the end of 2003. The average age of the owned fleet decreased from 12.6 years at the beginning of 2000, to just under 8 years at the end of 2003. The estimated useful life of a container ship was around 25 years. CP Ships reached an agreement during August 2003 to charter from Seaspan Container Lines, for a period of up to twelve years, a further nine 4,250 teu container ships to be built and delivered from the end of 2005 to mid-2007. The charter cost for these nine ships, constructed by Samsung Heavy Industries of Korea, was estimated to be close to CP Ships' equivalent cost of ownership, including financing.

On 1 January 2004, 34 per cent of CP Ships' container fleet was held under capital leases or sale and leaseback arrangements. CP Ships believed that owning containers was generally less expensive than hiring them under short-term leases. However, short-term leases provided CP Ships with the ability to reduce or otherwise adjust its container fleet in response to changing trade conditions or container imbalances in specific trade lanes. The company's objective was to increase over time the proportion of owned and long-term leased containers in its fleet, although they did not have any commitments at the time to purchase containers. CP Ships achieved significant efficiencies and cost savings by combining the management of various decentralised services, including container fleet, inland transport, marine operations, marine terminals, administration, information systems and insurance and risk management. The company were also looking at transferring processing activities from both Europe and the United States to India, and further consolidation of facilities in Europe and the United Kingdom.

On 25 March 2004, CP Ships and certain of its subsidiaries entered into a $525 million secured revolving credit facility with a syndicate of financial institutions represented by ING Bank NV, as agent and security trustee. The $525 million facility replaced CP Ships' previous $175 million and $350 million revolving credit facilities, which were cancelled. The facility had a five-year term, expiring in March 2009. Borrowing under the facility was by subsidiaries of CP Ships and was secured by twenty-five owned ships, and guaranteed by CP Ships, Lykes LLC, TMM LLC and CP Ships (UK).

In 2003, Contship Containerlines won Shipping Line of the Year, and Lykes Lines was a finalist. ANZDL and Cast both won Logistics Management Quest for Quality Awards. Cast also won SC Johnson's Carrier of the Year Award and was named as a Star Performer in the Lloyd's Loading List annual North Atlantic trade analysis. Lykes Lines was named Best Carrier to Africa by the Canadian International Freight Forwarders Association; Canada Maritime won three awards – Best European, Best Mediterranean and Best Overall Carrier, for the third time in a row. It also won the Ocean Carrier Award from *Canadian Transportation and Logistics* magazine and was recertified to Q1 Quality Status by the Ford Motor Group.

The container shipping industry has always been highly competitive. While the world's top twenty carriers controlled 63 per cent of global container capacity, the industry remained highly fragmented, with over 550 carriers operating worldwide. Within the trade lanes it served, CP Ships competed against a wide range of global, regional and niche carriers. However, CP Ships participated in joint service agreements with other container shipping companies in nearly all of its trade lanes.

On 21 August 2005, TUI AG offered to acquire CP Ships Limited for US$2 billion and merge it with its Hapag-Lloyd division. On 19 October that year, CP Ships and TUI AG jointly announced that 89.1 per cent of CP Ships' shareholders had accepted the offer for US$21.50 per share. The ships were renamed with Hapag-Lloyd names ending in 'Express'. TUI AG (Touristik Union International) is an Anglo-German multinational travel and tourism company, with its headquarters in Hannover, Germany, and is the largest leisure, travel and tourism company in the world. It owns travel agencies, hotels, airlines, cruise ships and retail stores, and is jointly listed on the Frankfurt Stock Exchange and the London Stock Exchange as a constituent of the FTSE 250 Index. It can be traced back to the industrial and transportation company Preussag AG, which was originally formed as a German mining company and was incorporated on 9 October 1923 as the Prussian Mine and Foundry Company. In 1927, it was merged with the Ruhr coal company Hibernia AG. Preussag AG had acquired Hapag-Lloyd AG in 1997, becoming a global enterprise in the service and leisure industry. Hapag-Lloyd held a 30 per cent interest in TUI, and this was increased to 100 per cent by 1999.

In 2002, Preussag renamed itself TUI AG and merged its travel division with the British tour operator First Choice in March 2007. This was approved by the European Commission on 4 June 2007, on the condition that the merged company sell Budget Travel in the Republic of Ireland. TUI Travel PLC, which began operations in September 2007, held a 55 per cent stake in the new company. In April 2008, TUI Travel expanded into Eastern Europe and Russia, but the shipping interests were kept separate under Hapag-Lloyd, where a majority stake of the shipping company was sold to the Albert Ballin consortium in March 2009 and February 2012 as TUI moved from shipping to optimise its tourism activities, with expansion in Russia, China and India.

In late 2012, Hapag-Lloyd announced that it was considering the possibility of a merger with Hamburg Süd. However, Hamburg Süd's shareholders and owners did not reach an agreement with Hapag-Lloyd stakeholders and remained a private, independent company until December 2016, when Maersk announced that it would purchase Hamburg Süd. The container business of Chile's Compañía Sudamericana de Vapores SA (CSAV) was taken over by Hapag-Lloyd

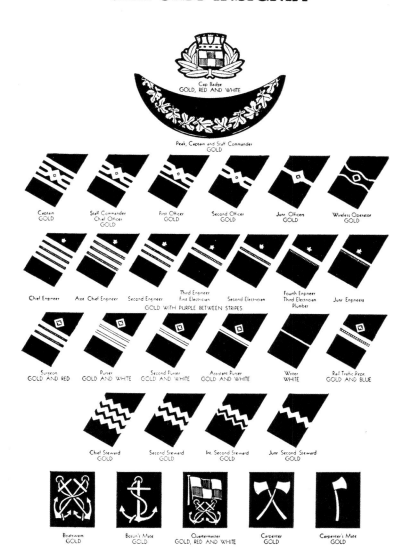

Canadian Pacific uniform insignia.

in 2014, making them the fourth largest container company in the world at the time. In 2016, Hapag-Lloyd merged with the United Arab Shipping Company (UASC), and the integration between the two companies was completed the following year. In 2012, the clothing company Eyecon Enterprises of Ontario was granted the Canadian Pacific Steamships trademark name along with the chequered flag logo. Canadian Pacific Steamships Limited was incorporated in Ontario, Canada, in 2013, and based in Newmarket, Ontario.

FLEET LIST

WHEN THE TRANSCONTINENTAL RAILWAY LINE was being built from Montreal to the Pacific coast, Canadian Pacific appointed Everett Frazar & Company as agents for the company in the Orient. During 1886, seven sailing vessels were chartered and sent from the Orient to Port Moody. *Abyssinia*, *Batavia* and *Parthia* were acquired in 1887 by the agents Adamson, Bell & Company and placed on the Pacific routes. As the traffic grew, other ships were chartered.

Abyssinia (1887–91)
1870
3,651grt
364 x 42 x 34ft
ID: 1063765
Single-screw, single-expansion engines by J. Jones & Son
11 knots
b. J. & G. Thomson, Clydebank
Passengers: 200 first, 1,050 third class
She was launched on 3 March 1870 for the Cunard Line and sailed on her maiden voyage from Liverpool to New York on 24 May that year. In 1880, she was taken over by J. & G. Thomson as part payment for *Servia* and *Catalonia*. In 1881, she was sold to S.B. Guion and re-engined in 1882 with compound engines. Her ownership was transferred to Sir William Pearce in 1885, and she was placed on Canadian Pacific service, managed by Adamson, Bell & Company. She made her final and seventeenth transpacific voyage from Vancouver on 28 January 1891. Following this voyage, she was returned to the Guion service from New York. On 18 December 1891, she was destroyed by fire on a voyage from New York to Liverpool. All passengers and crew survived.

Batavia (1887–91)
1870
2,549grt
327 x 39 x 26ft
ID: 1063756
Single-screw, compound engines by builder
11 knots
b. William Denny & Brothers, Dumbarton
Passengers: 54 first, 51 second, 624 third class
Launched on 1 February 1870 for the Cunard Line, it had been purchased on the stocks. She was Denny's first compound engine vessel. She sailed on her maiden voyage on 10 May 1870, and in February 1880 she made one sailing to Bombay for P&O. She was chartered for service as a transport for the Egyptian Expedition in 1882 and traded in to John Elder & Company two years later, in part payment for Etruria and Umbria. Her registered owner was shown as Sir William Pearce, MP, who also controlled the Guion Line. On 11 February 1887, she was placed on the Canadian Pacific transpacific route and left Vancouver on her fifteenth, and last, Canadian Pacific voyage. She was chartered to the Upton Line and taken over by the Northern Pacific Steamship Company in May 1892, becoming

Tacoma. Triple-expansion engines and new boilers were fitted in 1895 and she was sold to the North American Steamship Company in 1898. She was transferred to United States registry and in 1901 was acquired by the Northern Pacific Steam Ship Company. In February 1904, she was bought by the Northwestern Commercial Company, and registered in the name of the Northwestern Steam Ship Company. On 15 March 1905, she was seized by the Japanese during the Russo-Japanese war and was later purchased by R. Yamashina and renamed Shikotan Maru. She ran aground on 3 October 1924 and was lost.

Parthia (1887–91)
1870
3,167grt
361 x 40 x 34ft
ID: 1063797
Single-screw, compound engine by builder
11 knots
b. William Denny & Brothers, Dumbarton
Passengers: 200 first, 1,050 third class
Launched for the Cunard Line. In 1874 she was traded in to John Elder & Company in part payment for *Etruria* and *Umbria*. Her owner was

shown as Sir William Pearce, who controlled the Guion Line. She was fitted with triple-expansion engines in 1885. Two years later she was operating for Canadian Pacific, arriving at Vancouver on 4 July 1887. She completed twenty voyages for Canadian Pacific on 20 August 1891, and was returned to the Guion Line. The following year she was renamed *Victoria* and transferred to the Tacoma–Hong Kong service of the Northern Pacific Steamship Company, which was in competition with Canadian Pacific. In 1898, she was operating for the North American Mail Steam Ship Company and carried out trooping duties to Manila during the Spanish–American war. From 1901 to 1904, she reverted to the Northern Pacific Steam Ship Company. In 1904, she was sold to the Northwestern Steam Ship Company for the Alaska service. Four years later, the Northwestern fleet was taken over by the Alaska Steam Ship Company for the San Francisco–Seattle–Nome route. She was converted to oil fuel in 1924, and was laid up from 1936 to 1939. From 1941 to 1947, she was operated by the United States War Administration and made forty-six voyages to Alaska. In 1952, she was sold to Dulien Steel Products Company to be broken up, and in 1954 was acquired by the Straits Towing & Salvage Company of Vancouver and converted into a log-carrying barge. She was renamed *Straits No. 27*. Two years later, she was sold to Japanese breakers, and renamed *Straits Maru* for the voyage to Osaka, where she arrived on 16 October after eighty-six years in service.

Empress of India (1891–1914)

1890
5,905grt
456 x 51 x 33ft
ID: 1049345
Twin-screw, triple-expansion engines by builder
17½ knots
b. Naval Construction & Armament Company, Barrow-in-Furness
Yard No. 179
Passengers: 120 first, 50 second, 600 third class

Launched on 30 August 1890 by Lady Louise Egerton and sailed on her maiden voyage from Liverpool to Vancouver, via Suez and Hong Kong, on 8 February 1891. She was then employed on the Hong Kong–Shanghai–Nagasaki–Kobe–Yokohama–Vancouver service. She was painted white, with a clipper bow, two buff funnels with a black band at the top, with three lightweight schooner-type masts. On 17 August 1903, she collided with and sank the Chinese cruiser *Huang Tai*. On 19 December 1914, she was sold to the Maharaja of Gwalior and converted into a hospital ship for Indian troops, and renamed *Loyalty* the following year. On completion of this work she was sold to the Scindia Steam Navigation Company in March 1919, and inaugurated their Bombay–Marseilles service. The service was not profitable and was closed in 1920, when she was laid up at Bombay. She was sold to Maneckchand Jiyray in 1923, and broken up at Bombay.

Empress of Japan (1891–1925)

1891
5,905grt
456 x 51 x 33ft
ID: 1098911
Twin-screw, triple-expansion engines by builder
16 knots
b. Naval Construction & Armament Company, Barrow-in-Furness
Yard No. 180
Passengers: 120 first, 50 second, 600 third class

Launched on 13 December 1890 by Lady Alice Stanley, daughter-in-law of Lord Stanley, Governor General of Canada, and sailed on her maiden voyage to Vancouver, via Suez and Hong Kong, on 11 April 1891. *Empress of Japan*, under Captain Henry Pybus, gained the Blue Riband crossing the Pacific in nine days, nineteen hours and thirty-nine minutes in 1897. She held this record for twenty-two years. She was requisitioned by the Admiralty as an Armed Merchant Cruiser on 13 August 1914, based at Hong Kong. She was returned to her owners on transpacific service on 27 October 1915. In 1921, she was given a black hull and placed on an intermediate service, and was laid up at Vancouver the following year. In 1923, Canadian Pacific used the ship to house strike-breakers in a dispute with the Vancouver and District Waterfront Workers' Association. She was sold to V. Lamken of the United States in 1925, on behalf of Japanese interests, but remained at her berth in Vancouver. On 31 March 1926, she was sold to R.J. Christian & Company and broken up at Burrard Inlet, Vancouver. She had been in service for thirty-one years, and held the Pacific record for twenty-two years and crossed the Pacific 315 times. Her dragon figurehead was preserved at the Seawall in Stanley Park and was replaced with a fibreglass replica in 1960. The original figurehead was then restored and is now housed in the Vancouver Maritime Museum.

Empress of China (1891–1911)

1891
5,905grt
456 x 51 x 33ft
ID: 1098953
Twin-screw, triple-expansion engines by builder
16 knots
b. Naval Construction & Armament Company, Barrow-in-Furness
Yard No. 181
Passengers: 120 first, 50 second, 600 third class
Launched on 25 March 1891 by Lady Stafford Northcote, and sailed on her maiden voyage from Liverpool to Vancouver, via Suez and Hong Kong, on 15 July that year. The Archduke Franz Ferdinand of Austria boarded her at Yokohama on 25 August 1893 for a voyage across the Pacific to Vancouver. On 27 July 1911, she struck a rock in rough seas and thick fog, and was wrecked on Mera Reef, in Tokyo Bay, 35 miles from Yokohama. All passengers and crew were rescued by the Japanese cruisers *Aso* and *Soya*, who also removed the mail and baggage. She was refloated in September 1912 and sold and broken up at Yokohama by Sasso Shojiro.

Athenian (1897–1907)

1881
3,877grt
365 x 46 x 29ft
ID: 1082425
Single-screw, compound engine by builder
12 knots
b. Aitken & Mansel, Glasgow
Passengers: 120 first, 90 second, 50 third class
Launched on 7 December 1881, for the Union Steam Ship Company. She was the first ship to enter Cape Town's Robinson Graving Dock, on 22 October 1882. In 1887, she was re-engined with triple-expansion engines by T. Richardson & Sons, West Hartlepool, and was acquired by Canadian Pacific in 1897, with *Tartar*. On 12 February 1898, she left Southampton for Vancouver via Cape Horn and made the first Canadian Pacific call at Hawaii in December 1898. She was sold to shipbreakers at Osaka in 1907.

Tartar (1897–1907)

1883
4,339grt
377 x 47 x 30ft
ID: 1086336
Single-screw, compound engine by J. & G. Thomson, Clydebank
14 knots
b. Aitken & Mansel, Glasgow
Passengers: 170 first, 60 second, 50 third class
Launched on 25 January 1883, for the Union Steam Ship Company. In 1889, she was re-engined with triple-expansion engines by T. Richardson & Sons, West Hartlepool, and was purchased by Canadian Pacific in 1897. On 5 February 1898, she left Southampton for Vancouver, via Tenerife, Buenos Aires and Valparaíso. She was in collision with the *Charmer* on 17 October 1907, and was beached at English Bay. The following year she was sold and broken up at Osaka.

Lake Champlain/Ruthenia[1] (1903–16)

1900
7,392grt
446 x 52 x 28ft
ID: 1110650
Twin-screw, triple-expansion engines by builders
13 knots
b. Barclay Curle & Company, Glasgow
Yard No. 422
Passengers: 100 first, 80 second, 500 third class
Launched on 31 March 1900, and fitted with the first radio installation on a merchant ship in May 1901. On 14 April 1903, she left Liverpool on Canadian Pacific Lines' inaugural Atlantic sailing. She was renamed *Ruthenia* on 7 March 1913, and was transferred to the Trieste service. In November 1914, she was requisitioned by the Admiralty and fitted as a dummy battleship, HMS *King George V*. The following year, she reverted to *Ruthenia* and was used as a store ship. She was purchased by the

_____
1 Pictured in the colour section.

Admiralty in January 1916 and converted to an oil tanker, based at Hong Kong with the China fleet. In 1929, she was used as a naval oil hulk at Singapore. On 16 February 1942, she was scuttled when the Japanese took Singapore and was later raised and converted to a troop carrier as *Choran Maru*. In 1945, she was used to return Japanese prisoners of war to Japan. She left Singapore on 3 April 1949, in tow of the tug *Englishman* for the Clyde, and was broken up at Dalmuir.

Lake Erie/Tyrolia (1903–16)

1900
7,550grt
446 x 52 x 31ft
ID: 1110631
Twin-screw, triple-expansion engines by builder
13 knots
b. Barclay Curle & Company, Glasgow
Yard No. 420
Passengers: 100 first, 80 second, 500 third class
Launched on 21 November 1899, and was chartered to the Allan Line for several months in 1910. She was renamed *Tyrolia* on 29 March 1913, when she was transferred to the Trieste service. In October 1914, she was requisitioned by the Admiralty and fitted out as a dummy battleship, HMS *Centurion*. She later became a stores ship and was converted to carry oil as *Saxol*. On 27 June 1916, she was purchased by the Admiralty and transferred to Lane & MacAndrew Limited, becoming *Aspenleaf*. Transferred to the Shipping Controller. In 1919, she was acquired by the Anglo-Saxon Petroleum Company Limited, becoming *Prygona* in 1921. Sold to Petersen & Albeck of Copenhagen in 1925, and broken up.

Lake Manitoba (1903–18)

1901
8,850grt
469 x 56 x 32ft
ID: 1113497
Twin-screw, triple-expansion engines by Richardson & Westgarth

12 knots
b. C.S. Swan & Hunter Limited, Newcastle
Yard No. 263
Passengers: 120 first, 130 second, 500 steerage
Passengers 1909: 150 cabin, 1,000 steerage class
Launched on 6 June 1901, with her tonnage being increased to 9,674grt in 1903. On 26 August 1918, she suffered a serious fire at Montreal and was scuttled. She was refloated the following month and sold by the underwriters to the Bishop Navigation Company and refitted at Halifax, becoming *Iver Heath*. Purchased by Canada Steamship Lines Limited in 1921 and acquired by Stelp & Leighton Limited in 1923. She was broken up in 1924.

Lake Michigan (1903–18)

1903
8,200grt
469 x 56 x 32ft
ID: 1115252
Twin-screw, triple-expansion engines by Richardson & Westgarth
12 knots
b. C.S. Swan & Hunter Limited, Newcastle
Yard No. 264
Passengers: 350 second, 1,200 steerage class (increased to 2,150 in 1904)
Launched on 28 September 1901, on 21 February 1904 she was in collision with the *Matterhorn* and beached at Dungeness. She was refloated four days later and towed to Gravesend for repairs. She was mined off Brest on 15 November 1916, and towed to port. On 16 April 1918, she was torpedoed 93 miles north-west of Eagle Island by *U-100*.

Milwaukee (1903–18)

1897
7,317grt
470 x 56 x 32ft
ID: 1106834
Single-screw, triple-expansion engines by North East Marine Engineering Company Limited

12 knots
b. C.S. Swan & Hunter Limited, Newcastle
Yard No. 214
Launched on 7 November 1896, for Alfred Jones ownership, with Elder Dempster & Company as managers. Transferred to Elder Dempster ownership in 1898. On 16 September 1898, she went aground on rocks near Peterhead, Scotland, and explosives were used to break her in two at the bridge front. She was refloated on 21 October, minus 180ft of her stern. She was returned to her owners in 1899 following repairs, which included the fitting of a new fore part by her builders. She was acquired by Canadian Pacific on 6 April 1903, and was torpedoed by *U-105* on 31 August 1918, south-west of Fastnet.

Monmouth (1903–19)

1900
4,078grt
375 x 48 x 26ft
ID: 1113379
Single-screw, triple-expansion engines by Furness, Westgarth Limited
10 knots
b. Sir Raylton Dixon & Company, Middlesbrough
Yard No. 467
Launched on 1 May 1900, for Elder Dempster & Company, and delivered to the British & African Steam Navigation Company. She was transferred to Canadian Pacific in 1903, and on 16 November 1916, she was mined off Cherbourg and towed into port, and then to Portsmouth, where she was repaired. In 1919, she was sold to the Imperial Oil Company Limited of Toronto, and purchased by C.O. Stillman, Sarnia, in 1922. The following year she was acquired by Kishimoto Shokai K Ishimoto, Dairen, becoming *Shinzan Maru*. In 1929, she was purchased by Dalgosrybtrest of Vladivostok, and was renamed *Treti Krabolov*.

Montcalm[1] (1903–16)

1897
5,478grt
445 x 53 x 28ft
ID: 1106869
Single-screw, triple-expansion engines by builders
13 knots
b. Palmers Shipbuilding & Iron Company Limited, Jarrow
Yard No. 724
Passengers: 70 second, 1,800 third class
Launched on 17 May 1897 for the African Steam Ship Company, with Elder Dempster & Company as managers. On 6 April 1903, she was taken over by Canadian Pacific and passenger accommodation was added. Requisitioned by the Admiralty in October 1914, after service as a BEF transport and fitted out as a dummy battleship, HMS *Audacious*. She became a store ship in 1915 and was purchased by the Admiralty, with the Leyland Line as managers the following year. Later in 1916, she was operating for the Anglo-Saxon Petroleum Company, becoming *Crenella*, and was transferred to the Shipping Controller in 1917. On 26 November 1917, she was torpedoed off the south-west of Ireland but was able to reach port safely. She was returned to the Anglo-Saxon Petroleum Company in 1919, and to Velefa Steam Ship Company in 1920. On 20 June 1923, she was acquired by C. Nielsen & Company of Norway and converted to a whaling depot ship, becoming *Rey Alfonso*. In 1925 she was sold to H.M. Wrangell & Company and to the Anglo-Norse Company in 1927, becoming *Anglo-Norse*. In 1929, she was acquired by the Falkland Whaling Company, renamed *Polar Chief*, and was sold to the Ministry of War Transport in 1941, becoming *Empire Chief*. She was sold to the South Georgia Company Limited, and renamed *Polar Chief*, and arrived at Dalmuir on 29 April 1952 and was broken up.

---

1   Pictured in the colour section.

Monteagle/Belton (1903–26)

1899
5,498grt
445 x 52 x 28ft
ID: 1110554
Twin-screw, triple-expansion engines by builder
13 knots
b. Palmers Shipbuilding & Iron Company
Limited, Jarrow
Yard No. 738
Passengers: 97 cabin, 1,200 third class

Launched on 13 December 1898 for Elder
Dempster & Company, she became a Boer
War transport, HMT No. 87, in 1900. She was
transferred to Canadian Pacific in 1903, operating
on Atlantic routes until 1906, when she was
moved to Pacific services. On 18 September
1906, she was driven aground at Hong Kong by
a typhoon, breaking her stern post. The salvage
and repairs took six months to complete. In 1916
she was requisitioned at Vancouver, and sent to
Bombay to act as an Indian cavalry troopship
to Marseilles. The following year she returned
to the Hong Kong–Vancouver service and made
three voyages to Vladivostok in 1918 to collect
Austrian and Czecho-Slovak prisoners of war
and then returned to the Pacific service. In 1921,
she rescued the crew of the *Hsin Tien* off the
Amoy coast, and her captain received the French
Medaille d'Honneur. In 1922, she was operating
on Atlantic services, and was renamed *Belton* in
1923. She was laid up at Southend in 1924, and
was sold and broken up at Blyth two years later.

Monterey (1903)

1898
5,455grt
445 x 52 x 28ft
ID: 1109427
Single-screw, triple-expansion engines by builders
13 knots
b. Palmers Shipbuilding & Iron Company, Jarrow
Yard No. 728
Passengers: 70 second, 1,800 third class

Launched on 25 November 1897 for Elder
Dempster & Company, and placed on the
Tyne–Montreal–Avonmouth service. On
16 March 1900, she was requisitioned by the
Admiralty for Boer War transport duties. In
1903, she was transferred to Canadian Pacific
and on 14 July that year, she was wrecked on
Plata Point, Little Miquelon.

Montezuma (1903–15)

1899
7,345grt
485 x 59 x 31ft
ID: 1110604
Twin-screw, triple-expansion engines by builder
13 knots
b. A Stephen & Sons, Linthouse
Yard No. 383
Passengers: 500 third class (emigrants)

Launched on 11 July 1899 for Elder Dempster
& Company, and placed on Boer War duties.
In 1901, she was transferred to the British &
African Steam Navigation Company, and was
taken over by Canadian Pacific two years later.
She was converted to a dummy battleship,
HMS *Iron Duke* in 1914 and based at Scapa
Flow. Converted to an oil tanker the following
year, she was renamed *Abadol* and transferred
to Lane & MacAndrew Limited in 1917,
becoming *Oakleaf*. On 25 July 1917, she was
torpedoed by *UC-41*, 64 miles north-west of
the Butt of Lewis.

Montfort (1903–18)

1899
5,481grt
445 x 52 x 28ft
ID: 1110568
Twin-screw, triple-expansion engines by builder
12 knots
b. Palmers Shipbuilding & Iron Company
Limited, Jarrow
Yard No. 739
Passengers: 15 first class

Launched on 13 February 1899 for Elder
Dempster & Company, and operated as a
Boer War transport for three voyages on the
Liverpool–Cape Town service. In 1900 she was
owned by Elder Line Limited, and in July 1901,
she went aground on the Isle of Wight. Two years
later, she was transferred to Canadian Pacific
for the Atlantic service. On 1 October 1918, she
was torpedoed by *U-55*, 170 miles south-west of
Bishop Rock.

Montreal (1903–18)

1900
6,960grt
469 x 56 x 32ft
ID: 1113373
Twin-screw, triple-expansion engines by Wallsend
Slipway & Engineering Company Limited
12 knots
b. Swan & Hunter Limited, Newcastle
Yard No. 252
Passengers: 12

Launched on 28 April 1899 for the British &
African Steam Navigation Company, with Elder
Dempster as managers. Her tonnage became
6,870grt in 1901, and 8,644grt in 1904. She was
requisitioned as a Boer War transport in 1900,
carrying horses and mules from New Orleans
to Cape Town. In 1903, she was transferred to
Canadian Pacific. She was in Antwerp, with her
engines dismantled, on the outbreak of the First
World War in August 1914. Her cargo of coal
was transferred to the *Montrose* and she left in
tow before the port was captured by German
troops. Both vessels also carried refugees out
of Belgium on the voyage. On 1 April 1915,
she was requisitioned as a troop carrier, and on
29 January 1918, she was in collision with *Cedric*
off Morecambe Bay in convoy. She was taken in
tow and sank the following day, 14 miles from the
River Mersey. Two people lost their lives.

Montrose (1903–14)

1897
5,431grt
444 x 52 x 28ft
ID: 1108251
Single-screw, triple-expansion engines by
T. Richardson & Son, Hartlepool
13 knots
b. Sir Richard Dixon & Company, Middlesbrough
Yard No. 441
Passengers: 70 second, 1,800 third class

Launched on 17 June 1897 for Elder Dempster
& Company, and fitted with Linde refrigeration
for the carriage of dairy products from Canada.
In 1900, she was requisitioned as a Boer War
transport, HMT No. 93. She carried thirty
officers and 1,250 men. She was released from
trooping and transferred to Canadian Pacific
in 1903. On 20 July 1910, she left Antwerp for
Quebec with Dr Hawley Crippen and his lover,
Ethel Le Neve, on board. They were spotted
and their details were sent to Scotland Yard
by wireless. Detectives were sent on the faster
Laurentic and arrested the pair on *Montrose*'s
arrival off Quebec. It was the first time that a
ship's radio had been used to pursue a criminal.
On the outbreak of the First World War in
August 1914, she towed *Montreal* from Antwerp
before the Germans captured the port. Later
that year, she was sold to the Admiralty and was
prepared to be used as a blockship and extra
wharf at Dover. On 28 December 1914, she broke
loose from her moorings at Dover during a gale,
and was wrecked on the Goodwin Sands.

Mount Royal (1903–16)

1898
7,044grt
470 x 56 x 32ft
ID: 1109498
Single-screw, triple-expansion engines by Central
Marine Engineering Works, West Hartlepool
12 knots
b. C.S. Swan & Hunter Limited, Newcastle
Yard No. 230

Launched on 17 August 1898 for Elder Dempster
& Company, and used as a Boer War transport
the following year from Naples to Cape Town
with mules, and from New Orleans with horses.
In 1900, she was owned by the Elder Line
Limited and transferred to Canadian Pacific in
1903. On the outbreak of the First World War in
1914, she was converted into a decoy battleship as
HMS *Marlborough*, Special Services Squadron.
The following year she was converted to an oil
tanker with circular tanks, becoming *Rangol*. She
was placed under the management of Lane &
MacAndrews in 1916, and renamed *Mapleleaf*.
At the end of the war, she was acquired by British
Petroleum in 1919, and was renamed *British Maple*
the following year. In 1922, she became a bunker
depot ship at Southampton, and was anchored
off Hamble. In December 1932, she was sold and
broken up at Rosyth, where she had arrived on
25 January 1933.

Mount Temple (1903–16)

1901
8,790grt
485 x 59 x 30ft
ID: 1113496
Twin-screw, triple-expansion engines by the
Wallsend Slipway, Newcastle
12 knots
b. Sir W.G. Armstrong, Whitworth Limited,
Newcastle
Yard No. 709
Passengers: 500 third class (emigrants)

Launched on 18 June 1901 for Elder Dempster
& Company and transferred to Canadian Pacific
in 1903. On 1 December 1907, she went aground
on West Ironbound Island, LaHave, Nova Scotia,
and 600 people were saved by breeches buoy. She
was refloated the following year and taken to
Halifax for repairs. In 1914, she was requisitioned
for trooping duties, and returned to commercial
service the following year. On a voyage from
Montreal to Brest on 6 December 1916, she was
captured and sunk by the German raider *Möwe*,
620 miles off Fastnet.

Empress of Britain/Montroyal (1906–30)

1906
14,188grt
550 x 65 x 37ft
ID: 1120940
Twin-screw, quadruple-expansion engines by
builder
18 knots
b. Fairfield Shipbuilding & Engineering
Company, Glasgow
Yard No. 442
Passengers: 310 first, 470 second, 750 third class

Launched on 11 November 1905, and sailed from
Liverpool to Montreal on her maiden voyage
on 5 May 1906. She was the last of the British
high-speed liners with reciprocating machinery.
The contracts for *Empress of Britain* and *Empress
of Ireland* were delayed pending a decision as
to whether they should be designed to reach
Montreal. It was finally decided that they were

prevented from proceeding beyond Quebec until the channel had been deepened. They carried Canadian mail together with the Allan Line and occasionally berthed at Halifax on the way to Saint John. On 27 July 1912, she collided with and sank the *Helvetia* off Cape Madeleine and was requisitioned by the Admiralty in 1914 as an Armed Merchant Cruiser in the North Atlantic, and later as troop transport No. 628. She was returned to commercial service in 1919, and converted to oil fuel by her builders and placed on the Southampton, and, later, Antwerp routes. On 16 April 1924, she was renamed *Montroyal* and sold to the Stavanger Shipbreaking Company in 1930 to be broken up. It was reported that the smoke room from the ship was dismantled and incorporated into the Sola Strand Hotel, Stavanger, Norway.

Empress of Ireland (1906–14)

1906
14,191grt
550 x 65 x 37ft
ID: 1123972
Twin-screw, quadruple-expansion engines by builder
18 knots
b. Fairfield Shipbuilding & Engineering Company, Glasgow
Yard No. 443
Passengers: 310 first, 470 second, 750 third class
Launched on 27 January 1906, and sailed on her maiden voyage on 29 June from Liverpool to Montreal. On 29 May 1914, she left Quebec in patchy fog, carrying 1,477 passengers and crew, and collided with the Norwegian collier *Storstad* near Father Point, in the St Lawrence. *Empress of Ireland* heeled to starboard and sank within fifteen minutes of the collision. Most of her 1,057 passengers were asleep below, and 840 were lost, together with 172 of the 420 crew. The inquiry into the collision found *Storstad* entirely to blame.

Empress of Russia (1913–45)

1912
16,810grt
570 x 68 x 42ft
ID: 1135197
Quadruple-screw turbines by builders
19 knots
b. Fairfield Shipbuilding & Engineering Company, Glasgow
Yard No. 484
Passengers: 284 first, 100 second, 808 steerage class
Launched on 28 August 1912, and sailed on her maiden voyage on 1 April 1913 from Liverpool to Hong Kong via the Suez Canal. She then sailed from Hong Kong to Nagasaki and Vancouver in eight days, eighteen hours and thirty-one minutes, arriving on 29 May. On her call at Nagasaki, 3,200 tons of coal was loaded in six hours. The main, first-class public rooms were on the promenade deck, the dome of the forward lounge rising between the forward and second funnels, and that of the smoke room aft of the third stack. The veranda café was also on that deck, facing aft. Apart from these and the writing room, the promenade deck and the one below were devoted to first-class cabins, which were mainly two-berth. The shelter deck had a domed, 200-seat first-class dining room, the café and reception room forward; the second-class dining saloon and open decks for the second-class and steerage passengers were aft. The remainder of the cabins, both first and second class, were on the upper deck, the after part being devoted to steerage passengers.

In 1914, she was requisitioned by the Admiralty as an Armed Merchant Cruiser in the Indian Ocean. On 12 February 1916, she returned to commercial service and was taken over for trooping duties in 1918. On 12 January 1919, she left Liverpool for Hong Kong via Suez to be refitted, returning to her owners on 8 March. In the years between the two world wars, she completed 310 transpacific crossings before the Admiralty requisitioned her for service as a troopship on 28 November 1940, and she was refitted at Vancouver. On 8 September 1945, she was destroyed by fire at Barrow during an extensive refitting, and was broken up there by Thos W. Ward.

Empress of Asia (1913–42)

1913
16,908grt
570 x 68 x 42ft
ID: 1135226
Quadruple-screw turbines by builders
19 knots
b. Fairfield Shipbuilding & Engineering Company, Glasgow
Yard No. 485
Passengers: 284 first, 100 second, 808 third class
Launched on 23 November 1912, she sailed on her maiden voyage on 14 June 1913 from Liverpool to Cape Town and Hong Kong. She was requisitioned by the Admiralty in 1914 as an Armed Merchant Cruiser, and served in the Red Sea. On 20 March

1916, she returned to commercial service and was converted to carry troops in May 1918. When these duties were completed, she returned to service on 2 January 1919, when she left Liverpool for Hong Kong with a black hull and white band. She collided with and sank the *Tung Shing* on 11 January 1926. The following year, her hull was painted white again.

She was requisitioned by the Admiralty for trooping duties on 1 January 1941, and was sunk by Japanese aircraft off Singapore on 5 February 1942, with 2,600 people on board. She suffered five direct hits and was on fire when she ran aground on Sultan Shoal, west of Ayer Chawan island. Many troops of the 18th Division were taken on board the Australian corvette *Yarra*, which went alongside *Empress of Asia* as she heeled over. Others were rescued by Royal Navy patrol boats and the tug *Veruna*, belonging to the Singapore Harbour Board. Many of the survivors in several of her lifeboats escaped to Java, where most were later captured.

Missanabie (1914–18)

1914
12,469grt
501 x 64 x 38ft
ID: 1136705
Twin-screw, quadruple-expansion engine by builder
15 knots
b. Barclay, Curle & Company, Glasgow
Yard No. 510
Passengers: 520 cabin, 1,138 third class
Launched on 22 June 1914, she sailed on her maiden voyage from Liverpool to Quebec and Montreal on 7 October. *Missanabie* and her sister, *Metagama*, were specifically designed for cabin class. In 1916, they were on the Atlantic route to Canada. On 9 September 1918, on a voyage to Montreal, she was torpedoed by *U-87*, 52 miles south-east of Daunt Rock, Kinsale. She was on a commercial voyage for Canadian Pacific

with passengers and fifty-seven troops on board. Forty-eight people lost their lives. Most of these fatalities were caused by a funnel crashing into one of the boats.

Metagama (1915–34)

1915
12,420grt
501 x 64 x 38ft
ID: 1136791
Twin-screw, quadruple-expansion engine by builder
15 knots
b. Barclay, Curle & Company, Glasgow
Yard No. 511
Passengers: 520 cabin, 1,138 third class
Launched on 19 November 1914, she sailed on her maiden voyage on 26 March 1915 from Liverpool to Saint John, New Brunswick. On 26 May 1923, she collided with the *Baron Vernon* in the Clyde, and on 19 June the following year, she was in

collision with the *Clara Camas*. In May 1929, she was operating on the Antwerp–Southampton–Cherbourg–Quebec–Montreal route. She was laid up in 1930 because of the Great Depression and was sold in 1934 and broken up.

Mattawa/Berwyn (1915–28)

1912
4,874grt
398 x 52 x 27ft
ID: 1131444
Single-screw, triple-expansion engines by D. Rowan, Glasgow
10 knots
b. A. McMillan & Son Limited, Dumbarton
Yard No. 443
Launched on 15 June 1912, as *St Hugo* for the British & Foreign Steamship Company Limited and acquired by the Palace Shipping Company in 1915, becoming *Franktor*. On 10 September that year, she was sold to Canadian Pacific, and made one voyage as *Franktor* before being renamed *Mattawa*. In 1920, she was transferred to the Pacific route, and was operating on the Canada–West Indies service in 1922. She became *Berwyn* in 1923, and was sold to the Kintyre Steam Ship Company, of Liverpool, in 1928 and renamed *Kingarth*. In 1932, she became *Beppe*, owned by G. & F. Bozzo of Italy. On 19 October 1942, she was torpedoed by HMS *Unbending* off Lampedusa Island.

Medora (1915–18)

1912
5,135grt
410 x 52 x 29ft
ID: 1131438
Single-screw, triple-expansion engines by D. Rowan, Glasgow
11 knots
b. Russell & Company, Port Glasgow
Yard No. 632
Launched on 26 April 1912 as *Frankmount* for Palace Shipping, and acquired by Canadian

Pacific in 1915, becoming *Medora*. On 21 May 1917, on a voyage from Montreal to London, off the Lizard, she missed a torpedo from *U-31*. On a voyage from Liverpool to Montreal on 2 May 1918, she was torpedoed by *U-86*, 11 miles off the Mull of Galloway. Her master and two others were taken prisoner.

Allan Line was taken over by Canadian Pacific on 1 October 1915.

Alsatian/Empress of France (1914–34)

1914
18,481grt
571 x 72 x 42ft
ID: 1136266
Quadruple-screw turbines by builder
18 knots
b. W. Beardmore & Company Limited, Glasgow
Yard No. 509
Passengers: 287 first, 504 second, 848 third class

Launched on 22 March 1913, and sailed on her maiden voyage from Liverpool to Halifax and Saint John, New Brunswick (Captain Edmund Outram), on 17 January 1914. She was the fastest liner to be built before the First World War for the Canadian trade, and the first Atlantic liner to have motor lifeboats and the first with a cruiser stern. Her accommodation with public rooms and deluxe staterooms and suites was in line with the New York express mail liners, and she soon acquired a reputation on the route.

She was requisitioned by the Admiralty as an Armed Merchant Cruiser, joining the 10th Cruiser Squadron as flagship of Admiral de Chair. In 1914, she rescued the crew of the auxiliary cruiser *Oceanic* and collided with the Cunard liner *Ausonia* in the Mersey in May 1918. In December 1918, she was released from her commission, during which she had steamed 266,700 nautical miles and had examined 15,000 ships. She arrived at Glasgow in February 1919 for a refit at her builders, and was renamed *Empress of France* on 4 April.

She sailed on her first post-war voyage from Liverpool on 26 September 1919. After the appointment of the Duke of Devonshire as Governor General, in 1919 she carried the Duke and Duchess to Canada, with Captain Cook in command. In 1920, she made a record passage for the Canadian run of five days, twenty-three hours, and shortly after made round trips in fifteen days, five hours and five minutes. In 1921, she was transferred to the Southampton–Quebec service. On 30 May 1922, she inaugurated the Hamburg–Southampton–Cherbourg–Quebec service and made the first round-the-world cruise undertaken by a Canadian Pacific Atlantic liner. This was followed by a number of successful cruises in 1923. She was selected to carry HRH Prince Edward to Canada and was converted to oil fuel by her builders in 1924. On 31 October 1928, she left Southampton for the Pacific via Suez and returned to Liverpool from Hong Kong the following year. She was laid up on the Clyde on 28 September 1931, and sold to W.H. Arnott Young & Company for £35,000, and broken up at Dalmuir, where she arrived on 24 November 1934.

Calgarian (1914–18)

1914
17,515grt
569 x 70 x 42ft
ID: 1136277
Quadruple-screw turbines by builders
18 knots
b. Fairfield Shipbuilding & Engineering Company, Glasgow
Yard No. 487
Passengers: 280 first, 500 second, 900 third class

Launched on 19 April 1913, and sailed on her maiden voyage from Liverpool to Quebec on 8 May 1914. She was requisitioned by the Admiralty as an Armed Merchant Cruiser with the 10th Cruiser Squadron, and was involved in the blockade of the Tagus and Lisbon, where several German ships were anchored. On 16 July 1917, she was transferred to Canadian Pacific but did not actually sail for them commercially. On 1 March 1918, while guarding a convoy of thirty ships, she was torpedoed by *U-19* off Rathlin Island. Forty-nine people lost their lives.

Carthaginian (1915–17)

1884
4,214grt
386 x 45 x 22ft
ID: 1089990
Single-screw, compound engines by J. & J. Thompson, Glasgow
12 knots
b. Govan Shipbuilding Company, Glasgow
Yard No. 140
Passengers: 64 first, 32 second, 500 third class

Launched on 9 October 1884 and sailed on her maiden voyage on 6 December from Glasgow to Boston. She remained on commercial service during the First World War and was transferred to Canadian Pacific in October 1915. On a voyage from Liverpool to Montreal on 14 June 1917, she struck a mine 2½ miles north-west of Inishtrahull Light, County Donegal. The mines were laid by the German submarine *U-79*.

Corinthian (1916–18)

1900
6,227grt
430 x 54 x 28ft
ID: 1111257
Single-screw, triple-expansion engines by builders
12 knots
b. Workman, Clark & Company, Belfast
Yard No. 160
Passengers: 280 second, 900 third class
Launched on 19 March 1900 and sailed on her maiden voyage from Liverpool to Quebec and Montreal on 24 May. In 1908, she was converted to carry second and third class only (7,333grt). In August 1914, she carried troops of the First Canadian Expeditionary Force to Liverpool, and was taken over by Canadian Pacific in January 1916. On 14 December 1918, she was wrecked in the Bay of Fundy on Brier Island. Attempts were made to salvage her but these were abandoned.

Corsican/Marvale (1916–23)

1907
11,436grt
500 x 61 x 38ft
ID: 1124191
Twin-Screw, triple-expansion engines by builders
16 knots
b. Barclay, Curle & Company Limited, Glasgow
Yard No. 467
Passengers: 208 first, 298 second, 1,000 third class
Launched on 29 April 1907, replacing the wrecked *Bavarian*, and sailed on her maiden voyage from Liverpool to Saint John, New Brunswick, in November that year. In 1912, she collided with an iceberg near Belle Island, and in August 1914, she was requisitioned as a troopship, and taken over by Canadian Pacific in 1916. She helped to repatriate Canadian troops in November 1918, and was then placed on the London–Canada and Glasgow–Montreal routes. On 16 November 1922, she was renamed *Marvale*, following her conversion to a cabin-class vessel.

at Liverpool. She was wrecked on Freel Rock, off Cape Fine, Newfoundland, on 21 May 1923.

Grampian (1916–21)

1907
9,598grt
486 x 60 x 38ft
ID: 1124220
Twin-screw, triple-expansion engines by builders
15 knots
b. A. Stephen & Sons, Glasgow
Yard No. 422
Passengers: 210 first, 250 second, 1,000 third class
Launched on 25 July 1907 and placed on the Glasgow–Quebec–Montreal route. In August 1914, she completed one trooping voyage from Canada and carried out the same duties the following year. In 1916, she was taken over by Canadian Pacific. On 14 March 1921, while refitting at Antwerp, she caught fire and was destroyed, and was abandoned by the underwriters. She was broken up in 1926 at Rotterdam.

Ionian (1915–17)

1901
8,265grt
470 x 57 x 37ft
ID: 1113989
Twin-screw, triple-expansion engines by builders
14 knots
b. Workman, Clark & Company, Belfast
Yard No. 127
Passengers: 131 first, 160 second, 800 steerage class
1 funnel, 4 masts, 3 decks. Fitted with refrigerated machinery
Launched on 12 September 1901 and was taken over by Canadian Pacific in October 1915. She was wrecked by mines off Milford Haven on 20 October 1917. The mines had been laid by *UC-51*.

Pomeranian (1915–18)

1882
4,364grt
381 x 44 x 33ft
ID: 1085193
Single-screw, compound engines by builders
12 knots
b. Earle's Shipbuilding & Engineering Company Limited, Hull
Yard No. 241
Passengers: 40 first, 60 second, 1,000 third class
Launched on 6 May 1882, as *Grecian Monarch* for the Monarch Line (the Royal Exchange Shipping Company Limited). She was acquired by the Allan Line in 1887 and renamed *Pomeranian* for the London–Montreal route. In February 1893, she ran into a severe storm and the bridge, charthouse and fore deck saloon was carried away, and twelve people lost their lives. She then had to return to Glasgow for repairs. In 1900, she was used as a mule transport in the Boer War, and was returned to the Allan Line in 1902, when triple-expansion engines were fitted by Denny Brothers of Dumbarton. In 1908, the passenger accommodation was reduced to second and third class only, and she moved to Canadian Pacific in 1915. On 15 April 1918, on a voyage from London to Saint John, she was torpedoed by *UC-77*, 9 miles from Portland Bill.

Pretorian (1915–22)

1901
6,436grt
437 x 53 x 30ft
ID: 1113969
Single-screw, triple-expansion engines by Richardson & Westgarth, Hartlepool
13 knots
b. Furness, Withy & Company, Hartlepool
Yard No. 253
Passengers: 140 first, 200 second, 600 steerage class
Passengers 1908: 280 second, 900 third class

Launched on 22 December 1900, for the Liverpool–Quebec–Montreal service. She was taken over by Canadian Pacific in 1915 and by the Liner Requisition Scheme the following year. On 30 April 1917, she was chased by a German submarine off the south-west of Ireland and escaped. In 1919, she repatriated Belgian refugees, and took troops to Archangel and Murmansk during the Bolshevik revolution. Converted to cabin class in 1921, and was laid up at Gareloch the following year and broken up at Garston by J.J. King in 1926.

Sardinian (1915–20)

1875
4,376grt
400 x 42 x 35ft
ID: 1071695
Single-screw, compound engines by William Denny & Brothers, Dumbarton
13 knots
b. R. Steele & Company, Greenock
Yard No. 81
Passengers: 120 saloon, 850 third class
Launched on 3 June 1874, and sailed on her maiden voyage on 29 July 1875 from Liverpool to Quebec and Montreal. On 10 May 1878, she caught fire at Moville, scuttled and refloated. Triple-expansion engines were fitted in 1897 by William Denny & Brothers, Dumbarton, and she left Liverpool on 26 November 1901, with Guiseppi Marconi and his equipment, to set up a wireless station at St John's, Newfoundland. She joined the London–Montreal service in 1910. In 1915, she was transferred to Canadian Pacific and became a hulk at Vigo, Spain, in 1920. She was broken up at Bilbao in 1938.

Scandinavian (1915–23)

1898
11,394grt
555 x 59 x 39ft
ID: 1109441
Twin-screw, triple-expansion engines by builders
14 knots
b. Harland & Wolff Limited, Belfast
Yard No. 315
Passengers: 200 first, 200 second, 800 steerage class
Launched on 7 April 1898 as New England for the Dominion Line, for the Liverpool–Boston service. She was transferred to the White Star Line in November 1903, becoming Romanic, and made White Star's first sailing to Boston. In 1912, she was transferred to the Allan Line, and renamed Scandinavian. In 1915, she was transferred to Canadian Pacific and to F. Rijsdijk Industries, Rotterdam, Klasmann & Lentze, Emden in 1923 and broken up.

Scotian/Marglen (1915–26)

1898
10,319grt
515 x 60 x 24ft
ID: 1129547
Twin-screw, triple-expansion engines by builders
14 knots
b. Harland & Wolff Limited, Belfast
Yard No. 320
Passengers: 550 second, 1,150 third class

Launched on 7 May 1898 as Statendam for the Holland America Line. She was acquired by the Allan Line on 23 March 1911, and renamed Scotian. In 1914, she carried out trooping duties for the Canadian Army. She was transferred to Canadian Pacific in 1915 and was renamed Marglen in 1922. Laid up at Southampton on 11 April 1925, and was chartered for three winter round voyages to Bombay. Sold on 30 December 1926 to D.L. Pittaluga, Genoa, and broken up the following year.

Sicilian/Bruton (1916–23)

1899
6,224grt
430 x 54 x 28ft
ID: 1111225
Single-screw, triple-expansion engines by builders
12 knots
b. Workman, Clark & Company, Belfast
Yard No. 158
Passengers: 50 first, 150 second, 400 third class
Launched on 28 August 1899, on completion she was requisitioned as a Boer War transport. On 28 February 1901, she sailed on her maiden voyage for the Allan Line from Liverpool to Portland, Maine. Refitted as a cabin-class steamer in 1910, increasing her tonnage by 1,000 tons, and allocated to the London service. During the First World War she sailed mainly from Liverpool. She was taken over by Canadian Pacific in 1916, and was used to repatriate Belgian refugees from England to France in 1919. She operated on the Saint John–West Indies service in 1921 and was laid up at Falmouth the following year. In 1923, she made three voyages from Libau, Latvia–Southampton and was then reduced to cargo only. Her six lifeboats were removed. She became Bruton in 1923, and on 8 May 1925, she was sold and broken up by F. Gregorini in Italy.

Tunisian/Marburn (1915–28)

1900
10,576grt
500 x 59 x 40ft
ID: 1111248
Twin-screw, triple-expansion engines by builders
14 knots
b. A. Stephen & Sons, Glasgow
Yard No. 384
Passengers: 240 first, 220 second, 1,000 third class

Launched on 17 January 1900 for the Liverpool–Halifax–Portland, Maine, service. She was requisitioned by the Admiralty as a troopship and then for prisoner-of-war accommodation for German seamen taken prisoner in British ports when war was declared. She was taken over by Canadian Pacific in 1915 and was re-engined to burn oil fuel, and converted to cabin class in 1920. On 16 November 1922, she was renamed *Marburn* and was laid up at Southend in 1928. Following a voyage from Antwerp to Saint John, she was laid up at Southampton and sold to Soc A Co-operativa Ligure Demolitori Navi, Genoa, and broken up.

Victorian/Marloch (1915–28)

1905
10,629grt
520 x 60 x 38ft
ID: 1121216
Triple-screw turbines by Parsons
18 knots
b. Workman Clark & Company Limited, Belfast
Yard No. 206
Passengers: 346 first, 344 second, and 1,000 third class

Launched on 25 August 1904 for the Allan Line. *Victorian* and *Virginian* were pioneer ocean-going turbine-driven ships. It was originally intended to install triple-expansion engines but it was decided to fit them with turbines. In 1914, she was requisitioned by the Admiralty as an Armed Merchant Cruiser, and joined the 10th Cruiser Squadron. The following year she was taken over by Canadian Pacific, but the transfer was not completed until 1917 because of her duties for the Admiralty. In 1919, she was involved in the first wireless telephony tests at sea, transmitting messages 600 miles.

She was converted to oil fuel in 1921 and on 11 December 1922, she returned to service as *Marloch*. On 2 February 1926, *Marloch* was in collision with the *Whimbrel* (1910/1,655grt) of the British & Continental Steamship Company of Liverpool, near Flushing. *Whimbrel* was sunk but the crew of twenty-one men were rescued by a Dutch tug. The Belgian pilot and all of the crew were taken to a Flushing hotel; the *Marloch* anchored near the scene and was forced to keep her pumps working. Tugs were standing by but she eventually reached Antwerp. *Whimbrel* had been requisitioned by the Royal Fleet Auxiliary in 1914 as a Squadron Supply Ship, and on 12 May 1918, she was in collision 6 miles off the Lizard and sank the *Ibis*. In 1928, *Marloch* was laid up at Southend, sold to Thos W. Ward and broken up at Pembroke Dock the following year.

Virginian (1916–20)

1905
10,757grt
520 x 60 x 38ft
ID: 1121219
Triple-screw turbines by Parsons
18 knots
b. A. Stephen & Sons, Glasgow
Yard No. 405
Passengers: 426 first, 286 second, 1,000 third class
Passengers 1923: 532 cabin, 854 third class

Launched on 22 December 1904 for the Liverpool–Saint John, New Brunswick, service. However, the direct-acting turbines in *Victorian* and *Virginian* gave initial problems. The three small propellers driven at a high speed of 280rpm caused cavitation and strumming vibration aft. The efficient speed of the turbine was far too fast for the propeller and the design of the hull; as a result, coal consumption was excessive. On 14 April 1912, when *Titanic* sank, *Virginian* heard her SOS and made her way to the scene before Cunard's *Carpathia* reported that she was only 57 miles away. She was requisitioned by the Admiralty in 1914 as a troop carrier and, later, Armed Merchant Cruiser, attached to the 10th Cruiser Squadron. In 1916, she was taken over by Canadian Pacific, with the transfer being completed the following year. She was declared surplus and placed on the for-sale market in 1918, and she was sold to the Swedish America Line and renamed *Drottningholm*. De Laval single-reduction, 10,500shp geared turbines were installed, which gave her a service speed of 17 knots.

During the Second World War, she and *Gripsholm* were used by the International Red Cross for the exchange of diplomatic personnel, civilians and wounded prisoners of war. In 1948, she was delivered to Home Lines, a company in which the Swedish America Line had a half share, and was renamed *Brasil* for South Atlantic Lines Incorporated. She was placed on the Naples–New York route in 1950 and modernised in Italy the following year, being renamed *Homeland* for the Hamburg–Southampton–Halifax–New York service. The following year she was transferred to the Naples–Genoa–New York route. She arrived at Trieste on 29 March 1955, and was broken up.

Miniota (1916–17)

1913
4,928grt
420 x 55 x 24ft
ID: 1135311
Single-screw, triple-expansion engines by Central Marine Engineering Works, Hartlepool
b. William Gray & Company, West Hartlepool
Yard No. 834
Passengers: 12

Launched on 27 November 1913, as *Hackness* for Pyman Brothers, London & Northern Shipping Company. Acquired by Canadian Pacific in 1916 and renamed *Miniota*. On 31 August 1917, on a voyage from Montreal, she was torpedoed by *U-19* 30 miles off Start Point. Three people lost their lives.

Methven/Borden (1917–24)

1905
4,928grt
390 x 53 x 27ft
ID: 1120650
Single-screw, triple-expansion engines by builders
12 knots
b. D. & W. Henderson & Company Limited, Glasgow
Yard No. 448
Launched on 1 December 1905, as *Heliopolis*, for the Alliance Steam Ship Company, with Harris & Dixon as managers. In 1908, she was transferred to the Century Shipping Company, and was purchased by the Admiralty for conversion into a naval hospital ship in 1913. It was intended to call her *Mediator*, but she was renamed *Maine* and the conversion was not completed. In 1916, she reverted to *Heliopolis* and was acquired by Canadian Pacific the following year, becoming *Methven*. In 1919, she inaugurated the new Vancouver–Singapore service and was transferred to the Atlantic route in 1923, as *Borden*. She was laid up at Falmouth in 1924 and sold to G.E. Kulukundis in 1926, becoming *Perseus*. She was transferred to Atlanticos Steam Ship Company the following year and broken up at Genoa by Febo Amadeo Bertorello.

Montcalm (2)/*Bolingbroke* (1917–29)

1917
6,608grt
420 x 53 x 36ft
ID: 1140349
Single-screw, triple-expansion engines by North East Marine Engineering Company, Newcastle
11 knots
b. Northumberland Shipbuilding Company, Newcastle
Yard No. 238
Launched on 7 June 1917, for the London–Quebec–Montreal service. In 1920, she was renamed *Bolingbroke*, and was laid up at Falmouth in 1929. On 27 December 1933, she was sold to W.H. Arnott, Young & Company, and broken up at Troon in 1934.

Melita (1918–35)

1918
3,967grt (15,183 in 1925)
520 x 67 x 42ft
ID: 1136367
Triple-screw, triple-expansion engines with turbine by Harland & Wolff Limited, Belfast
17 knots
b. Barclay Curle & Company Limited
Yard No. 517
Passengers: 550 cabin, 1,200 third class
Laid down for Hamburg America Line and launched on 21 April 1917 as *Melita* for

Canadian Pacific. She was towed to Harland & Wolff at Belfast for engine installation and completion. She was employed on the Liverpool–Canada route. On 26 July 1918, she was attacked by gunfire from *U-140*, and escaped after returning gunfire onto the submarine. Later that year, she was used for troop repatriation to India and Canada. She collided with the Belgian vessel *General Lemon* in 1924. In 1926, she was modernised by Palmers at Jarrow, and fitted with superheaters (15,200grt, Passengers: 206 cabin, 545 tourist, 588 third class). Transferred with *Minnedosa* to the Glasgow service two years later. Laid up in the early 1930s because of the Great Depression and in 1935 she was sold and towed by Smit Zwarte Zee to Genoa for demolition. However, she was taken over by the Italian Government for the Abyssinian war and renamed *Liguria*, operated by Lloyd Triestino. In July 1940, she was damaged off Tobruk by British torpedo bombers. On 22 January 1941, she was scuttled, raised in 1950, and on 19 August 1950, she was towed to Savona by *Ursus* and broken up.

Montezuma (2)/*Bedwyn*/*Balfour* (1918–28)

1918
5,038grt
405 x 53 x 27ft
ID: 1142423
Single-screw, triple-expansion engines by J.G. Kincaide & Company, Greenock
11 knots
b. Robert Duncan & Company Limited, Glasgow
Yard No. 330
Launched on 28 March 1917 as *Camperdown* for Glen & Company, Glasgow, and acquired by Canadian Pacific prior to completion. She was named *Montezuma*, managed by Canadian Pacific Steamships. On 14 May 1923, she was renamed *Bedwyn*, and after one voyage she became *Balfour* for the Montreal–West Indies route. On 4 February 1928, she was sold to the

Lyle Steamship Company of Glasgow, becoming *Cape Verde* (2). In June 1935 she was sold to Fan Shien Ho of Shanghai, becoming *Shang Ho*, and was acquired by Miyachi Kisen K.K., and renamed *Kizan Maru*. On 27 September 1943, she was destroyed by Allied underground forces at Singapore.

Holbrook/Bredon/Brandon (1918–28)

1917
6,655grt
412 x 55 x 27ft
ID: 1140409
Single-screw, triple-expansion engines by Blair & Company, Stockton
11 knots
b. J.L. Thompson & Sons Limited, Sunderland
Yard No. 524

Launched on 17 July 1917, as *Holbrook* for the Century Shipping Company, with Harris & Dixon as managers. When delivered she was used as a military nitrate carrier and was acquired by Canadian Pacific in 1918. On 2 March 1923, she was renamed *Bredon*, and *Brandon* two months later. She was sold to Christian Salvesen on 3 March 1928 for their grain trade from Hudson Bay or River Plate–United Kingdom routes. On a voyage in ballast from Cardiff to Port Everglades, she was torpedoed by *U-48* 150 miles off Land's End. Nine people lost their lives, and forty-three were saved by the naval escort.

Dunbridge/Brecon (1918–28)

1917
6,650grt
412 x 55 x 27ft
ID: 1142305
Single-screw, triple-expansion engines by Blair & Company, Stockton
11 knots
b. J.L. Thompson & Sons Limited, Sunderland
Yard No. 525
Sister of *Holbrook*

Launched on 1 October 1917 for the Century Shipping Company and acquired by Canadian Pacific in 1918. She was renamed *Brecon* in 1923 and was sold to Goulandris Brothers, Andros, in 1928, becoming *Frangoula B*. On a voyage from Cork to St Thomas in ballast on 26 June 1940, she was torpedoed by *U-26* south-west of Cape Clear. The sinking was not reported by the submarine, which was sunk the following day by HMS *Gladiolus*. Six crew lost their lives and thirty-two were rescued by a Spanish fishing boat and taken to San Sebastian.

Mottisfont/Bawtry (1918–27)

1917
5,692grt
400 x 52 x 33ft
ID: 1140262
Single-screw, triple-expansion engines by North East Marine Engineering Company, Newcastle
10 knots
b. W. Dobson & Company, Newcastle
Yard No. 197

Launched on 11 November 1916 and delivered to Harris & Dixon, London. She was acquired by Canadian Pacific in 1918 and became *Bawtry* in 1923. On 22 February 1927, she was sold to N.G. Livanos, Piraeus, owned by the Arbor Shipping Company, and renamed *Archangelos*. In 1935, she was transferred to Theofano Maritime Company (same owners) and in 1950 she was acquired by Kemal Sadikoglu, Galata, Turkey, and renamed *Sadikoglu*. She was damaged and laid up in 1957 and broken up at Kalafatyeri, Turkey in 1961.

Batsford (1918–27)

1914
4,782grt
388 x 54 x 27ft
ID: 1136641
Single-screw, triple-expansion engines by J. Dickinson & Sons, Sunderland

11 knots
b. J.L. Thompson & Sons, Sunderland
Yard No. 503

Launched on 11 December 1913 for the Century Shipping Company, with Harris & Dixon as managers. In 1914, she was used as an Admiralty collier, and then later by the French Government, Army Transport D 816. She was acquired by Canadian Pacific in 1918, and spent time laid up between 1924 and 1926. On 18 January 1927, she was sold to Turnbull Coal & Shipping Company, Cardiff, becoming *Hamdale*. In 1937, she was acquired by the Barry Shipping Company, Cardiff, and renamed *St Mellons*. Later that year, she became *Tozan Maru* of Seiichi Okada, Osaka. On 6 March 1938, on a voyage from Yawata to Keelung in ballast, she was wrecked in fog on the Gotō Islands.

Minnedosa (1918–35)

1925
15,186grt
1925: 15,186grt
520 x 67 x 42ft
ID: 1142717
Triple-screw, triple-expansion engines with turbines by Harland & Wolff Limited, Belfast
17 knots
b. Barclay, Curle & Company Limited, Glasgow
Yard No. 518
Passengers: 550 cabin, 1,200 third class

Laid down for Hamburg America Lines North Atlantic service and launched on 17 October 1917, she was towed to Harland & Wolff at Belfast for completion, where she arrived on 2 May 1918. She was delivered to Canadian Pacific following her requisition by the Admiralty and was used to repatriate Canadian troops. Following an overhaul, and the fitting of superheaters by Cammell Laird at Birkenhead, she was sent to Hawthorn, Leslie & Company at Newcastle to be modernised. During this work she suffered a fire in the officer's accommodation, which caused £5,000 of damage. In 1931, she was laid up at Glasgow and was sold to Ricuperi Metallici at Turin for £30,500, and it was intended to scrap her. *Shipping and Transport* magazine, September 1935, stated:

> These two ships (*Melita* and *Minnedosa*) were, in fact, purchased under the clause 'for breaking up purposes', but later the private Italian purchasers approached the Canadian Pacific Railway Company in order to have the original contract altered so that the ships might be used for further trading. To this, the Canadian Pacific Railway Company has since agreed against payment of a further substantial sum.

She was taken over by the Italian Government and brought into service as a troopship, named *Piemonte*, for the Abyssinian war, with Lloyd Triestino as managers. In 1938, she was operating on Lloyd Triestino's Far East service, and in November 1942, she was torpedoed near Messina and badly damaged, but survived and was sent to Messina. While berthed there she was hit several times by Allied bombs and on 15 August 1943, she was scuttled. In 1949, she was raised and left Messina on 27 July in tow for Spezia and broken up.

Bosworth (1919–28)

1919
6,660grt
412 x 55 x 27ft
ID: 1143043
Single-screw, triple-expansion engines by
J. Dickinson, Sunderland
10 knots
b. J.L. Thompson & Sons, Sunderland
Yard No. 527
Launched as *War Peridot* for the Shipping Controller (Standard 'F' type) and acquired by Canadian Pacific in 1919. The following year she was renamed *Bosworth*, and was sold to H.M. Thomson in 1928, retaining the same name. On 4 September 1944, she was sunk as part of the Mulberry harbour operations and was later scrapped by W.H. Arnott, Young & Company.

Bothwell (1919–33)

1918
6,723grt
412 x 55 x 27ft
ID: 1143057
Single-screw, triple-expansion engines by builders
11 knots
b. W. Doxford & Sons Limited, Sunderland
Yard No. 533
Launched on 7 December 1918 as *War Pearl* for the Shipping Controller and acquired by Canadian Pacific in 1919. The following year she became *Bothwell* and was laid up in 1929 at

Falmouth. On 27 November 1933, she was sold to the Tramp Shipping Development Company, and to Tower Shipping Company the following year, becoming *Tower Crown*. In 1937, she was purchased by Kulukundis Shipping Company and renamed *Mount Ossa*. Two years later, she was acquired by Robert Bornhofen GmbH, Hamburg, becoming *Robert Bornhofen*. In 1940, she became the German naval supply ship *Sperrbrecher III*, later *Sperrbrecher A*, and then *Sperrbrecher 14*. On 9 September 1942, she was sunk by a mine off Honningsvåg, Norway.

Montreal (2) (1920–28)

1906
9,720grt
476 x 55 x 30ft
ID: 1143162
Twin-screw, quadruple-expansion engines by builders
16 knots
b. Blohm & Voss, Hamburg
Yard No. 184
Passengers: 332 cabin, 990 third class
Passengers 1922: 229 cabin, 240 third class
Launched as *Konig Friedrich August* for the Hamburg America Line for their South American service. On 6 November 1920, she was bought by Canadian Pacific, becoming *Montreal*, and became cabin class only in 1923. On 22 May 1927, she was laid up off Southend and was sold

to Cyprien Fabre, Marseilles, on 4 May 1928, becoming *Alesia*. In 1931, she was laid up at Marseilles and arrived at Genoa on 3 November 1933 and was broken up.

Empress of China (3)/Empress of India (2)/Montlaurier/Monteith/Montnairn (1921–29)

1907
17,500grt
590 x 68 x 39ft
ID: 1144402
Triple-screw, quadruple-expansion engine by builders
16 knots
b. J.C. Tecklenborg AG, Geestemünde
Yard No. 211
Passengers: 416 first, 338 second, 1,000 third class
Launched 21 October 1907 as *Prinz Friedrich Wilhelm* for the North German Lloyd (Norddeutscher Lloyd). On the outbreak of the First World War in August 1914, she was cruising to Norway, grounded and took refuge in the Norwegian port of Odda. In 1916, she attempted to sail for Germany but went ashore on the coast of Denmark. She was salvaged and returned to Kiel. In 1919, she was used to repatriate United States troops and was managed by Canadian Pacific for the Shipping Controller. In 1921, she was acquired by Canadian Pacific, refurbished, renamed *Empress of India*, and used as a reserve

ship. In 1922, she operated as an intermediate vessel on the Liverpool–Cobh–Quebec route, and made one trooping voyage to Turkey. She was renamed *Montlaurier* on 13 December 1922. On 26 February 1925, she stranded at Cobh and suffered rudder damage, which was repaired at Cammell Laird at Birkenhead. On 18 June that year, she was renamed *Monteith* but did not sail under that name, as she appeared as *Montnairn* on 2 July on the Antwerp–Quebec route. On 7 October 1928, she arrived at Southampton, was laid up off Netley and was sold on 23 December 1929 for breaking up by Soc Anon Co-operativa Ligure Demolitori Navi at Genoa.

Montcalm (3) (1922–42)

1922
16,418grt
546 x 70 x 40ft
ID: 1145903
Twin-screw, geared turbines by builders
16 knots
b. John Brown & Company Limited, Glasgow
Yard No. 464
Passengers: 542 cabin, 1,268 steerage class
Launched on 3 July 1920 and sailed on her maiden voyage on 17 January 1922 from Liverpool to Halifax–Saint John, New Brunswick. On this voyage she rescued survivors from the Norwegian *Mod*. On 6 December 1928, she arrived at Harland & Wolff, Belfast, for re-engining with six single-reduction geared turbines. In 1932, she operated a cruise programme out of Liverpool and stranded at the entrance to the Mersey in 1933 in a snowstorm. She was requisitioned by the Admiralty in 1939, and converted into an Armed Merchant Cruiser, renamed HMS *Wolfe*. In 1941, she was used as a troopship and was converted into a submarine depot ship the following year when she was purchased by the Admiralty, serving with the 3rd Submarine Flotilla. In 1943, she became a destroyer depot ship, and was transferred to the Eastern Fleet at Trincomalee

the following year. In 1950, she was laid up in the reserve fleet and was sold to Metal Industries on 7 November 1952, and broken up at Faslane.

Empress of Scotland (1921–30)

1905
24,581grt
678 x 77 x 50ft
ID: 1144375
Twin-screw, quadruple-expansion engines by builder
17 knots
b. Vulcan Werke AG, Stettin
Yard No. 264
Passengers: 459 first, 478 second, 536 third class
Passengers 1921: 459 first, 478 second, 960 third class (25,037grt)
Laid down as *Europa* and launched on 29 August 1905 for the Hamburg America Line as *Kaiserin Auguste Victoria*, the largest ship in the world until *Mauretania* of 1907. In 1919, she was ceded to Great Britain and chartered to the United States Shipping Board to repatriate troops back to America. The following year she was chartered to the Cunard Line, and operated on the Liverpool–New York service. She was returned to her builders and converted to oil burning. On 13 May 1921, she was transferred to Canadian Pacific and sailed on her first voyage for them on 22 January 1922, as *Empress of Scotland*. She was sold to Hughes Bolckow at

Blyth on 2 December 1930, to be broken up. She caught fire on 10 December, was gutted and later sank at her berth. In May 1931, she was raised and broke in two on 1 June.

Empress of Canada (1922–43)

1922
21,516grt
625 x 78 x 42ft
ID: 1146215
Twin-screw, 2 sets of geared turbines, 26,000shp by builders
18 knots
b. Fairfield Shipbuilding & Engineering Company, Glasgow
Yard No. 528
Passengers: 453 first, 126 second, 168 intermediate, 926 third class

Launched on 17 August 1920, at a cost of £1.7 million, and sailed on her maiden voyage from Falmouth–Suez Canal–Hong Kong and then on the transpacific service. In 1923, she raced the *President Jackson* across the Pacific and arrived twelve hours ahead of the American vessel. Her record passage from Yokohama to Vancouver took eight days, ten hours and fifty-three minutes. She left New York on Canadian Pacific's first 'Round the World' cruise on 30 January 1924. In 1928, she was re-engined by her builders, and made one round voyage Southampton–Quebec, then returned back to the Pacific via the Panama Canal. On 18 September 1933, her captain reported her leaking and she returned to Yokohama and entered a dry dock.

She was requisitioned by the Admiralty in 1939 and carried out trooping duties. In August 1941, she took part in the Spitsbergen raid with HMS *Aurora*, *Nigeria*, *Icarus*, *Tartar*, *Anthony* and *Antelope*. They were also accompanied by the oil tanker *Oligarth* and evacuated 2,000 Russian mine workers and Norwegian and Soviet citizens from Barentsburg to Murmansk, where the miners disembarked. The Canadian troops who were disembarked at Barentsburg were then responsible for wrecking the coal mines. Operation Gauntlet was organised to destroy coal mines and fuel stocks that might have been of use to the enemy. During the operation, Bear Island was also visited to destroy a German weather station. The two cruisers, *Nigeria* and *Aurora*, were diverted to intercept a German convoy and *Nigeria* sank the German training ship *Bremse*, but suffered serious damage to her bow, possibly from a mine. *Empress of Canada* then brought Canadian troops to the United Kingdom.

On 1 March 1943, she left Durban with 1,800 people on board, including 200 Polish released from Russia and 400 Italian prisoners of war. Because of her speed she was out of convoy, avoiding the usual German submarine routes, and sailed towards the Antarctic before heading around Tristan da Cunha. On 12 March, she was ordered to call at Takoradi to pick up another 300 Italian prisoners of war. At 23.45 on 13 March, she was torpedoed 1,000 miles off the coast of Africa by the Italian submarine *Da Vinci*. The following day she was struck by a second torpedo, and sank quickly, with a loss of 392 lives (340 passengers, 8 gunners and 44 crew). The lifeboats were located by a Catalina aircraft and were picked up by the destroyer HMS *Boreas* and the sloop HMS *Petunia*, which took them to Freetown. At Freetown they were accommodated on the *Edinburgh Castle*, and brought back to the United Kingdom by Cunard's *Mauretania*.

Montmorency/Montrose (2) (1922–40)

1922
16,401grt
546 x 70 x 40ft
ID: 1145919
Twin-screw, geared turbines by builders
16 knots
b. Fairfield Shipbuilding & Engineering
Company, Glasgow
Yard No. 529
Passengers: 542 cabin, 1,268 third class
Laid down as *Montmorency* and launched on
14 December 1920 as *Montrose*. She sailed on
her maiden voyage from Liverpool to Quebec
and Montreal on 5 May 1922. In 1931, she was
re-engined by Harland & Wolff at Belfast, and
employed as a cruise ship. She was requisitioned
by the Admiralty on 3 September 1939 as an
Armed Merchant Cruiser, becoming HMS *Forfar*,
and deployed on the Northern Patrol out of Scapa
Flow and Loch Ewe. On 2 December 1940, she
was torpedoed off the west coast of Ireland by the
German submarine *U-99*.

Empress of China (2)/*Empress of Australia* (1921–52)

1913
21,860grt
590 x 75 x 41ft
ID: 1145300
Twin-screw, turbines by builders
17 knots

b. Vulcan-Werke AG, Stettin
Yard No. 333
Passengers: 400 first, 144 tourist, 632 third class
Launched on 20 December 1913 as *Admiral von
Tirpitz* for the Hamburg America Line, her name
was shortened to *Tirpitz* in February the following
year. In March 1919, she was handed over to the
British as part of the Reparations Commission
and the following year she was engaged in troop
replacement work, with P&O as managers, and
then laid up at Immingham. On 25 July 1921, she
was acquired by Canadian Pacific and renamed
Empress of China, returning to her builders for a
refit of her engines. She then proceeded to John
Brown's yard on the Clyde for fitting out for
service with Canadian Pacific. On 2 June 1922,
she was renamed *Empress of Australia* and sailed
from the Clyde on 16 June to the Pacific service
via the Panama Canal. She was at Yokohama on
1 September 1923 when the earthquake struck
and was damaged after colliding with the *Lyons
Maru*. However, she was able to help in providing
humanitarian assistance, and over 3,000 people
were rescued by the ship's boats.

In August 1926, she was re-engined by her
builders with Parsons steam turbines, and emerged
the following year with a white hull. On 25 June
1927, she carried the Prince of Wales, Prince
George and Prime Minister Stanley Baldwin
from Southampton to Quebec. She was a very
popular cruise ship, and in January 1935 she left
Southampton on an extended cruise, taking mail
and cargo to the Pacific island of Tristan da
Cunha. On 4 April 1935, her commander, Captain
E. Griffiths, brought her into Southampton on his
last voyage before retiring after having commanded
every large passenger vessel in the Canadian Pacific
fleet and having forty-eight years at sea, during
which he sailed around the world three times and
crossed the Atlantic 700 times. On 6 May 1939,
she carried King George VI and Queen Elizabeth
from Portsmouth to Quebec, and later that year
she was requisitioned by the Admiralty and

converted to carry troops. On 7 May 1952, she was
sold to the British Iron and Steel Corporation
and broken up by Thos W. Ward at Inverkeithing,
where she arrived on 10 May.

Montclare (1922–42)

1922
16,314grt
546 x 70 x 40ft
ID: 1145964
Twin-screw, geared turbines by builders
16 knots
b. John Brown & Company Limited, Clydebank
Yard No. 465
Passengers: 542 cabin, 1,268 third class
Laid down as *Metapedia* and launched as
Montclare on 18 December 1921, she sailed on
her maiden voyage from Liverpool to Quebec
and Montreal on 18 August 1922. She went
ashore on 22 March 1931 at Little Cumbrae,
and 300 passengers were disembarked. She left
Glasgow on 21 August 1931, which was the final
ex-Allan Line direct Glasgow–Montreal sailing.
On 28 August 1939, she was requisitioned by
the Admiralty, becoming an Armed Merchant
Cruiser, and later a submarine depot ship as
HMS *Montclare*. She was decommissioned in
1954 and transferred to Portsmouth the following
year. However, on 4 February on a voyage, she

broke adrift from the Admiralty tugs *Warden* and *Enforcer* 25 miles west of the Scillies and was recovered. In January 1958, she was towed by *Englishman* and *Merchantman* to Inverkeithing, where she arrived on 3 February and was broken up by Thos W. Ward.

Beaverburn (1927–40)

1927
9,874grt
503 x 62 x 38ft
ID: 1160187
Twin-screw, geared turbines by builders
14 knots
b. William Denny & Brothers Limited, Dumbarton
Yard No. 1192
Passengers: 12
Launched on 27 September 1927 for the London–Canada weekly service, she was the first ship to be fitted with Erith-Roe automatic stokers, and cost £262,823. On 5 February 1940, in convoy OA84, she was torpedoed by *U-41* and sank. The U-boat was then sunk by the convoy escorts.

Beaverford (1928–40)

1928
10,042grt
503 x 62 x 38ft
ID: 1149983
Twin-screw, geared turbines by Parsons Marine Steam Turbine Company

14 knots
b. Barclay, Curle & Company Limited, Glasgow
Yard No. 617
Passengers: 12
Launched on 27 October 1927 and sailed on her maiden voyage from Glasgow to Canada on 21 January 1928. She was requisitioned by the Admiralty on 22 February 1940. She was sunk by the *Admiral Scheer* in the North Atlantic on 5 November 1940.

Beaverdale (1928–41)

1928
9,957grt
503 x 62 x 38ft
ID: 1149987
Twin-screw, geared turbines by Parsons Marine Steam Turbine Company
14 knots
b. Sir W.G. Armstrong, Whitworth & Company, Newcastle
Yard No. 1019
Passengers: 12
Launched on 28 September 1927, and sailed from Newcastle to Saint John, New Brunswick via Antwerp on 1 February 1928 on her maiden voyage. Requisitioned by the Admiralty on 13 September 1939 and torpedoed on 1 April 1941 in convoy SC26. She was then shelled by *U-48* and twenty-one lost their lives and thirty-seven were wounded.

Beaverhill (1928–44)

1928
10,041grt
503 x 62 x 38ft
ID: 1160362
Twin-screw, geared turbines by Parsons Marine Steam Turbine Company
14 knots
b. Barclay, Curle & Company Limited
Yard No. 618
Passengers: 138 berths fitted in October 1944

Launched on 8 November 1927 and sailed on her maiden voyage on 18 February 1928 from Glasgow to Canada. She was requisitioned by the Admiralty on 3 May 1940 and fitted to carry 138 passengers in October 1941. On 24 November 1944, she went aground on Hillyard's Reef, Saint John, New Brunswick, where she broke in two. On 11 December 1946, her stern half was refloated and towed into Saint John, where it sank at its berth. It was later refloated and towed out to sea and scuttled off Grand Manan Island.

Beaverbrae (1928–41)

1928
10,041grt
503 x 62 x 38ft
ID: 1160386
Twin-screw, geared turbines by Parsons Marine Steam Turbine Company
14 knots
b. Sir W.G. Armstrong Whitworth & Company Limited, Newcastle
Yard No. 102
Passengers: 12

Launched on 24 November 1927 and sailed on her maiden voyage from Newcastle to Antwerp, Halifax and Saint John on 15 March 1928. She was requisitioned by the Admiralty on 1 March 1940, and sunk by enemy aircraft in the North Atlantic on 25 March 1941.

Duchess of Bedford/ Empress of France (2)[1] (1928–60)

1928
20,123grt
582 x 75 x 42ft
ID: 1160482
Twin-screw, six geared turbines by builders
18 knots
b. John Brown & Company Limited, Glasgow
Yard No. 518
Passengers: 580 cabin, 486 tourist, 510 third class

[1]   Pictured in the colour section.

Launched on 24 January 1928 by Mrs Stanley Baldwin, wife of the prime minister, and sailed on her maiden voyage from Liverpool to Quebec and Montreal on 1 June. In August of that year, she set up a new record from Liverpool to Montreal of six days, nine and a half hours, reducing the previous record by nearly twenty-four hours. Although her twin-screw machinery was intended to give a service speed of 17 knots, she consistently exceeded an average of 18 knots, and even managed 20 knots on occasions.

The three sisters were identical in appearance, and claimed to have all the latest modern improvements in British shipbuilding and decoration. Spacious accommodation was provided and promenade space on three decks. Revolving glass doors led into the entrance hall, a large observation drawing room, lounge, ballroom in stately Empire style, and dining room in ivory and oak grey, with card room, writing room, nursery and gymnasium provided for the comfort of passengers.

In November 1932, *Duchess of Bedford* made her record passage from Montreal to Greenock in six days and one hour, at an average speed of 18½ knots. In February 1933, she was chartered by Furness Withy to run alongside *Monarch of Bermuda* prior to the arrival of the new *Queen of Bermuda*. On 27 November 1933, she was held up in the St Lawrence River by snow, ice and fog, together with twelve other steamers, and it was rumoured that she had foundered after striking an iceberg off Newfoundland. On 29 August 1939, she was requisitioned by the Admiralty as a troopship. In February 1942, she left Singapore five days before the surrender, her decks packed with refugees, having taken 4,000 Indian troops and forty Indian nurses into the British colony. In 1945, she took liberated Russian troops to Odessa and brought back Allied prisoners who had been released by the Russian advance. From the outbreak of war to July 1946, she carried 231,000 troops and covered 344,000 miles.

She was decommissioned and left Liverpool on 2 March 1947 for Govan, where she was refitted by Fairfield Shipbuilding and Engineering Company, and emerged as *Empress of France*. Pepperpot funnels were fitted in 1958, and on 19 December 1960, she left Liverpool and was broken up by John Cashmore at Newport, Monmouthshire.

Duchess of Atholl (1928–42)

1928
20,119grt
582 x 75 x 42ft
ID: 1160505
Twin-screw, geared turbines by builder
18 knots
b. W. Beardmore & Company Limited, Dalmuir
Yard No. 648
Passengers: 580 cabin, 486 tourist, 510 third class
Launched on 23 November 1927, she sailed on her maiden voyage on 13 July 1928 from Liverpool to Quebec and Montreal. She left Liverpool on a cruise on 29 March 1933, visiting Morocco, Italy, French Riviera, Spain and the Balearic Islands. In December that year, she brought over Canadian bullion gold worth £1.5 million for the Mint. Captain A.H. Hall of the *Beaverburn* was appointed her commander in December 1934. On 30 December 1935, she lost her rudder and arrived at Liverpool three days late, having used her screws as steerage. When off Liverpool, tugs attempted

to tow her in but owing to a gale and heavy seas, the tow ropes snapped and she remained out at sea until the weather eased, and was then brought in and safely berthed in dock. On 30 December 1939, she was requisitioned by the Admiralty and used as a troopship. On 5 May 1942, she was part of convoy WS17 and took part in the Madagascar landings at Courier Bay, Diego Suarez, intending to stop the Japanese from cutting the lifeline to the Middle East. She was torpedoed by *U-178* 200 miles east of Ascension Island on 10 October 1942, homeward bound from Durban.

Duchess of Richmond/Empress of Canada (2) (1929–53)

1929
20,022grt
582 x 75 x 42ft
ID: 1160631
Twin-screw, geared turbines by builders
18 knots
b. John Brown & Company Limited, Glasgow
Yard No. 523
Passengers: 580 cabin, 486 tourist, 510 third class
Launched on 18 June 1928, she carried out a cruise to the Canary Islands for her maiden voyage on 26 January 1929. In April 1934, she carried to Gallipoli 700 veterans with their families and anchored in Kheli Bay. The veterans, who included two generals, visited the thirty-six

British cemeteries scattered over the Gallipoli peninsula. She carried the Duke and Duchess of Kent on their honeymoon cruise on 25 January 1935, and was requisitioned by the Admiralty on 14 February 1940 and operated as a troopship.

She arrived at Fairfield Shipbuilding & Engineering Company in May 1946 for refurbishment, and returned to service on 12 July 1947 as *Empress of Canada*, sailing on her and her owner's first post-war voyage on 16 July 1947. On 25 January 1953, fire broke out on her in Gladstone Dock, Liverpool, and she was declared a total loss. On 6 March 1954, she was righted and towed to Gladstone Graving Dock on 30 June. In August 1954, she was bought by the Cantiere Portovenere of Genoa for scrapping, and left Liverpool in tow of the Dutch tug *Zwarte Zee*, arriving at Spezia on 10 October 1954.

Duchess of Cornwall/Duchess of York (1929–43)

1929
20,021grt
582 x 75 x 42ft
ID: 1161202
Twin-screw, geared turbines by builder
18 knots
b. John Brown & Company Limited, Glasgow
Yard No. 524
Passengers: 580 cabin, 486 tourist, 510 third class

She was ordered as *Duchess of Cornwall* and launched on 9 September 1928 as *Duchess of York*, and sailed from Liverpool on her maiden voyage on 22 March 1929. On 7 March 1940, she was requisitioned by the Admiralty and operated as a troopship. On 11 July 1943, on a voyage from the Clyde to Freetown, she was set on fire by air attack from long-range bombers off Morocco. Eleven lives were lost.

Empress of Japan (2)/Empress of Scotland (2)[2] (1930–57)

2   Pictured in the colour section.

1929
26,032grt
644 x 84 x 45ft
ID: 5142322
Twin-screw, geared turbines by builder
21 knots
b. Fairfield Shipbuilding & Engineering
Company, Glasgow
Yard No. 634
Passengers: 458 first, 205 tourist, 100 third,
510 steerage class

Launched on 17 December 1929, she sailed on her maiden voyage on 14 June 1930 from Liverpool to Quebec and then to Southampton. She left Southampton for Hong Kong via Suez, and then to Yokohama and Vancouver. She incorporated a palm court, long gallery, foyer, green and black swimming pool, and a Cipollino marble-decorated dining saloon and sun deck. In April 1931, she sailed from Yokohama to Victoria in seven days, twenty hours and fifteen minutes at 22¼ knots. This crossing remains the fastest transpacific passage of any commercial vessel.

Requisitioned for trooping duties on 26 November 1939, following the attack on Pearl Harbor she was renamed *Empress of Scotland*. On 3 May 1948, she arrived at Liverpool and was converted to North Atlantic duties. She operated her first post-war sailing on 9 May 1950 from Liverpool–Greenock–Quebec, and in winter she

cruised from New York to the West Indies. For two years she sailed to Quebec, until her masts were shortened by 40ft, which enabled her to pass under the Quebec Bridge and make Montreal her terminal. She arrived at Liverpool on 25 November 1957 and was sold to the Hamburg America Line on 13 January 1958, becoming *Hanseatic*.[1] On 7 September 1966, she caught fire at New York and was towed to Hamburg for repairs by the tugs *Atlantic* and *Pacific*. Following inspection at Howaldtswerke Shipyard it was decided that she was beyond economic repair and was sold for scrapping at Hamburg.

Empress of Britain (2) (1931–40)

1931
42,348grt
761 x 98 x 56ft
ID: 1162582
Quadruple-screw, geared turbines by builders

---

1   Pictured in the colour section.

24 knots
b. John Brown & Company Limited, Glasgow
Yard No. 530
Passengers: 452 first, 260 tourist, 470 third class

Empress of Britain was laid down on 28 November 1928 and launched on 11 June 1930 by Edward, Prince of Wales, and sailed on her maiden voyage on 27 May 1931 from Southampton to Cherbourg to Quebec. Her departure was witnessed by the Prince of Wales and the crossing was a record of four days, nineteen hours and thirty-five minutes from Cherbourg to Father Point. She cost almost £3 million to build, of which about £750,000 was spent in machinery equipment. She was propelled by four sets of single-reduction, geared turbines on four shafts, these being arranged in two separate engine rooms with a watertight bulkhead between. The two inner screws were driven from the forward engine room, and the other two outer screws from the aft engine room. The whole of the auxiliary machinery of the ship was electrically driven, supplied by a group of diesel engines driving generator sets.

She was designed to carry out round-the-world cruises in the winter and her length, breadth and draught had to be kept as low as possible to enable her to enter the maximum number of ports and transit the Panama Canal. The Empress room, or ballroom, was decorated by Sir John Lavery, and was fitted with a complete stage and loudspeaker system. The Salle Jacques Cartier was the dining room and was decorated by Frank Brangwyn. The main lounge was decorated by Charles Allom, and was also equipped with a complete concert stage. The Mall stretched from Mayfair to the Empress room, which was a gallery designed by P.A. Staynes, and Eastern imagery, lacquer and porcelain inspired the design of the Cathay Lounge smoking room designed by Edmund Dulac. The Olympian-sized swimming pool of translucent terrazzo glass combined to give the impression of luxury and beauty which had never been seen before on the Canadian service.

She was the largest ship to appear south of the Equator. In November 1934, she made a round trip from Southampton to Quebec and back in eleven days, four hours and forty-seven minutes, which included twenty-six hours and two minutes at Quebec. Captain R.G. Latta was appointed general superintendent of the line in November 1934. He had retired the previous year as the *Empress of Britain*'s first commander and had steamed over 300,000 miles in her, including three round-the-world cruises. In June 1935, she arrived at Southampton thirty-six hours late through fog in the St Lawrence after having collided with the *Kafiristan* shortly after leaving Quebec. The following month, Sir Edward W. Beatty, president of Canadian Pacific, stated that it was the intention of the company to build a sister ship to her in the near future. Later that year, Captain Latta was appointed general manager of the company, replacing Captain James Gillies, who retired from the position due to ill health. On 17 June 1939, she left Conception Bay with King George VI and Queen Elizabeth on board on their return to Britain.

Her last commercial departure from Southampton took place on 2 September 1939, and she was requisitioned on 25 November 1939 to operate as a troopship. On 26 October 1940, she was 75 miles west of the Aran Islands when she was attacked by a long-range Focke-Wulf 200 enemy aircraft and set on fire. The first bomb hit her amidships and the second fell aft among the anti-aircraft armament. She was taken in tow by the Polish destroyer *Burza* and the tugs *Marauder* and *Thames*. However, she was torpedoed twice by *U-32* on 28 October and sank with a loss of forty-five lives. *U-32* was sunk by the destroyer *Harvester* two days later. *Empress of Britain* was the largest liner sunk during the Second World War.

Beaverdell/Mapledell (1946–63)

1946
9,901grt
476 x 64 x 40ft
IMO: 5214292
Single-screw, turbo-electric machinery by Parsons Marine Steam Turbine Company
16 knots
b. Lithgows Limited, Port Glasgow
Yard No. 1001
Launched 27 August 1945, she sailed on her maiden voyage from Liverpool to Saint John, New Brunswick, on 28 February 1946, and then operated from London (Royal Albert Dock) to Montreal. The winter service was to Saint John. On 28 August 1952, she was transferred to a new service from Vancouver–Japan–China–Manila and was renamed *Mapledell*. On 24 June 1954, she left Vancouver for London, where she then operated on the North Atlantic route. She reverted back to *Beaverdell* on 21 December 1956, and was sold to Giacomo Costa fu Andrea of Genoa on 11 January 1963, becoming *Luisa Costa*. On 24 March 1971, she arrived at La Spezia and was broken up the following year.

Beaverburn (2) (1946–60)

1944
9,875grt
476 x 64 x 40ft
ID: 5041463
Single-screw, geared turbines by Parsons Marine

Steam Turbine Company
15 knots
b. Caledon Shipbuilding & Engineering Company, Dundee
Yard No. 404
Passengers: 12
Launched on 25 February 1944 as *Empire Captain* for the Ministry of War Transport and acquired by Canadian Pacific on 15 May 1946, becoming *Beaverburn*. On 25 March 1960, she was sold to the Ben Line, and renamed *Bennachie*. She caught fire on 7 July and was towed into Singapore, and sold to the Atlantic Navigation Company of New York, becoming *Silvana*. In 1969, she was owned by the Outerocean Navigation Company, Kaohsiung, Taiwan, arriving there on 15 April 1971 and was broken up.

Beaverglen (1946–63)

1945
9,824grt
476 x 64 x 40ft
ID: 1180858
Single-screw, turbo-electric machinery by Parsons Marine Steam Turbine Company
16 knots
b. Lithgows Limited, Port Glasgow
Yard No. 1002
Launched on 10 December 1945, she sailed from Liverpool on her maiden voyage on 24 May 1946. She was sold to Hibiscus Limited of Hamilton, Bermuda, on 29 September 1963, becoming *Bermuda Hibiscus*, registered in London and *Ping An* in April 1965, when she was acquired by Teh-Hu Steam Ship Company, Hong Kong. On 24 November 1965, she went aground near the Hook of Holland and broke her back, and was broken up by Heuvelman NV.

Beaverford (2) (1946–62)

1944
9,881grt
476 x 64 x 40ft
ID: 5156660
Single-screw, geared turbines by Metropolitan
Vickers Limited
15 knots
b. Caledon Shipbuilding & Engineering
Company, Dundee
Yard No. 406
Passengers: 12

Launched on 18 August 1944 as *Empire
Kitchener* for the Ministry of War Transport,
with Canadian Pacific Steamships as managers.
She was acquired by Canadian Pacific on
12 June 1946, and renamed *Beaverford*. On
6 September 1956, she was briefly requisitioned
by the Admiralty during the Suez crisis, but
was released later that month. She was laid up
at Antwerp on 29 August 1962 and purchased
by the Alliance Maritime Corporation,
Hong Kong, becoming *Hulda*. In 1966,
her owners were the International Marine
Development Corporation of Monrovia. On
18 August 1969, she was driven ashore outside
Gulfport, Mississippi, by hurricane Camille,
and abandoned as a total loss. She was sold
and broken up by Coastal Metal Processors
Incorporated, P&W Industries Limited.

Beaverlake (1946–62)

1946
9,824grt
476 x 64 x 40ft
ID: 5044154
Single-screw, turbo-electric machinery by Parsons
Marine Steam Turbine Company
16 knots
b. Lithgows Limited, Port Glasgow
Yard No. 1003

Launched on 20 May 1946, she sailed on her
maiden voyage from Liverpool on 25 October.
On 18 June 1962, she was sold to Lloyd Tirrenico
S p A., Genoa, becoming *Bice Costa*. She arrived
at La Spezia on 23 April 1971 and was broken up
next to her sister, *Beavercove/Maplecove*.

Beavercove/Maplecove (1947–63)

1947
9,824grt
476 x 64 x 40ft
ID: 5420114
Single-screw, turbo-electric machinery by Parsons
Marine Steam Turbine Company
16 knots
b. Fairfield Shipbuilding & Engineering
Company, Glasgow
Yard No. 728

Launched on 16 July 1946, she sailed on her
maiden voyage from London on 3 September
1947. She was renamed *Maplecove* on 22 July
1952, arriving at Vancouver on 15 August. On
8 December 1952, she lost her rudder in a storm
and was towed to safety by the *Island Sovereign*.
She reverted back to the North Atlantic route
in December 1956, becoming *Beavercove* again,
and was sold to Costa on 19 August 1963 and
renamed *Giovanni Costa*. She was sold on
24 March 1971 for demolition at La Spezia.

Beaverbrae (2) (1947–54)

1939
9,034grt
469 x 60 x 35ft

ID: 5030854
Single-screw, diesel-electric engine
16 knots
b. Blohm & Voss Limited, Hamburg
Yard No. 518
Passengers: 35–58 (according to season)

Launched on 15 December 1938 as *Huascaran* for
the Hamburg America Line's South American
service. In the Second World War she served in the
German Navy as a submarine workshop ship, was
ceded to Britain on 14 November 1945, and taken
over by the Canadian War Assets Corporation. On
2 September 1947, she was acquired by Canadian
Pacific, refitted at Sorel, and fitted with 775 berths
for the carriage of immigrants. She was renamed
Beaverbrae. She operated her first Canadian
Pacific sailing on 8 February 1948, on the Saint
John–Antwerp–Hamburg route. On 1 November
1954, she was sold to the Compagnia Genovese
d'Armamento, Genoa, and renamed *Aurelia*. She
was acquired by Chandris Cruises in 1970, and
renamed *Romanza*, and transferred to Armadores
Romanza SA., of Panama. On 17 October 1979,
she grounded on Dhenousa Island in fog and her
passengers were evacuated. She was refloated two
days later and towed into Syroa for repairs. She was
renamed *Romantica* in 1991 by New Ambassador
Leisure Cruises, Cyprus. On 4 October 1997 she
suffered a fire and was beached near Limassol. She
was broken up at Alexandria the following year.

Beaverlodge (1952–60)

1943
9,904grt
476 x 64 x 40ft
ID: 5041035
Single-screw, geared turbine engines
15 knots
b. Furness Shipbuilding Company Limited,
Haverton Hill, Stockton-on-Tees
Yard No. 335
Passengers: 12

Launched as *Empire Regent* for the Ministry of War Transport, with Furness, Withy & Company as managers, on 13 August 1946, she was acquired by Furness Withy, and renamed *Black Prince*. In 1949, she was renamed *Zealandic*, on long-term charter to Shaw, Savill & Albion, and purchased by Canadian Pacific on 3 October 1952, becoming *Beaverlodge*. On 16 March 1960, she was sold to the Ben Line, and renamed *Benhiant*. She became *Venus* in 1970, owned by Witty Cia Naviera SA, Limassol, and arrived at Kaohsiung, Taiwan, on 14 July 1971 and was broken up.

Empress of Australia (2) (1953–56)

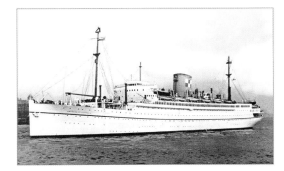

1924
17,707grt
552 x 72 x 42ft
ID: 1185887
Twin-screw, geared turbine engines
16 knots
b. Cammell Laird & Company Limited,

Birkenhead
Yard No. 886
Passengers: 500 cabin class

She was laid down at the yard as the *Suffren* in 1920 and was launched on 23 February 1924 as *De Grasse*. She was actually completed at St Nazaire because of a strike of workers at Birkenhead and sailed on her maiden voyage from Le Havre to New York on 21 August 1924. However, the 463 passengers were forced to return to Le Havre two days later when the shaft on one of the electric fans broke in the aft boiler room. That fan was repaired then, the following day, the fan on the forward boiler room also broke. *De Grasse* arrived back at Le Havre on 24 August and, when the fan was repaired, sailed again three days later.

On 10 November 1929, she hit the *Pequonnock* in New York but was not damaged. Her tonnage was reclassed as 18,435grt in 1932, when some of her passenger accommodation was removed. Following the introduction of *Normandie* in 1935, *De Grasse* was laid up. In 1938, it was announced that she would be reconditioned to carry out a series of West Indies cruises. A swimming pool, double-deck dining room and a new sun deck were installed for the cruises to Havana, Nassau, Miami, Haiti and Jamaica.

The following year she arrived at New York equipped with a gun turret fitted to her foredeck and 75mm guns mounted. She had sailed in complete secrecy from Le Havre on 7 October 1939, with 281 passengers on board. She was painted grey and in 1940 was laid up at Bordeaux, where she was captured by the Germans and subsequently used as an accommodation ship. She spent the rest of the war at this berth and was sunk by a depth charge on 30 August 1944 as German troops withdrew from Bordeaux.

De Grasse was refloated exactly one year later and towed to St Nazaire, where she was refitted and returned to service on 12 July 1947. When she arrived at New York on 25 July, she was the first French Line vessel to berth since the outbreak

of the war, and was welcomed by whistles and fireboats. There was a bittersweet atmosphere that day as when *De Grasse* arrived, the *Normandie* was in her final stages of being scrapped at a nearby pier.

In 1952, *De Grasse* sailed from Le Havre to the West Indies and was sold the following year to become the *Empress of Australia* for Canadian Pacific Steamships. The line required a passenger vessel to replace the *Empress of Canada*, which had been lost following a dockside fire at Liverpool's Gladstone Dock. She sailed on her maiden voyage for Canadian Pacific from Liverpool to Quebec on 28 April 1953 and served the line until 1956, when she was sold to Sicula Oceanica, Palermo, and renamed *Venezuela*.

Venezuela was placed on their Naples–La Guaira migrant service and in 1960 was refitted with a new bow, which increased her length to 187 metres, and she was certified to carry 180 first-, 500 tourist- and 800 third-class passengers. On 17 March 1962, she stranded on rocks near Cannes and her passengers and crew were taken off the ship. The following month she was refloated; following an inspection it was decided that it was uneconomical to repair her and she was sold to ship-breakers at Le Spezia.

Empress of Britain (3) [1] (1956–64)

1956
25,516grt
640 x 85 x 48ft
IMO: 5103924
Twin-screw, geared turbines by builders
20 knots
b. Fairfield Shipbuilding & Engineering Company, Glasgow
Yard No. 731
Passenger: 160 first, 894 tourist class

Empress of Britain was launched by Her Majesty Queen Elizabeth on 22 June 1955 and sailed from Liverpool to Quebec and Montreal on her maiden

---

1   Pictured in the colour section.

voyage on 20 April 1956. She was chartered to the Travel Savings Association in 1963 and sold to the Greek Line on 16 November the following year, being renamed *Queen Anna Maria* by Her Majesty at a ceremony at Piraeus on 15 March 1965. She sailed on their transatlantic service until 1975, when she was laid up at Piraeus. In December that year, she was sold to the Carnival Cruise Line and renamed *Carnivale*, becoming *Fiesta Marina* in 1994, and later, *Olympic*. In 1997, she became *Topaz*, operating as a cruise ship for Thomson Cruise Line, and then was chartered as the Peace Boat until 2008, when she was laid up at Singapore. She was sold to ship-breakers at Alang, India, later that year.

Empress of England[1] (1957–70)
1957
25,585grt
640 x 85 x 48ft
IMO: 5103948
Twin-screw, geared turbines by builder
20 knots
b. Vickers-Armstrong Shipbuilders, Walker-on-Tyne
Yard No. 155
Passenger: 160 first, 894 tourist class
Empress of England sailed on her maiden voyage from Liverpool to Quebec and Montreal on 18 April 1957, when she replaced the *Empress of Scotland*. In December 1962, she broke adrift in Gladstone Dock, Liverpool, and collided with the *Hindustan*. In unusually fierce gales she tore a bollard out of the dockside and swung round on her bow moorings, striking the knuckle between the entrance to the Hornby Dock and the Gladstone Dock, causing a 20ft gash in her side forward of the bridge. Due to the heavy storm continuing, it was impracticable to move her and she was made fast in the position where she came to rest until after the gale abated. This blocked

both the river entrance and the Hornby Dock for about twelve hours. Both ships were damaged in the collision.

In 1963, *Empress of England* was chartered by the Travel Savings Association and sailed on her first cruise for them on 28 October from Cape Town. In 1964, she returned to the Canadian Pacific Steamships route Liverpool to Montreal and was involved in a collision with a Norwegian tanker in the St Lawrence on 8 November 1965, when she was forced to return to Quebec for repairs. In February 1966, she encountered a hurricane off the North African coast while on a sixteen-day cruise. She maintained the North Atlantic route from Liverpool until 1970, when she was sold to the Shaw, Savill & Albion Line and renamed *Ocean Monarch*.

She made one round sailing from Liverpool to Southampton and Australia, and then returned to Cammell Laird for refitting into a one-class liner. She sailed from Merseyside on 17 September 1971 but as she was delayed due to industrial action, the line was forced to cancel twelve cruises she was due to make that summer. She made only one Mediterranean cruise that year, leaving Southampton on 16 October.

On 5 November, she left Southampton for Barbados, Curaçao, Panama, Acapulco, Los Angeles, Vancouver, Honolulu, Tokelau Islands, Fiji and Auckland. She was employed on a cruising programme out of Sydney in 1973 but as she suffered serious mechanical problems, in 1974 she returned to Britain and completed a series of cruises from Southampton. *Ocean Monarch* arrived at Southampton on her last cruise on 5 June 1975, and sailed to the ship-breakers at Kaohsiung the following week.

Empress of Canada (3)[2] (1961–72)
1961
27,300grt
650 x 76 x 48ft
IMO: 5103936
Twin-screw, Parsons steam turbines by builder
20 knots
b. Vickers-Armstrong Shipbuilders, Walker-on-Tyne
Yard No. 171
Passengers: 192 first, 856 tourist class
Empress of Canada sailed on her maiden voyage from Liverpool to Quebec and Montreal via Greenock on 24 April 1961. In April 1967, on a crossing of the North Atlantic she encountered a hurricane, which delayed her for eight hours. During the period of bad weather she rammed a whale, which became fixed to her bow. In the late 1960s, various rumours circulated regarding the sale of the *Empress of Canada*, and it was reported that she may be sold to Shaw Savill and become *Dominion Monarch*.

On 23 November 1971, she arrived at Liverpool, ending Canadian Pacific's North Atlantic service after sixty-eight years. She sailed from Liverpool on 14 December for Tilbury and was laid up. It was reported that Home Lines were interested in purchasing her and engaged consultants to prepare a detailed conversion proposal. However, nothing came of the plan and she was sold to the Carnival Cruise Line in 1972, becoming *Mardi Gras*, then *Olympic* in 1993, *Star of Texas* in 1994, and *Apollon* in 1996, when she returned to the Mersey for a series of sailings by Direct Cruises. She was sold to ship-breakers in 2003.

1   Pictured in the colour section.

2   Pictured in the colour section.

Beaverfir (1961–72)

1961
4,539grt
374 x 51 x 25ft
IMO: 5039020
Single-screw, 2SA 6-cylinder engine by
Burmeister & Wain
14½ knots
b. Sarpsberg Mek, Verksted A/S, Greaker,
Oslofjord
Yard No. 32
Beaverfir was acquired by Canadian Pacific in
March 1961 to operate to the Great Lakes via the
St Lawrence Seaway. She was sold on 21 April
1972, becoming *Arion*, and then *Manaure II* in
1975 and *Anden* in 1981. On 20 September 1982,
she dragged her anchor during a storm while
lying off Acajutla, El Salvador, and was blown
ashore on Barra de Santiago. Sixteen of her crew
of twenty-six were lost.

Beaverpine/CP *Explorer*[3] (1962–73)

1962
4,514grt
371 x 53 x 24ft
IMO: 5039044
Single-screw, Fairfield-Sulzer 2SA 6-cylinder engine
14 knots

3   Pictured in the colour section.

b. Burntisland Shipbuilding Company,
Burntisland, Fife
Yard No. 403
Launched 18 June 1962, *Beaverpine* sailed on
her maiden voyage on 23 October from London
to *Montreal*. She was built to Lloyd's Register
Class +100A1 with Class II Ice Strengthening.
She was fitted out to meet the requirements of
the St Lawrence Seaway Authority, having Port
Colborne fairleads, landing booms, navigating
lights and a stern anchor. Three of the four
holds and tweendecks were positioned forward
of the machinery space, and all the living
accommodation was situated in the midships
superstructure. A section of No. 4 tweendeck was
allocated for the carriage of special cargo, and
the forecastle space could also be used for this
purpose. She was converted to a container ship
in 1971 and renamed CP *Explorer*. She became
Moira in 1973, *Trade Container* in 1981, and
arrived at Kaohsiung on 29 December 1986 to be
broken up.

Beaverelm (1962–71)

1960
3,959grt
355 x 49 x 30ft
IMO: 5039018
Single-screw, 2SA 7-cylinder engine by
Burmeister & Wain
14 knots
b. Moss Vaerft & Dokk A/S, Moss, Norway
Yard No. 144

Launched on 5 May 1960 as *Roga* for Akties,
Asplund, Moss and acquired by Canadian Pacific
on 9 August 1962, becoming *Beaverelm* for the
Great Lakes service with Ellerman's Wilson Line.
On 28 September 1971, she was sold and renamed
Hengshan, and *Yong Kang* in 1977. She was deleted
from the register in 1992.

Beaverash (1963–69)

1958
4,529grt
375 x 50 x 23ft
IMO: 5401558
Single-screw, 2SA 7-cylinder engine by
Burmeister & Wain
15 knots
b. A/B Ekensberg Varv, Stockholm
Yard No. 214
Launched on 19 May 1958 as *Mimer* for
M. Thorviks Rederi A/S, Oslo, and acquired by
Canadian Pacific on 10 January 1963, becoming
Beaverash. She was sold in 1969, renamed *Zanet*,
then *Agios Nikolaos* in 1980, and *Nissaki* in 1984.
She arrived at Pakistan in May 1985 and was
broken up.

Anders Rogenaes and *N.O. Rogenaes*, owned by Nils
Rogenaes, were chartered by Canadian Pacific
to operate container services to the Great Lakes.
They were renamed *Medicine Hat* and *Moose Jaw*,
and were painted in CP colours. Each ship carried
cargo and twelve containers on deck.

Medicine Hat (1960/4,186grt)

IMO: 5016200
1960: *Concordia Anders*
1962: *Anders Rogenaes*
1968: *Helgoland*
1972: *Furka*
1973: *Yacu Guagua*
1980: *Yanmar*
1 February 1981: Stranded, and arrived at Brownsville on 7 May 1981 and broken up.

Moose Jaw (1963/7,302grt)

IMO: 5421546
1968: *Hoegh Beaver*
1978: *Copihue*
1981: *Sheng Li*
5 November 1984: Arrived at Gadani Beach and broken up.

Beaveroak/CP *Ambassador* (1965–73)

1965
6,165grt
408 x 58 x 33ft
IMO: 6511790
6-cylinder, Clark-NEM-Sulzer diesel
16 knots
b. Vickers-Armstrong Shipbuilders, Walker-on-Tyne
Yard No. 182
Launched on 3 March 1965 for the Antwerp–London–Montreal–Great Lakes service. She was strengthened beyond Lloyd's Class 1 Ice,

and her icebreaker bow and strengthened shell enabled her to sail up the St Lawrence as far as Montreal in the winter. She was designed for both dry and container trade and was built with an air-conditioned control room in the engine room, with duplicate controls on the bridge, and data logging of instrumentation was incorporated. Her cargo gear was designed for short in-port periods and to give forklift trucks maximum freedom of movement below decks, and the refrigerated cargo installation was fully automated. The ice strengthening required an extra 180 tons of steel above normal construction. She was lengthened in 1970 at Rotterdam and converted into a container ship, returning to service as CP *Ambassador*. She became *Atalanta* in 1973, then *Zim Atlanta* in 1980, *New Penguin* in 1981, and *Flamingo* the following year. She arrived at Karachi on 30 April 1984 and was broken up at Gadani Beach.

CP *Voyageur* (1970–82)

1970
15,680grt
548 x 84 x 30ft
IMO: 7027394
Single-screw, 2SA 8-cylinder engines by Burmeister & Wain
18 knots
b. Cammell Laird & Company Limited, Birkenhead
Yard No. 1343
Launched on 19 August 1970 and sailed on her maiden voyage from Liverpool to Canada on 29 November. She became *Andes Voyager* for one voyage in 1983, reverting back to CP *Voyageur*. The following year she was named *Andes Voyager* again, and *Louisane* and *Cedar Voyager* in 1985. She was acquired by Mid Atlantic Shipping in 1986, becoming *Biokovo*, *Montreal Venturer* in 1993, *Canmar Valiant* in 1994, MSC *Rebecca* in 1995, and *Biokovo* in 1997. She arrived at Alang on 19 December 1997 and was broken up.

CP *Trader*/*Andes Trader*[1] (1971–82)

1971
15,680grt
548 x 84 x 30ft
IMO: 7046015
Single-screw, 2SA 8-cylinder engines by Burmeister & Wain
18 knots
b. Cammell Laird & Company Limited, Birkenhead
Yard No. 1344
Launched on 28 January 1971, and towed to Verolme Dockyard, Cork, for completion due to industrial action at the yard. In 1982 she was operating as *Andes Trader* for Compañía Chilena de Nav., then *Cedar Trader* in 1985, *San Lorenzo* in 1986, and *Canmar Spirit* in 1994. She arrived at Alang on 12 March 2001 and was broken up.

CP *Discoverer*/*Andes Discoverer*[2] (1971–82)

1971
15,680grt
548 x 84 x 30ft
IMO: 7102352
Single-screw, 2SA 8-cylinder engines by Burmeister & Wain
18 knots
b. Cammell Laird & Company Limited, Birkenhead
Yard No. 1345

---

1 Pictured in the colour section.
2 Pictured in the colour section.

Launched on 26 March 1971 and sailed on her maiden voyage from Liverpool on 28 July and then moved to the Rotterdam–Quebec route and Felixstowe in 1981. Renamed *Andes Discoverer* in 1982, then *Mississippi* two years later, *Cedar Discoverer* in 1985, and *Canmar Venture* in 1986. She arrived at Alang on 20 June 2001 and was broken up.

CP *Hunter* (1980–81)

1979
13,348grt
536 x 75 x 45ft
IMO: 7636559
Single-screw, 2s.sa engines by MAN, Ghent
16 knots
b. Boelwef SA, Tamise
She was built as *E.R. Brussel* and was chartered by Canadian Pacific from Ernst Russ of Hamburg on 16 January 1980 for six round voyages.

CP *Ambassador* (2) (1981–86)
1971
29,398grt
28,037dwt
232 x 31 x 11ft
IMO: 7032210
Single-screw, 2s.sa Sulzer engines by G. Clark & NEM Limited, Wallsend, Tyne and Wear
23 knots
b. Swan Hunter Shipbuilders Limited, Newcastle
Yard No. 15

Launched on 14 October 1970 for the Dart Container Line Limited, owned by the Bristol City Line and entered service as *Dart Atlantic*. On 18 August 1981, she became CP *Ambassador* on charter to Canadian Pacific, owned by Trinity Finance Limited. She was renamed *Canmar Ambassador* in 1985, remaining on charter to Canadian Pacific. She arrived at Alang on 19 March 1995, and was beached on 13 April and broken up.

TANKERS AND BULK CARRIERS

R.B. *Angus* (1965–67)
1958
9,371grt
503 x 62 x 30ft
IMO: 5421481
Single-screw, 2s.sa engines by SA Fiat SGM, Turin
15 knots
b. Brodogradilište, Split, Yugoslavia
Yard No. 147
Launched as *Sunrise*, becoming *Modena* in 1963, and *R.B. Angus* in 1965, when acquired by Canadian Pacific (Bermuda) Limited. On 25 November 1967, she left Chemainus, British Columbia, for Tokyo, and on 17 December, during a storm, she developed a leak in Nos 3 and 4 holds, and was abandoned. She sank 620 miles north-east of Japan. All crew were saved.

Lord Mount Stephen[3] (1966–85)
1966
41,521grt
758 x 118 x 57ft
IMO: 6618304
Single-screw, 2s.sa Sulzer engines by builder
b. Mitsubishi Heavy Industries, Nagasaki
Yard No. 1623

Launched on 3 August 1966 for Canadian Pacific (Bermuda) Limited and placed on long-term charter to the Shell Petroleum Company. She was sold in 1985, becoming *Pedoulas*, and arrived at Alang on 22 April 1992 and broken up.

Lord Strathcona (1967–85)
1966
41,521grt
758 x 118 x 57ft
IMO: 6702313
Single-screw, 2s.sa Sulzer engines by builder
b. Mitsubishi Heavy Industries, Nagasaki
Yard No. 1624
Launched on 15 November 1966 and placed on long-term charter to the British Petroleum Company. She was sold in 1985 to Acanthus Cia Naviera SA, Cyprus, renamed *Breeden* and arrived at Mangalore on 3 March 1992 and broken up.

H.R. MacMillan[4] (1968–78)
1967
21,461grt
594 x 96 x 52ft
IMO: 6802589
Single-screw, 2s.sa engines by builder
14½ knots
b. Mitsubishi Heavy Industries, Hiroshima
Yard No. 191
Launched on 31 October 1967 and placed on a ten-year charter to MacMillan Bloedel. She was sold in July 1978 to the Pender Shipping Corporation, Panama, becoming *Grand Reliance*. She was detained at Basrah with a cargo of rice between March 1976 and March 1978, and arrived at Huangpu, China, on 13 October 1985 and broken up.

3 Pictured in the colour section.

4 Pictured in the colour section.

J.V. Clyne (1968–79)

1968
21,461grt
594 x 96 x 52ft
IMO: 6810122
Single-screw, 2s.sa engines by builder
14½ knots
b. Mitsubishi Heavy Industries, Hiroshima
Yard No. 192

Launched on 2 February 1968, sailing on her delivery voyage from Hiroshima to Port Alberni, British Columbia, on 26 April. On 31 March 1979, she was sold to the Korean Shipping Corporation, Panama, becoming *West Sunori*, and arrived at Ulsan, South Korea, in October 1986 and was broken up.

N.R. Crump (1969–79)

1969
21,461grt
594 x 96 x 52ft
IMO: 6913431
Single-screw, 2s.sa engines by builder
14½ knots
b. Mitsubishi Heavy Industries, Hiroshima
Yard No. 204

Launched on 8 March 1969 and managed by CP Steamships, she was the first Canadian Pacific ship to carry the new green-designed funnel. She sailed on her delivery voyage from Hiroshima to Nanaimo on 31 May 1969. Sold to Baruca (Panama) SA on 27 February 1979, she became *West Jinori*, and transferred to the Korea Shipping Corporation the following year. She became *Texistepec* in 1980 and was owned by NAVIMIN in 1982. In August 1983, she ran aground and caught fire in the Gulf of Mexico. She was towed to Cartagena, Colombia, as *Yoshito Venture* and broken up.

Fort St John (1969–81)

1969
10,324grt
487 x 70 x 40ft
IMO: 6924351
Single-screw, 2s.sa Sulzer engines by Sumitomo Shipbuilding & Machinery Company, Tamashima
15 knots
b. Sanoyasu Dockyard Company, Osaka
Yard No. 275

Launched on 8 July 1969 as *Pacific Logger*, she sailed on her maiden voyage from Osaka–Seattle on 5 September. On 18 December 1974, her shaft was damaged during a gale, and she was towed to the builders for repairs. On 28 March 1977, she was renamed *Fort St John*, and in 1981 she became *Shanta Rohan*, owned by Hede Navigation (Pvt) Limited, Bombay. She was laid up off Bombay on 5 September 1988, and in July the following year she took on a list and became waterlogged. She was abandoned and scrapped in 1990.

T. Akasaka (1969–85)

1969
33,328grt
744 x 102 x 58ft
IMO: 7002203
Single-screw, 2s.sa Burmeister & Wain-type 7K84EF engine
15 knots
b. Nippon Kokan K.K., Yokohama
Yard No. 860

T. Akasaka was launched on 15 August 1969, with a hinged main mast for passing under bridges on her route. She was placed on charter to Marubeni-Lida Kabushiki Kaisya, and was sold to Thenamaris on 8 July 1985, becoming *Seaboss*. In 1986, she was sold to Waterdiamond Marine, Cyprus. She arrived at Alang on 17 August 1994, and work began on 3 September to break her up.

W.C. Van Horne (1970–85)

1970
33,328grt
744 x 102 x 58ft
IMO: 7013745
Single-screw, 2s.sa Burmeister & Wain-type 7K84EF engine
15 knots
b. Nippon Kokan K. Waterdiamond, Yokohama
Yard No. 861

Launched on 11 March 1970, she sailed on her delivery voyage from Yokohama to Vancouver on 10 June. She was sold to Peninsula Shipping Company Limited, Hong Kong, on 13 December 1985, and was renamed *Pratincole*, then *Hope Sea* in 1994, and arrived at Alang on 11 September 1998, where she was broken up by the Ashwin Corporation.

Port Hawkesbury (1970–86)

1970
133,699grt
1,109 x 170 x 88ft
IMO: 7016125
Single-screw, 2s.sa Burmeister & Wain-type 9K98FF engine
15½ knots
b. Nippon K.K.
Yard No. 2

Launched on 26 October 1969, she sailed on her maiden voyage from Yokohama to Mina al Ahmadi, Persian Gulf, on 16 July 1970. On 4 February 1986, she was sold to Mill Reef Shipping, Hong Kong, renamed *Porthmeus*, and acquired by Popham Shipping, Hong Kong, later that year, becoming *Red Sea Pioneer*. She arrived at Alang on 18 August 1993, and was broken up by the Ghasiram Gokalchand Ship Breaking Company.

T.G. Shaughnessy (1971–82)

1970
133,701grt
1,109 x 170 x 88ft
IMO: 7034892
Single-screw, 2s.sa Burmeister & Wain-type 9K98FF engine
15½ knots
b. Nippon Kokan K. Goaltend
Yard No. 4
Launched on 4 April 1970 and loaded for her voyage from Mina al Ahmadi to the Port Tupper Refinery, Nova Scotia, on 29 January 1971. She was sold on 9 February 1982 to Shinwa Kaiun K.K., Japan, becoming *Shin en Maru*, and to Aurica Shipping, Cyprus, in 1986, where she was renamed *Shining Star*. She arrived at Gadani Beach on 21 September 1993 and was broken up.

G.A. Walker (1973–88)

1973
18,774grt
560 x 85 x 47ft
IMO: 7225702
Single-screw, 2s.sa Burmeister & Wain 6K74EF engines

15 knots
b. Van der Giesen-Noord N.V., Krimpen, Netherlands
Yard No. 888
Launched on 2 September 1972, she sailed on her maiden voyage from Rotterdam to Salem on 20 March 1973. She was chartered to the Ministry of Defence on 12 April 1982, and used as a fuel tanker at Port Stanley. She was returned to Canadian Pacific on 27 September 1984. Acquired by Bergvall & Hudner in April 1988, and renamed *Inver Alke* in 1988, and *Alex* in 1990. She arrived at Chittagong on 31 October 2000.

W.A. Mather (1973–88)

1973
18,774grt
650 x 85 x 47ft
IMO: 7304429
Single-screw, 2s.sa Burmeister & Wain 6K74EF engines
15 knots
b. Van der Giesen-Noord N.V., Krimpen, Netherlands
Yard No. 889
Launched on 28 July 1973 and placed on charter to Shell Petroleum. She was sold to Bergvall & Hudner in April 1988, and arrived at Gadani Beach on 17 February 1999 and broken up.

E.W. Beatty (1973–87)

1973
69,904grt
853 x 137 x 78ft
IMO: 7327677
Single-screw, 2s.sa Burmeister & Wain-type 9K84EF engines
15 knots
b. Nippon Kokan K.K.
Yard No. 893
Launched on 22 June 1973, she sailed on her maiden voyage from Yokohama to Port Hedland. She was laid up at Brixham on 8 July 1982.

On 14 April 1986, she was transferred to the Isle of Man Register, and sold to Windsor Bulk Incorporated on 5 October 1987, becoming *Solita*. In 1991, she was renamed *Apostolos Andreas 4*, and *Apollo Sea* in 1993. She foundered north-west of Robben Island.

R.A. Emerson (1973–89)

1973
18,774grt
560 x 85 x 47ft
IMO: 7325370
Single-screw, 2s.sa Burmeister & Wain 6K74EF engines
15 knots
b. Van der Giesen-Noord N.V., Krimpen, Netherlands
Yard No. 890
Launched on 7 July 1973 and entered service on 2 November on a voyage from Rotterdam to Portland. In 1989, she was sold to Ceres Hellenic Shipping Limited, Piraeus, becoming *Clearventure*, and then *Strength* in 1994. She arrived at Alang on 18 October 1997 and was broken up.

D.C. Coleman[1] (1974–84)

1974
69,904grt
853 x 137 x 78ft
IMO: 7355296
Single-screw, 2s.sa Burmeister & Wain-type 9K84EF engines
15 knots
b. Nippon Kokan K.K.
Yard No. 894

Launched on 17 January 1974, she entered service with CP (Bermuda). She was sold on 6 December 1984 to Dawn Sky Limited, Hong Kong, becoming Golden Commander, and then Philippine Commander, owned by the Crimson Navigation Company, Panama. In 1988, she was acquired by Coresol Ventures Incorporated and renamed Delantera, then El Delantero in 1989, owned by Delantero KS. She became Ocean Flare in 1992, Kartal 4 in 1993, and Art 54 in 1998. She arrived at Gadani Beach on 3 April 1998, and was broken up.

Fort Macleod (1974–88)

1974
18,774grt
560 x 85 x 47ft
IMO: 7332139
Single-screw, 2s.sa Burmeister & Wain 6K74EF engines
15 knots
b. Van der Giesen-Noord N.V., Krimpen, Netherlands
Yard No. 893

Launched on 1 March 1973, she entered service on 4 March 1974, sailing from Rotterdam to Port Jefferson. She was sold in 1988 to the Bergvall & Hudner Group, becoming Osco Macle for Macle Shipping Limited, Macle in 1989, and Macler in 2000. She arrived at Chittagong on 6 October 2003, and was broken up.

I.D. Sinclair (1974–86)

1974
133,679grt
1,109 x 170 x 88ft
IMO: 7374709
Single-screw, 2s.sa Burmeister & Wain-type 9K98FF engine
15½ knots
b. Nippon Kokan K.K.
Yard No. 27

Launched on 23 March 1974, and positioned in ballast to Dubai on 20 July, for service to the Point Tupper Refinery. In March 1986, she was sold to Mill Reef Shipping Limited, Hong Kong, becoming Fidius, managed by Barber Ship Management. She was transferred to the Isle of Man Register on 1 May 1986, and was renamed Happy Master by K/S A/S Norman Tankers, then Nor Master in 1989 and Assimina in 1992. She arrived at Chittagong on 20 July 1999, and was broken up.

W.M. Neal (1974–86)

1974
69,904grt
853 x 137 x 78ft
IMO: 7380576
Single-screw, 2s.sa Burmeister & Wain-type 9K84EF engines
15 knots
b. Nippon Kokan K.K.
Yard No. 899

Launched on 7 May 1974, she sailed from Yokohama to Port Hedland, Western Australia, on 8 August. She was sold to Rochefort Maritime Incorporated on 17 December 1986, and renamed Channel Commander, then Lady Bird in 1988, River Plate in 1990, and Iolcos Pioneer in 1995. She arrived at Ky Ha, Vietnam, on 9 June 1998, and was broken up.

Fort Steele (1974–90)

1974
18,774grt
560 x 85 x 47ft
IMO: 7368267
Single-screw, 2s.sa Burmeister & Wain 6K74EF engines
15 knots
b. Van der Giesen-Noord N.V., Krimpen, Netherlands
Yard No. 894

Launched on 27 July 1974, she sailed from Rotterdam to Ventspils, Latvia, on 30 November. She was sold to Elcrown Incorporated in April 1990, and renamed Crestventure L, then Courage in 1994, Wawasan Courage in 1996, and Kithira in 1999. She arrived at Xinhui, China, on 6 July 2002, and was broken up.

Fort Edmonton (1975–87)

1975
18,774grt
560 x 85 x 47ft
IMO: 7381714
Single-screw, 2s.sa Burmeister & Wain 6K74EF engines
15 knots
b. Van der Giesen-Noord N.V., Krimpen, Netherlands
Yard No. 900

Launched on 20 October 1974, she sailed from Rotterdam to Callao, Peru, on 1 March 1975. She was placed on charter to the Ministry of Defence on 2 November 1982 to act as a fuel tanker at Port Stanley. She was returned to Canadian Pacific on 30 August 1983, and was transferred to the Isle of Man Register on 10 September 1986. She was sold to the Edmonton Shipping Company on 6 October 1987, becoming Edmonton, then Osco Edmo in 1989, and Edmo the following year. She arrived at Chittagong on 19 July 1999, and was broken up.

---

1 Pictured in the colour section.

Fort Kipp (1975–88)

1975
18,774grt
560 x 85 x 47ft
IMO: 7381726
Single-screw, 2s.sa Burmeister & Wain 6K74EF
engines
15 knots
b. Van der Giesen-Noord N.V., Krimpen,
Netherlands
Yard No. 901
Launched on 8 March 1975, she sailed from
Rotterdam to Gibraltar on 3 July. She was
transferred to the Isle of Man Register on
2 October 1986, and was sold to the Bergvall &
Hudner Group in 1988. She was acquired by Tiki
Shipping Limited in 1988, becoming *Iver Tiki*,
and *Nike* in 1990. On 19 July 1999, she arrived at
Chittagong, and was broken up.

Fort Nelson (1975–88)

1975
21,894grt
604 x 92 x 51ft
IMO: 7375571
Single-screw Burmeister & Wain-type 7K67GF
engines
15 knots
b. Sanoyasu Dockyard Company, Osaka
Yard No. 3
Launched on 28 May 1975, she sailed from Osaka
to Suez on 12 August. She was transferred to the
Hong Kong Register on 26 April 1984, and was

sold to the Bergvall & Hudner Group in April
1988, becoming *Elso*, then *Ismini* in 1994, *Petalis*
in 1999, and *Pacific No. 1* in 2005. She arrived at
Alang on 8 February 2009, and was broken up.

Fort Coulonge (1976–88)

1976
18,872grt
650 x 85 x 47ft
IMO: 7381738
Single-screw, 2s.sa Burmeister & Wain 6K74EF
engines
15 knots
b. Van der Giesen-Noord N.V., Krimpen,
Netherlands
Yard No. 902
Launched on 18 October 1975, she sailed
from Rotterdam to Amuay Bay, Venezuela, on
20 February 1976. She was transferred to the
Isle of Man Register on 14 September 1986, and
renamed *Coulonge*. In April 1988, she was sold
to the Bergvall & Hudner Group, and became
Ulan Trader and then *Ulan* in 1989. Following a
collision at Kandla, India, on 9 June 1998, she was
laid up, and arrived at Gadani Beach on 23 May
the following year, and was broken up.

Fort Calgary (1976–88)

1976
21,893grt
604 x 92 x 51ft
IMO: 7375595
Single-screw, Burmeister & Wain-type 7K67GF
engines
15 knots
b. Sanoyasu Dockyard Company, Osaka
Yard No. 345
Launched on 18 December 1975, she sailed from
Osaka to Tripoli on 26 March 1976. She was
transferred to the Hong Kong Register on 6 June
1986, and in April 1988 she was acquired by the
Bergvall & Hudner Group, becoming *Calga*
for Calga Shipping Limited, Hong Kong, the

following year. She became *Galea 1* and *Galea* in
1994, *Ekaterina A* in 1996, and *Blue Lady* in 1998.
She arrived at Chittagong on 28 April 2002, and
was broken up.

Fort Kamloops (1976–86)

1976
17,281grt
604 x 92 x 51ft
IMO: 7420857
Single-screw, Burmeister & Wain-type 7K67GF
engines
15 knots
b. Sanoyasu Dockyard Company, Osaka
Yard No. 357
Launched on 22 July 1976 as the first of three
ships, she sailed from Osaka to Vancouver on
28 October. The ships were delivered to Canadian
Pacific (Bermuda) Limited, and registered
in Hong Kong. On 25 November 1986, *Fort
Kamloops* was sold to Addship Trading Company
Limited, who also purchased *Fort Carleton*
and *Fort Hamilton*. She was renamed *Kamloops
Progress*, and became *Kamo* in 1988, owned by
the Kamo Shipping Corporation, Monrovia. She
became *Huldra* in 1994, *Angeliki B* in 1995, *Amelia*
in 2002, and *Iris S* in 2008. She arrived at Alang
on 8 June 2010, and was broken up.

Port Vancouver (1977–86)

1977
35,716grt
738 x 106 x 59ft
IMO: 7423938
Single-screw, 2s.sa-type 7K80GF engines
15½ knots
b. Burmeister & Wain, Copenhagen
Yard No. 871
Launched on 11 November 1976, she sailed from
Copenhagen to Tubarão on 14 January 1977.
She was acquired by the Mill Reef Shipping
Company, Hong Kong, on 27 June 1986 and
renamed *Vancouver*, then became *Stacouver* in

1988, owned by Stamer Bulk Investments, Oslo, Helmer Staubo & Company. She was renamed *Vancouver* again in 1990, and arrived at Alang on 10 July 2001, and was broken up.

Fort Victoria (1977–88)

1977
17,281grt
568 x 84 x 47ft
IMO: 7420869
Single-screw, Burmeister & Wain-type 7K67GF engines
15 knots
b. Sanoyasu Dockyard Company, Osaka
Yard No. 358
Launched on 15 November 1976, she sailed from Osaka to Marseilles on 28 February 1977. She was sold to Mill Reef Shipping Limited on 17 September 1986, becoming *Victus*, and was acquired by the Bergvall & Hudner Group in April 1988 and renamed *Tusa*, owned by the Tusa Shipping Corporation, Monrovia. In 1994, she became *Ionia*, then *Ionis* in 1995, *Blue Angel* in 1998, *Mandy* in 1999, *Sino Smart* in 2001, and *Da Shen* in 2005. She arrived at Jiangyin on 24 May 2013, and was broken up.

Port Quebec (1977–86)

1977
35,716grt
738 x 106 x 59ft
IMO: 7423940
Single-screw, 2s.sa-type 7K80GF engines
15½ knots
b. Burmeister & Wain, Copenhagen
Yard No. 873
Launched on 17 February 1977, she sailed from Copenhagen to Contrecoeur on 18 April 1977. She was sold to Mill Reef Shipping Limited, Hong Kong, on 19 June 1986, becoming *Quebec*, and then *Kali L* in 1989, owned by Elprimero Incorporated, Piraeus, *Prodigy* and *Aerosmith* in 1995, *Pine Royal* in 2000 and *Santa Cruz II* in 2008. She arrived at Chittagong on 22 March 2012 and was broken up.

Fort Yale (1977–88)

1977
17,281grt
604 x 92 x 51ft
IMO: 7420845
Single-screw, Burmeister & Wain-type 7K67GF engines
15 knots
b. Sanoyasu Dockyard Company, Osaka
Yard No. 359
Launched on 17 March 1977, *Fort Yale* sailed from Osaka to Newcastle, NSW, on 2 August 1977. During a storm on 27 December 1981, in Latakia Roads, Syria, *Bravo Neck* was in collision with the *Wu Men* and then collided with *Fort Yale*, causing considerable damage. The *Bravo Neck* later sank. In April 1988, *Fort Yale* was sold to the Bergvall & Hudner Group, and chartered to BHP Transport (USA) Incorporated and renamed *Copper Yale*, then *Master Panos* in 1992, *Sonito* in 1998, *Lazos* in 1999, *Kiki P* in 2008, and *South Star* in 2009. She arrived at Chittagong on 11 October 2011, and was broken up.

Fort Walsh (1978–84)

1978
14,088grt
528 x 75 x 44ft
IMO: 7631559
Single-screw, 2s.sa engines Burmeister & Wain-type 6L55GF by Mitsui Zōsen, Tamano
15½ knots
b. Sanoyasu Dockyard Company, Osaka
Yard No. 364
Launched on 27 July 1977, she sailed from Osaka to Karachi on 17 January 1978. She was registered at Hong Kong, owned by Canadian Pacific (Bermuda) Limited as a self-trimming bulk carrier with deck capacity for 126 containers. She was the first of a class of three, which were a slightly smaller version of the Fort Kamloops class. She was sold on 25 July 1984 to Guyana Timbers Limited, Bahamas (Guybulk Shipping Limited as agents), becoming *Manaka*, then *Pany R* in 1992, *Zebra* in 2004, and *Orient Fortune* in 2007. She arrived at Aliaga, Turkey, on 15 July 2009, and was broken up.

Fort Carleton (1978–86)

1978
14,088grt
528 x 75 x 44ft
IMO: 7631561
Single-screw, 2s.sa engines Burmeister & Wain-type 6L55GF by Mitsui Zōsen, Tamano
15½ knots
b. Sanoyasu Dockyard Company, Osaka
Yard No. 365
Launched on 14 October 1977, she sailed from Osaka to Suez on 15 March 1978. She was sold to the Addship Trading Company, Hong Kong, on 19 November 1986, and renamed *Carleton Progress*. In April 1988, she was purchased by the Bergvall & Hudner Group, becoming *Carle*, then *Danis Koper* in 1994, *Mert V* in 2001, and *Mert E* in 2007. She arrived at Chittagong on 4 December 2009, and was broken up.

Fort Hamilton (1978–86)

1978
14,088grt
528 x 75 x 44ft
IMO: 7631573
Single-screw, 2s.sa engines Burmeister &
Wain-type 6L55GF by Mitsui Zōsen, Tamano
15½ knots
b. Sanoyasu Dockyard Company, Osaka
Yard No. 366
Launched on 23 December 1977, she sailed
from Osaka to New York on 27 March 1978.
She was sold to Addship Trading Company on
4 December 1986, becoming *Hamilton Progress*.
In April 1988, she was sold to the Bergvall
& Hudner Group, becoming *Hami*, and then
Greveno in 1994. She arrived at Alang on
30 December 2008, and was broken up.

Fort Norman (1979–84)

1968
29,304grt
714 x 97 x 42ft
IMO: 6805517
Single-screw, 2SA Burmeister & Wain engines by
builder
15½ knots
b. Eriksberg M/V A/B, Gothenburg
Yard No. 614
Launched on 21 December 1967 as *Rona* for
A/S Kosmos, A/S Agnes in 1972, and the Owen
Corporation, Liberia in 1978, becoming *Pilot
Trader* in 1978, then *Norman Trader*, and *Fort
Norman* in 1979. She arrived at Kaohsiung on
6 February 1984, and was broken up by the Shyeh
Sheng Fuat Steel & Iron Works Company.

Fort Fraser (1980–84)

1967
42,446grt
74,422dwt
825 x 106 x 45ft
IMO: 6707856

Single-screw, 2s.sa Burmeister & Wain-type
engines by builder
b. Mitsui Zōsen, Tamano
Yard No. 769
Launched as *Fernie* for the P&O subsidiary
Trident Tankers, with Hain-Norse as managers.
On 1 October 1971, she was transferred to P&O
Bulk Shipping Division, and was acquired by
Alcyone Shipping, Liberia, becoming *Alcyone* in
January 1979. She was purchased by Canadian
Pacific in February 1980, and renamed *Fort Fraser*,
registered in Hong Kong. On 17 January 1985, she
arrived at Kaohsiung with a cargo of coal, and was
then broken up by Cheng Yong Enterprises.

Fort Douglas (1980–81)

1968
52,706grt
105,439dwt
820 x 134 x 49ft
IMO: 6815744
Single-screw, 10-cylinder 2s.sa Sulzer-type
engines by builders at Aio works
15½ knots
b. Ishikawajima-Harima Heavy Industries, Kure,
Japan
Yard No. 156
Launched on 19 April 1968 as *Sidney Spiro*
for General Ore International Corporation &
International Marine Owners Limited, Monrovia,
in 1979 she was owned by Docynia Shipping
Corporation, becoming *Docynia* the following
year. She was acquired by Canadian Pacific in
1980 and renamed *Fort Douglas*. On 21 August
1981, she was sold to the Daeyang Shipping
Corporation Limited, South Korea, becoming
Daeyang Glory. She arrived at Zhangjiagang,
China, on 15 October 1992, and was broken up.

Fort Erie (1980–81)

1967
33,586grt
57,567dwt
743 x 102 x 39ft
IMO: 6712825
Single-screw, 8-cylinder 2s.sa Sulzer by Uraga
Heavy Industries, Tamashima
16½ knots
b. Nippon Kokan K.K., Tsurumi
Yard No. 835
Launched as *Jasaka* for Anders Jahre, Norway,
with a docking television camera mounted on the
ore mast. In 1978, she was acquired by the Arion
Shipping Corporation, Monrovia, becoming
Nemesis, and was owned by the Nemesis Shipping
Corporation the following year. In 1980, she was
sold to Canadian Pacific (Bermuda) Limited, and
renamed *Fort Erie*, registered at Hong Kong. She
was sold to Orient Rose Shipping Incorporated,
Monrovia, in 1981 and became *Orient Rose*. She
arrived at Kaohsiung on 15 May 1986 and was
broken up by the Tong Hing Steel & Iron Works
Company Limited.

Leda/Fort St John (2)/Leda/Fort Nanaimo (1980–88)

1975
19,498grt
35,414dwt
604 x 92 x 51ft
IMO: 7375583
Single-screw, 7-cylinder Burmeister & Wain-type
7K67GF engines
15 knots
b. Sanoyasu Dockyard Company, Osaka
Yard No. 344
Laid down as *Leda* for the Canadian Pacific
subsidiary Atlanta Ship Management Services
Limited, London, and launched on 12 September
1975, she sailed on her maiden voyage on
5 December, registered as *Fort St John*. In March

1980 as *Leda*, she was transferred to Canadian Pacific, and renamed *Fort Nanaimo*, registered at Hamilton, Bermuda. She was delivered at Tampa, Florida, and sailed from there on her first voyage for Canadian Pacific on 24 March. In April 1988, she was sold to the Bergvall & Hudner Group, and became *Naimo* for the Naimo Shipping Corporation, Monrovia. She became *Leo* in 1994 and arrived at Alang on 30 August 2000 and was broken up.

Fort Assiniboine (1980–89)

1980
19,982grt
31,766dwt
525 x 89 x 48ft
IMO: 7904073
Single-screw, 6-cylinder 2s.sa Burmeister & Wain-type engines by Mitsui Engineering & Shipbuilding Company, Tamano
15 knots
b. Sanoyasu Dockyard Company, Mizushima Yard No. 1033
She was launched on 7 December 1979 for Canadian Pacific (Bermuda), and sailed on her maiden voyage from Osaka to Kwinana. She was sold to Ceres Hellenic Enterprises Limited, Piraeus, in 1989, becoming *Conquestventure L*, then *Conquestventure* in 1998, *Canso* in 2002, *Tireless* in 2003 and *Nikos A* in 2004. She arrived at Chittagong on 5 October 2006 and was broken up.

Fort Garry (1980–89)

1980
19,982grt
31,766dwt
525 x 89 x 48ft
IMO: 7904085
Single-screw, 6-cylinder 2s.sa Burmeister & Wain-type engines by Mitsui Engineering & Shipbuilding Company, Tamano
15 knots

b. Sanoyasu Dockyard Company, Mizushima Yard No. 1034
Launched on 14 March 1980, and delivered on 12 September that year. She was sold to Ceres Hellenic Shipping Enterprises Limited in 1989, and was renamed *Crystalventure 1*, then owned by Elcrystal Incorporated, being renamed *Crystalventure* in 1997, *Cataumet* in 2002, *Kesaria* in 2003, and *Romeo* in 2006. She arrived at Chittagong on 1 June 2007 and was broken up.

Fort Rouge (1980–89)

1980
19,982grt
31,766dwt
525 x 89 x 48ft
IMO: 7913804
Single-screw, 6-cylinder 2s.sa Burmeister & Wain-type engines by Mitsui Engineering & Shipbuilding Company, Tamano
15 knots
b. Sanoyasu Dockyard Company, Mizushima Yard No. 1035
Launched on 29 May 1980, she sailed on her maiden voyage from Osaka to Kwinana on 11 December that year. She was chartered to the Ministry of Defence on 29 July 1982 for service in the Falkland Islands. On 22 December 1986, she was transferred to the Isle of Man Register, and was sold to Elconcept Incorporated in 1989, becoming *Courageventure L*, *Courageventure* in 1998, *Chebucto* in 2002, and *Fair Rainbow* in 2003. She arrived at Chittagong on 22 December 2006 and was broken up.

Fort Toronto (1981–91)

1980
19,982grt
31,766dwt
525 x 89 x 48ft
IMO: 7913816
Single-screw, 6-cylinder 2s.sa Burmeister & Wain-type engines by Mitsui Engineering &

Shipbuilding Company, Tamano
15 knots
b. Sanoyasu Dockyard Company, Mizushima Yard No. 1036
Launched on 28 August 1980, she sailed on her maiden voyage from Kashima to Australia on 21 February 1981. She was chartered to the Ministry of Defence on 10 April 1982, as a freshwater supply tanker in the Falkland Islands and was returned to Canadian Pacific two years later. In 1991, she was sold to Ceres Hellenic Shipping Enterprises Limited, Piraeus, becoming *Clipperventure L*, then *Clipperventure* in 1997, *Casco* in 2002, and *Kasco* in 2003. She arrived at Chittagong on 23 June 2009 and was broken up.

Fort Providence (1982–88)

1982
36,391grt
64,584dwt
736 x 106 x 59ft
IMO: 8102256
Single-screw, 7-cylinder 2s.sa Burmeister & Wain 7L67GFCA engines by builder
b. Hyundai Heavy Industries, Ulsan, South Korea Yard No. 188
Launched on 3 April 1982, she sailed to Port Kembla, NSW, on 30 July, with coal. In April 1988, she was sold to the Bergvall & Hudner Group, and placed on charter to Stena Line, becoming *Stena Africa*. She was then sold to El Seguro Incorporated of Pireaus in 1988, and renamed *Captain George L*, then *Captain George I* in 2003, *Grand George* in 2007, and *Grand* in 2009. She arrived at Jiangyin on 17 April 2012 and was broken up.

Fort Resolution (1982–89)

1982
36,391grt
64,584dwt
736 x 106 x 59ft
IMO: 8102402

Single-screw, 7-cylinder 2s.sa Burmeister & Wain 7L67GFCA engines by builder
b. Hyundai Heavy Industries, Ulsan, South Korea
Yard No. 189
Launched on 3 April 1982, she sailed on her maiden voyage on 27 October that year, registered at Hong Kong. She was sold to Elmotores Incorporated in 1989, becoming *Captain John L*, and then *Fortune* in 2003. She was broken up in 2012.

Fort Dufferin (1983–88)
1983
35,008grt
63,880dwt
738 x 106 x 59ft
IMO: 8101991
Single-screw, 4-cylinder 2s.sa Burmeister & Wain L90-GFCB engines by builde
b. Burmeister & Wain, Copenhagen
Yard No. 898
Launched on 10 June 1983, she sailed on her maiden voyage from Narvik with iron ore to Indonesia. In April 1988, she was sold to the Bergvall & Hudner Group, becoming *Annitsa L* for La Fontana Blanca Limited, Navarino, in 1995, and then *La Donna I* in 2006. She arrived at Chittagong on 21 August 2011 and was broken up.

Fort Frontenac (1984–88)
1984
35,008grt
63,880dwt
738 x 106 x 59ft
IMO: 8102000
Single-screw, 4-cylinder 2s.sa Burmeister & Wain L90-GFCB engines by builder
b. Burmeister & Wain, Copenhagen
Yard No. 899
Launched on 30 September 1983 for Canadian Pacific (Bermuda), and registered at Hong Kong. In April 1988, she was sold to the Bergvall & Hudner Group, becoming *Peter L*, then *Captain*

George L in 1995, and *Panostar* in 2010. She arrived at Chittagong on 29 September 2012 and was broken up.

Repap Enterprise (1986–92)
1972
10,999grt
533 x 64 x 24ft
IMO: 7208209
Twin-screw, 8-cylinder 4s.sa Pielstick engines by builder
b. O/Y Wartsila, Turku, Finland
Yard No. 1197
Delivered as *Mont Royal* for A/B Svenska Amerika Linien, Gothenburg. She was lengthened and converted to ro-ro in 1978 as *Mount Royal*, became *Atlantic Premier* in 1984, then *Incotrans Premier*, *Atlantic Premier* and *Atlantic Star* in 1985. She was sold to Bore Line in 1985, becoming *Canada Maritime*, and was acquired by Canadian Pacific in 1986 and renamed *Repap Enterprise*, owned by the Ozmillion Shipping Corporation, Monrovia. She became *New Enterprise* and *Neptune Princess* in 1992, and *Marmara Princess* in 1995. She was broken up in India in 2004.

COASTAL SHIPS

Canadian Pacific Navigation Company (CPR) acquired the company and fourteen vessels.

Amur (1901–11)
1890
907grt
570n
216 x 28 x 11ft
ID: 1098073
Single-screw, 3-cylinder, triple-expansion by North East Marine Engineering Company
12 knots

b. Strand Slipway Company, Sunderland
Yard No. 86
Sold to Lombard Steam Ship Company in 1895 and the Klondyke Mining Company in 1899. She was acquired by Canadian Pacific on 11 January 1901, and sold to Coastwise Steam Ship & Barge Company in 1911. In February 1924, she was sold to A. Berquist, Vancouver, and renamed *Famous*. She was wrecked on the Skeena River in 1926, and later salvaged. In 1929, she was scrapped and sank in the North Arm of Burrard Inlet.

Beaver (1901–19)
1898
545grt
140 x 28 x 5ft
ID: 1107096
Sternwheeler, 1-cylinder, horizontal direct-acting engine
b. Albion Iron Works, Victoria, BC
She was purchased by Canadian Pacific on 11 January 1901, as one of four sternwheelers on the Upper Fraser River to Chilliwack. She also made one annual sailing with stores to Hudson Bay's Fort Douglas. In 1919, she was sold to the Government of British Columbia, and converted for passenger service on the Fraser River. She was broken up in 1930.

Charmer (1901–35)
1887
1,081grt
497n
200 x 42 x 13ft
ID: 2150413
Single-screw, 3-cylinder, triple-expansion engines by builder
13 knots
b. Union Iron Works, San Francisco
Yard No. 6
Passengers: 40 berths, 350 deck passengers
Delivered as *Premier* for CPNC, but flew the United States flag with E.W. Spencer of Portland,

Oregon, as owner. On 18 October 1892, she collided with the collier *Willamette* and was beached at Bush Point. Her passengers were taken to Seattle, and she was towed to Victoria. To prevent any US legal action, she was transferred to the British Registry and renamed *Charmer*. On 11 January 1901, she was acquired by Canadian Pacific. On 17 October 1907, she collided with the *Tartar*, and on 26 February 1916, she rammed and sank the *Quadra* in fog off Nanaimo. In 1933, she was withdrawn from service and became the dressing rooms for bathers at Newcastle Island. She was broken up in 1935 by the Capital Iron & Metals Company, Vancouver, and her hull was burned off Albert Head.

Danube (1901–05)
1869
887grt
561n
215 x 28 x 11ft
ID: 1062279
Single-screw, 2-cylinder, compound inverted engines by builder
9½ knots
b. Randolph, Elder & Company, Glasgow
Yard No. 99
Delivered to D.R. MacGregor, Glasgow. She was reboiled in 1880 and sold to the Scottish Oriental Steam Ship Company, and chartered to Canadian Pacific in 1888 for the Vancouver–Portland route, with connections to San Francisco transpacific service. She was sold to CPN on 2 August 1890, and was acquired by Canadian Pacific on 11 January 1901. She was sold to the British Columbia Salvage Company on 20 October 1905, renamed *Salvor*, and converted into a salvage vessel. On 3 August 1918, she was purchased by J.P. Davies of Montreal, became *Nervion* in 1920, owned by A. Menchaca, Bilbao. She was scrapped in 1936.

Islander (1901)
1888
1,495grt
478n
240 x 42 x 14ft
ID: 1095093
Twin-screw, 2 x triple-expansion engines by Dunsmuir & Jackson, Glasgow
12 knots
b. Napier, Shanks & Bell, Glasgow
Yard No. 41
Passengers: 200
Delivered to the Pioneer Line, which was part of Canadian Pacific Navigation Company but operated under the Pioneer Line, based at Victoria. She left the Clyde on 22 September 1888, arriving at Victoria on 9 December. In 1890, when the Pioneer Line ceased, she became a member of the CPN, based at Victoria. She was acquired by Canadian Pacific on 11 January 1901, and on 15 August she collided with an iceberg in the Lynn Channel and sank within seventeen minutes, with a loss of forty-two lives. She was raised in April 1934 and beached on Admiralty Island.

Maude (1901–03)
1872
175grt
54n
113 x 21 x 9ft
Paddle engines by the Albion Iron Works, Victoria
b. Burr & Smith, San Juan Island, Washington State
Launched on 4 January 1872 for the East Coast Mail Line, Puget Sound, Olympia–Tacoma–Seattle route and was converted to single-screw compound engine in 1885. In 1890, she was purchased by CPN and was acquired by Canadian Pacific in 1901, and used as a collier and gunpowder carrier. She was sold to the British Columbia Salvage Company in 1903 and dismantled in 1914. Her hull was used as a barge.

Otter (1901–31)
1900
366grt
232n
128 x 24 x 11ft
ID: 1107832
Wooden
Single-screw, 2-cylinder compound engine by T. Gowen, Victoria, BC. Engine from *Rainbow* (1887)
8 knots
b. Canadian Pacific Navigation Yard, Victoria
Passengers: 44 in two-berth cabins on main deck
Acquired by Canadian Pacific in 1901, she went ashore south of Sidney Island on 7 October 1915, and was salvaged and reconditioned. In 1928, she was laid up, and sold to Gibson Brothers, Vancouver Island, in 1931. On 12 May 1937, she was lost by fire at anchor at Malkscope Inlet, Vancouver Island.

Princess Louise (1901–06)
1869
932grt
544n
180 x 30 x 13ft
Side-wheel paddler, 1 vertical cylinder, overhead beam, direct-acting engines by J. Roach & Sons, New York
10 knots
b. J. Inglis, New York
Delivered as *Olympia* for the Oregon Steam Navigation Company, and was renamed *Princess Louise* in 1879, she was transferred to CPN in 1883, for the Victoria–Vancouver service. In 1901, she was acquired by Canadian Pacific, introducing the 'Princess' nomenclature naming system. She was sold to Marpole McDonald in 1906, and converted into a barge by the Vancouver Dredging & Salvage Company. In 1916, she was owned by the Britannia Mining and Smelting Company, and sank at Port Alice in 1919.

Queen City (1901–16)

1894
391grt
244n
116 x 27 x 10ft
ID: 1103482
Wooden schooner
b. R. Brown & Company, Vancouver

She was purchased by CPN in 1897, and fitted with a 2-cylinder compound engine by the Albion Iron Works Company, Victoria, the following year. Acquired by Canadian Pacific in 1901, and damaged by fire at Victoria on 19 September 1916. She was sold to Victoria Dredge & Salvage Company, and to the Pacific Line in 1917, when she was rebuilt and re-engined. In 1918, she was owned by the Kingsley Navigation Company, and was converted into a barge in 1920. On 11 November 1920, in tow by Prospective, the No. 2 tank exploded off Beaver Cove, Vancouver Island. She was declared a total loss.

R.P. Rithet (1901–09)

1882
686grt
117 x 33 x 8ft
ID: 1085316
Wooden sternwheeler
2-cylinder, compound C2cy engine
8 knots
b. A. Watson & Company, Victoria
Passengers: 200 (including 24 berths)

Launched on 20 April 1882 for Captain J. Irving's Pioneer Line, which was amalgamated into the Canadian Pacific Navigation Company in 1883. On 28 July 1885, she collided with and sank the paddle steamer Enterprise, and was acquired by Canadian Pacific in 1901. She was sold to the Terminal Steam Navigation Company in 1909, becoming Baramba, and the Pacific Line Company in 1917, and was converted to a barge. In 1918, she was owned by the Kingsley Navigation Company and was sold to J. Wray in

1922, Captain G. Smith in 1923, and was beached at Sturt Bay, Texada Island, British Columbia.

Tees (1901–18)

1893
679grt
441n
165 x 26 x 11ft
ID: 1095929
Single-screw, 3-cylinder, triple-expansion engines by Blair & Company, Stockton
9 knots
b. Richardson, Duck & Company, Thornaby-on-Tees
Yard No. 408
Passengers: 16

Delivered for the Union Steam Ship Company, Newcastle, and sold to the Hudson Bay Company in 1896, she was then transferred to CPN. Acquired by Canadian Pacific in 1901, and sold to the Pacific Salvage Company, becoming Salvage Queen in 1925. She was sold to the Island Tug & Barge Company and renamed Island Queen. She was damaged in a storm in 1937, and broken up.

Transfer (1901–09)

1893
264grt
122 x 24 x 5ft
ID: 1100794
Wooden sternwheeler
2-cylinder, compound C2cy engine
8 knots
b. A. Watson & Company, New Westminster Yard
Passengers: 200 (including 24 berths)

Delivered for CPN's Fraser River service. In 1894, with record flood levels on the Fraser River, Transfer was able to reach inland areas where none had been before, and was able to rescue people and cattle who were at risk. It was reported that one person boarded her by gangway from his upstairs window. She was transferred to Canadian Pacific in 1901 and allocated to

the New Westminster–Lardner–Steveston daily service. In 1909, she was sold to Robert Jardine, New Westminster, and was converted into a power plant for a cannery at Redonda Bay, British Columbia.

Willapa (1901–02)

1882
373grt
245n
136 x 22 x 17ft
ID: 2085730
Wooden
Single-screw, 2-cylinder, compound engines by Pusey & Jones, Wilmington
10 knots
b. Ilwaco Navigation Company, Portland, Oregon

Launched as General Miles, and renamed Willapa in 1891 to operate Puget Sound ports to British Columbia. On 19 March 1896, she stranded on Regarth Reef and was salvaged. She was acquired by CPN in 1898 and Canadian Pacific three years later. In 1902, she was sold to the Bellingham Bay Transportation Company, becoming Bellingham, and then to the Island Navigation Company in 1912. She was laid up and her engines and boilers were removed in 1915, and she was used as a United States Army barge. She was tied up in a sinking condition at San Juan Island Dock in 1919. Bellingham survived until 1950, when she was burned at the Seattle Sea Fair.

Yosemite (1901–06)

1862
1,525grt
1,055n
282 x 35 x 12ft
ID: 5700797
Wooden side-wheeler paddle steamer
1-cylinder engines by Allaire Works, New York
9 knots
b. J.W. North, San Francisco
Passengers: 500 night, 1,500 day excursion work

Delivered for the Central Pacific Railroad Company's California Steam Navigation Company for the San Francisco–Sacramento service. She was sold to J. Irving in 1883, and to CPN in 1890. Acquired by Canadian Pacific in 1901, and purchased by T. Grant in 1906. On 9 July 1909, she was wrecked near Bremerton Wash, and was declared a total loss.

Princess May[1] (1901–19)

1888
1,394grt
892n
250 x 34 x 18ft
ID: 1109860
Twin-screw, 2 x triple-expansion T6cy IS engines by builder
15 knots
b. Hawthorn, Leslie & Company, Newcastle
Passengers: 150

Launched on 29 February 1888 as *Cass* for the Formosa Trading Company, Taipeh–Shanghai service. In 1894, she was acquired by the Government of Formosa, becoming *Arthur*, and later, *Cass*. In 1896, she was renamed *Ningchow* for the Government of China, and became *Hating* in 1899. She was acquired by Canadian Pacific in 1901, and was renamed *Princess May*. She was rebuilt in 1905 for the Alaska service and went aground on 5 August 1910 on Sentinel Island. She was salvaged on the next high tide and sold to the Princess May Steam Ship Company, managed by the Standard Fruit Company, in August 1919, for service in the Caribbean. She was scuttled in 1930, off Kingston.

Princess Beatrice (1904–29)

1903
1,290grt
635n
193 x 37 x 15ft
ID: 1116405
Single-screw, triple-expansion T3cy IS engines by Bow, McLachlan & Company, Paisley
13 knots
b. British Columbia Marine Railway Company, Victoria

Taken over on the stocks by Canadian Pacific and operated on the Victoria–Seattle service. In January 1929, she was sold to B.L. Johnson, and used as a cannery on the West Coast.

Princess Victoria (1903–52)

1903
1,943grt
428n
300 x 40 x 15ft
ID: 1115953
Twin-screw, two triple-expansion engines by Hawthorn, Leslie & Company, Newcastle
19½ knots
b. Swan & Hunter, Newcastle
Passengers: 1,900

Launched on 18 November 1902, she arrived at Victoria on 28 March 1903, where her superstructure was built by Robertson & Hackett, Vancouver. She entered service on 17 August 1903 on the Victoria–Vancouver service. On 21 July 1906, she collided with and sank the tug *Chehalis* off Burnaby, and on 26 August 1914 she collided with the *Admiral Sampson* in the Puget Sound. *Admiral Sampson* sank with a loss of twelve lives. In 1930, *Princess Victoria* was converted to carry fifty cars, and was used as a floating hotel at Newcastle Island in 1934. On 21 August 1950, she completed her last voyage on the Vancouver–Nanaimo route and was laid up at Victoria. She was sold to Tahsis & Company, Vancouver, in February 1952, as a fuel delivery barge, *Tahsis No. 3*. On 10 March 1953,

while in tow of the tug *Sea Giant*, she struck a rock in Welcome Passage and sank.

In 1905, Canadian Pacific acquired the Esquimalt & Nanaimo Railway Company, Victoria, together with the following three vessels.

City of Nanaimo (1905–12)

1891
761grt
518n
159 x 32 x 9ft
ID: 1096995
Twin-screw, 2 x 2-cylinder, compound engines by J. Doty Engine Company, Toronto
13 knots
b. McAlpine & Allen, Vancouver

Delivered to the Mainland & Nanaimo Steam Navigation Company, she was sold to the Terminal Steam Navigation Company, Vancouver, in 1912, and was renamed *Bowena*. She became *Cheam*, of the Union Steam Ship Company, in 1922, and operated day excursion work out of Vancouver. She was sold to US interests in 1926 and used as a bunkhouse.

Joan (1905–14)

1892
821grt
544n
177 x 30 x 11ft
ID: 1100635
Twin-screw, 2 x 2-cylinder, compound C4cy IS engines by builder
Wood
13 knots
b. Albion Iron Works, Victoria

Joan was taken over by Canadian Pacific in 1905, operating on the Vancouver–Nanaimo route. She was sold to the Terminal Steam Navigation Company in 1914, and was renamed *Ballena*. On 13 November 1920, she burnt out at Vancouver, and was sold to the Vancouver Dredging & Salvage Company and broken up.

---

1   Pictured in the colour section.

Czar (1905–14)

1897
152grt
93n
101 x 21 x 11ft
ID: 1103907
Single-screw, quadruple-expansion 4-cylinder engines by Hinckly, Spear & Hayes, San Francisco
Wooden
10 knots
b. T.H. Trakey, Victoria

Czar was delivered as a tug operating at Victoria, and was acquired by the Esquimalt & Nanaimo Railway Company in 1902 for barge towing. She was taken over in 1905 by Canadian Pacific, remaining at Victoria. In 1914, she was sold to Greer Coyle & Company and to the Imperial Munitions Board, Vancouver, in 1918, for towing explosive-laden barges. The following year she was owned by the Pacific Construction Company, and sold to the Dominion Tug & Barge Company in 1927. She was broken up by the Pacific Construction Company in 1930.

Princess Ena (1907–31)

1907
1,368grt
827n
195 x 38 x 15ft
ID: 1122387
Single-screw, 2-cylinder, compound engines by Crabtree & Company, Great Yarmouth
10½ knots
b. Garston Graving & Ship Building Company, Liverpool

Princess Ena was launched on 22 September 1907 and sailed on her maiden voyage on 31 October, from Liverpool to Vancouver via Montevideo. She arrived at Victoria on 22 January 1908, and was used to carry munitions from Vancouver to Vladivostok in 1916. In 1926, she was fitted with steel tanks to carry 75,000 gallons of fish oil, and was acquired by F. Millard & Company in 1931.

She stranded at the entrance to Jedway, British Columbia, on 14 October 1933, and was laid up from 1935 to 1936. She was broken up in 1938 by the Dulien Steel Works, Seattle.

Princess Royal (1907–31)

1907
1,997grt
981n
228 x 40 x 16ft
ID: 1121988
Single-screw, triple-expansion T3cy IS engines by Bow McLachlan & Company, Paisley
15 knots
b. British Columbia Marine Railway Company, Victoria
Passengers: 700

Launched on 1 September 1906 for the British Columbia Marine Railway Company, and operated on the Vancouver–British Columbia coastal ports–Alaska service. In 1931, her hull was stripped down and she was used as a sawdust carrier, and was broken up by H.B. Elworthy & Company in 1932.

Nanoose (1908–46)

1908
305grt
165n
116 x 24 x 14ft
ID: 1122397
Single-screw, 2-cylinder, compound engines by builder
12 knots
b. British Columbia Marine Railway Company, Victoria

She was delivered to operate as a Canadian Pacific tug at Victoria. She was withdrawn from service in 1940, laid up and sold to Comox Logging & Railway Company in 1946, and sunk as a breakwater.

Princess Charlotte[2] (1909–49)

1908
3,844grt
1,999n
330 x 46 x 23ft
ID: 1126236
Twin-screw, 2 x triple-expansion, 6 single boilers by builder
19½ knots
b. Fairfield Ship Building & Engineering Company, Glasgow
Passengers: 1,500/15 motor cars

Launched on 27 June 1908 and operated on the Channel and Puget Sound and coastal ports between Seattle and Skagway. During a 1926 refit, a ballroom was installed. On 30 August 1927, she struck Vichnefski Rock, Wrangell, and was in collision with *Chelhosin* on 4 February 1935. She also collided with *Caverhill* on 7 March 1941. She was withdrawn on 14 June 1949 and sold to Typaldos Brothers, Piraeus, becoming *Mediterranean*. She was converted into a cruise ship for the Venice–Piraeus–Istanbul route, and broken up at Perama, Greece, in 1965.

---

2 Pictured in the colour section.

Princess Adelaide (1911–49)

1910
3,061grt
1,910n
290 x 46 x 17ft
ID: 1126948
Single-screw, triple-expansion, 4-cylinder by builders
18 knots
b. Fairfield Shipbuilding & Engineering Company, Glasgow
Yard No. 474
Passengers: 1,200/6 motor cars

Launched on 10 July 1910, she left Glasgow on 4 October via the Strait of Magellan, arriving at Victoria on 24 January 1911. She was converted to coal burning in 1920. On 19 December 1928, she was holed by *Hampholm*, and was towed to Vancouver. She was withdrawn on 14 October 1948 and sold to Typaldos Brothers, Piraeus, and renamed *Angelika* for the Venice–Piraeus route. She was laid up in 1967 and broken up at Genoa, Italy.

Princess Mary (1910–52)

1910
1,697grt
1,011n
210 x 40 x 14ft
ID: 1126950
Twin-screw, 2 x triple-expansion, T6cy 2S engines by builder
15 knots
b. Bow, McLachlan & Company, Paisley
Yard No. 261
Passengers: 700

Launched on 21 September 1910, she sailed on 22 November via the Strait of Magellan, arriving at Victoria on 15 February 1911. She was lengthened in 1914 (248ft/75.59m) and operated cruises out of Vancouver in 1926. She was withdrawn in November 1951 and sold to the Island Tug & Barge Company the following year,

and the Union Steam Ship Company in 1953, becoming *Bulk Carrier No. 2*. Her superstructure was removed and became a restaurant at Victoria. On 19 April 1954, while being towed by *Chelan* in a gale, the tow line broke and she started to drift ashore. *Chelan* attempted to put a line aboard and take the crew off the ship. Both vessels were wrecked on Cape Decision, Alaska, with the loss of all aboard.

Will W. Case (1910–24)

1878
538grt
143 x 31 x 17ft
Wooden, 3-masted barque rig
b. S. Sterrett, Rockland, Maine

Acquired by Canadian Pacific in 1910, and operated as a towed collier to service smaller British Columbia ports. She was sold to the Canadian Government in 1924, and sunk as a breakwater at Sydney, British Columbia.

Melanope (1911–46)

1876
1,686grt
258 x 40 x 24ft
ID: 1074550
Iron sailing ship
b. W.H. Potter & Company, Liverpool

Delivered to the Australian Shipping Company, which was taken over by Gracie, Beazley & Company in 1882. In December 1898, she was acquired by a captain-owner at Antwerp, who brought his wife aboard. She died at Panama and a few days later the captain jumped overboard. The mate continued the voyage to San Francisco and the ship was sold to J. Melanie Moore, to enable the crew to be paid off. It was reported that the crew blamed the incidents on a curse that was bestowed on the ship by a woman apple seller, who had been forcibly removed. Her new captain was N.K. Wills. In December 1906, she was abandoned in a storm, but the crew were

able to reboard her later. The following year she was converted into a coal barge, and steam cranes replaced her masts. She was acquired by Canadian Pacific in 1911 for use as a coal hulk, and was sold to Comox Logging & Railway Company in 1946 and sunk as a breakwater at Royston, British Columbia.

Princess Alice (1911–49)

1911
3,099grt
1,910n
290 x 46 x 14ft
ID: 5003643
Single-screw, triple-expansion, 4 cylinder by Wallsend Slipway Company
18 knots
b. Swan Hunter & Wigham Richardson, Newcastle
Yard No. 883
Passengers: 1,200 + 6 motor cars

Princess Alice was launched on 29 May 1911 as a near sister to *Princess Adelaide* and carried the Prince of Wales (later King Edward VIII) in 1919 from Victoria to Vancouver during his Empire tour. She was laid up in June 1947 and sold to Typaldos Brothers two years later, becoming *Aegaeon*. On 2 December 1966, in tow of the tug *Eyforia* she broke adrift and was wrecked at Civitavecchia, Italy, on her way to be broken up at La Spezia.

Qualicum (1911–46)

1904
200grt
98n
96 x 22 x 12ft
ID: 11901
Single-screw, 2-cylinder, compound engines by builder
b. Neafie & Levy, Philadelphia

Delivered as tug *Colima* (US Army Construction Corps), and in 1907 she was engaged in the construction of the Panama Canal. She was acquired by Canadian Pacific in 1911, becoming *Qualicum*, and used to tow *Will W. Case*. In 1946, she was sold and sunk as a breakwater.

Princess Patricia (1911–37)
1902
1,157grt
558n
270 x 32 x 11ft
ID: 1115685
Five screws on three shafts, 3 turbines, by Parsons Steam Turbine Company, Newcastle
b. Denny Brothers, Dumbarton
Yard No. 970
Passengers: 900 deck in two classes
Launched on 2 April 1902, and delivered as *Queen Alexandra* for Turbine Steamers Limited, she operated on the Ardrossan–Campbeltown service. In September 1910, she was gutted by fire at Greenock and abandoned to the underwriters. She was acquired by Canadian Pacific the following year and reconditioned by her builder; screws were reduced to one per shaft, and she was renamed *Princess Patricia*. She left the Clyde on 12 January 1912 via Cape Horn for Victoria. The voyage took forty-three days and twenty-one hours, and her first sailing was from Vancouver to Nanaimo on 11 May. In 1928, she was replaced by *Princess Elizabeth*, which released her for summer excursion duties, and was laid up at Esquimalt in 1932. She was sold to the Capital Iron & Metals Company in May 1937, and her hull was burnt to remove all but the metalwork.

Princess Sophia (1912–18)
1911
2,320grt
1,466n
245 x 44 x 24ft
ID: 1130620
Single-screw, triple-expansion, T3cy IS engines by builders

14½ knots
b. Bow, McLachlan & Company, Paisley
Yard No. 272
Passengers: 350
Launched on 8 November 1911 for the Vancouver–Victoria night service, summer Alaska route. On 24 October 1918, she left Skagway for Vancouver on the last southbound sailing of the season with 218 men, 35 women, 17 children and 75 members of crew on board. She ran into a snowstorm, went off course and grounded at 02.00 on 25 October. She went ashore on the Vanderbilt Reef in the Lynn Channel. As she was high and dry, the passengers remained on board for forty hours waiting for the snow to abate. Two anchors held her to the shore and ships from Juneau stood by. The next high tide brought a gale with strong winds and the ships giving assistance were sent to shelter. A lighthouse tender came near the ship and stood by to give aid. *Princess Sophia* was suddenly washed off the reef into deeper water, where there were rocks near the surface. The ship then broke up in heavy seas, with a loss of all 345 people aboard. It was reported that the last message from her was, 'For God's sake come. We are sinking.' The lighthouse tender *Cedar* reported: 'Sophia driven over reef during night. Only masts showing. No survivors. Blowing storm. Started snowing this morning. King and Wing assisting.' The maritime author Duncan Haws' great-uncle, Richard Calvert Haws, was a ship's engineer, and was aboard as a passenger. His pocket watch, when recovered, had stopped at 06.50, when the ship sank. It was the worst North Pacific coastal service disaster. An attempt at salvage was made the following year, and all that was recovered was the purser's safe, which contained $12,000.

Princess Maquinna (1913–53)
1912
1,777grt
979n
232 x 38 x 14ft
ID: 1133769
Single-screw, triple-expansion, T3cy IS engines by Bow, McLachlan & Company, Paisley
b. British Columbia Marine Railway Company, Esquimalt
Passengers: 440
Launched on 24 December 1912, she entered service in July the following year. She was laid up in 1952 at Vancouver and was sold to the Union Steam Ship Company and converted into an ore-carrying barge, becoming *Taku* for the Alaska–Trail Smelter Plant service. She was broken up by the General Shipbreaking Company at False Creek, Vancouver, in July 1962.

Nitinat (1914–24)
1885
322grt
58n
149 x 26 x 14ft
ID: 1091255
Single-screw, 2-cylinder, compound engines by builder
9 knots
b. J. Readhead & Company, South Shields
Yard No. 219
Delivered as *William Joliffe* for W.T. Joliffe, Liverpool, as the world's most powerful tug. In 1907, she was sold to the British Columbia Salvage Company and fitted as a salvage vessel. She was acquired by Canadian Pacific in 1914, and renamed *Nitinat* for barge towing and salvage work. She was purchased by the Pacific Salvage Company in 1924, becoming *Salvage Chief*. On 7 February 1925, she was wrecked on Merry Island, Welcome Pass.

Princess Irene (1914)

1913
5,934grt
2,234n
395 x 54 x 28ft
ID: 6104902
Twin-screw, 2 steam turbines by builder
22½ knots
b. William Denny & Company, Dumbarton
Yard No. 1006
Passengers: 1,500

Launched on 20 October 1914, she was requisitioned by the Admiralty on 20 January the following year with her sister *Princess Margaret*, and converted into a minelayer for 400 mines. On 27 May 1915, she was completing final commissioning at Sheerness Dockyard and was destroyed by an explosion. A memorial was unveiled outside Sheerness Railway Station to the fifty-three crew and seventy-seven civilians who lost their lives. It was reported that if the accident had happened the next day, more than 400 people would have been working on or around the vessel. On 11 September 1962, two boilers were recovered.

Princess Margaret (1914)

1914
5,934grt
2,234n
395 x 54 x 28ft
ID: 5603800
Twin-screw, 2 steam turbines by builder
22½ knots
b. William Denny & Company, Dumbarton
Yard No. 1005
Passengers: 1,500

Princess Margaret was launched on 24 June 1914 and carried out her trials in Canadian Pacific livery, but with the Denny house flag. On 26 December 1914, she was requisitioned by the Admiralty and converted into a minelayer, operating off the Belgium coast and Heligoland Bight. In 1918, she acted as a hospital transport

vessel for soldiers and later for sick refugees. She was purchased by the Admiralty in 1919, and fitted out as an Admiralty yacht for the North Atlantic with hospital capability in 1921. She was laid up in 1927, arrived at Blyth on 2 July 1929, and was broken up by Hughes, Bolckow & Company, and never actually operated on Canadian Pacific service.

Dola (1917–33)

1907
176grt
96 x 22 x 11ft
ID: 1122517
Wood
Single-screw, triple-expansion, T3cy IS engines by McKie & Baxter, Glasgow
b. Wallace Shipyard, Vancouver
Yard No. 43

Delivered to the Vancouver Tug & Barge Company, Vancouver, and acquired by Canadian Pacific in 1917. She was sold to Dola Tug Boats Limited, Vancouver, in 1933. On 28 October 1953, she sank in Howe Sound, in collision with the *Lady Cynthia*.

Island Princess (1918–30)

1913
339grt
203n
116 x 25 x 8ft
ID: 5083241
Wood
Single-screw, triple-expansion, T3cy IS engines by S.F. Hodge, Detroit
b. M. McDowell, Tacoma
Passengers: 140

Delivered as *Daily*, operating in the Puget Sound on the Seattle (West Passage)–Tacoma service. She was acquired by Canadian Pacific in 1918, becoming *Island Princess* for the Gulf Islands service. In 1930 she was sold to the Gulf Islands' Ferry Company, and renamed *Cy Peck*.

In 1951, she was owned by Gavin Mouat, and was rebuilt in 1956, with a car capacity of forty. On 1 September 1961, she was taken over by British Columbia Toll Highways Authority, and went to British Columbia Ferries in 1964. In 1966, she was sold to J.H. Todd & Company, Vancouver, as a supply store for fishermen. In 1975 she was owned by J.W. Russell, and in 1980, she was purchased by Dale Forsberg for Canada Sea Life College.

Princess Louise (2)[1] (1921–63)

1921
4,032grt
2,449n
327 x 48 x 34ft
ID: 5284883
Single-screw, triple-expansion engines by builder
17½ knots
Wallace Ship Building Company, Vancouver
Yard No. 108
Passengers: 1,000 + 14 motor cars

Launched on 28 August 1921 for the Vancouver–Alaska service, and operated as a cruise ship to the Alaskan fjords in 1950. It was intended to use her as a restaurant at the ferry terminal at Tsawwassen in 1963 but she was sold and used for the same purpose at Los Angeles, and later at San Pedro. She was acquired by Shoreline Holdings, Vancouver, on 26 February 1964, and her engine and boilers were removed. In 1966, she was owned by the Princess Louise Corporation, and left Vancouver in June that year in tow of the tug *La Pointe* for Los Angeles. Capsized at San Pedro 30 October 1989, raised 30 May 1990. Sank in tow 20 June 1990

Motor Princess (1923–55)

1923
1,243grt
779n
165 x 43 x 9ft

---

1   Pictured in the colour section.

ID: 5412959
Wood
Twin-screw, 4SA 12cyl 4s.sa engines by McIntosh, Seymour & Company, Auburn, New York
14 knots
b. Yarrows Limited, Esquimalt, Victoria
Yard No. 18
Passengers: 250/370 (two staterooms), 45 cars (32 on main deck + 13 upper deck aft reached by a ramp)
Launched on 31 March 1923 as a car ferry with capacity for 45 cars. Forward vehicle side-loading doors. She was the first motor vessel built for Canadian Pacific and was operated by British Columbia Coast Steamship Services. She was sold to the Gulf Islands Ferry Company (1951) Limited in 1955, re-engined and remodelled and given two Fairbanks-Morse 525hp engines. She was acquired by the British Columbia Ferry Company (BC Toll Highways) in 1961, and renamed *Pender Queen* in 1963. Laid up in 1979 at Dea Dock, Fraser River, and sold in 1981 to Clark & Small for use as a floating hotel at Rivers Inlet, British Columbia, for fishermen.

Kyuquot (1924–62)
1919
419grt
135 x 29 x 14ft
ID: 1143307
Single-screw, triple-expansion engines by Fawcett, Preston & Company, Liverpool
10 knots
b. J. Crichton & Company, Saltney, Cheshire
Yard No. 286
10 knots
Delivered as *St Florence* for the Admiralty, and acquired by Canadian Pacific in 1924, becoming *Kyuquot* and left Leith for Victoria via Panama on 25 January 1925. She ran aground in 1931 and was salvaged the following year. Laid up at Victoria in 1957 and arrived at Vancouver on 11 July 1962, and was broken up.

Princess Kathleen (1925–52)
1925
5,875grt
2,719n
352 x 60 x 26ft
ID: 1150908
Twin-screw, 2 x 2 single-reduction geared turbines by builder
22½ knots
b. John Brown & Company, Glasgow
Yard No. 504
Passengers: 600 in berths, 900 deck, 3 vehicles
Launched on 27 September 1924 and sailed from the Clyde to Vancouver, via Panama, on 15 January 1925. During the Second World War she operated as a troopship, and resumed her Vancouver–Seattle–Victoria service on 22 June 1947. On 30 August 1951, she collided with the *Prince Rupert* and both ships returned to port safely. On 7 September 1952, she ran aground at Lena Point, and when the tide rose the water swamped her stern and she sank. All passengers and crew were saved.

Princess Marguerite (1925–42)
1925
5,875grt
2,719n
352 x 60 x 26ft
ID: 1150910
Twin-screw, 2 x 2 single–reduction, geared turbines by builder
22½ knots
b. John Brown & Company, Glasgow
Yard No. 505
Passengers: 600 in berths, 900 deck, 3 vehicles
Launched on 29 November 1924, and sailed to Vancouver via Panama on 25 March the following year. On 29 May 1939, she carried King George VI and Queen Elizabeth from Vancouver to Victoria. She operated as a troop carrier during the Second World War, and on 17 August 1942, en route from Port Said to Famagusta she was torpedoed. She was carrying around 1,000 troops and 49 people lost their lives.

Nootka (1926–50)
1919
2,069grt
1,201n
251 x 44 x 20ft
ID: 1141486
Single-screw, triple-expansion engines by builder
11 knots
b. Port Arthur Ship Building Company, Port Arthur, Ontario
Yard No. 41
Delivered as *Canadian Adventurer* for Canadian Government Merchant Marine, becoming *Emperor of Port McNicoll* in 1925, purchased by Canadian Pacific in 1926, and was renamed *Nootka*. She was converted to oil fuel and fitted with a 171,000-gallon/778,500-litre olive oil cargo tank for the pilchard fish canning industry. She was later fitted with three lifeboats port side and two starboard when she began to carry workers to and from the canneries. She was sold in 1950, becoming *Iquitos*, and to Cia de Nav y Comercio Amazonas, Lima, in 1957, reverting to *Nootka*. She was broken up in 1960 in Peru.

Princess Elaine (1928–63)
1928
2,125grt
725n
299 x 48 x 16ft
IMO: 5284845
Triple-screw, 3 single-reduction geared Brown-Curtis steam turbines by builder
19½ knots
b. John Brown & Company, Glasgow
Yard No. 520
Passengers: 1,200 + 60 vehicles
Launched on 26 October as Canadian Pacific's first ship designed for the carriage of motor cars. Vehicles were side loaded over special gangways onto the car deck. Doors were located fore and aft so that the vessel was drive-through, and a turntable was also fitted. On 13 October 1955, she collided with the barge *VT 25* at the entrance to

Vancouver Harbour, and also collided with *Alaska Prince* on 11 January 1960. She was withdrawn on 1 October 1962 and towed to Blaine, Washington, the following year to become a floating restaurant. In 1967, she was owned by Mrs T. Rogers and was towed to Seattle as a restaurant. She was broken up in 1977.

Princess Norah (1929–58)

1928
2,731grt
1,519n
262 x 48 x 26ft
ID: 5059836
Single-screw, triple-expansion T4cy IS engines by builder
b. Fairfield Ship Building & Engineering Company, Glasgow
Yard No. 632
Passengers: 450 + 9 vehicles

Launched on 27 September 1928, she arrived at Vancouver on 23 January the following year to operate on the West Coast ports of Vancouver Island service. From 1942 to 1944 she was used as a United States troopship between Seattle and Alaska, and was operating from Vancouver to Alaskan ports in 1949. She was renamed *Queen of the North* for the Portland Canal–Kitimat joint service with Canadian National Railways in 1955, reverting to *Princess Norah* in 1957, when the joint service was withdrawn. In July 1958, she was sold to the Northland Navigation Company, becoming *Canadian Prince*. In October 1964, her engines and boilers were removed and she was towed to Kodiak by *Hecate Prince* for use as a restaurant, and renamed *Beachcomber*.

Princess Elizabeth (1930–60)

1930
5,251grt
3,023n
366 x 52 x 28ft
ID: 5272866

Twin-screw, 2 x 4-cylinder quadruple-expansion engines by builder
16 knots
b. Fairfield Ship Building & Engineering Company, Glasgow
Yard No. 638
Passengers: 1,000 + 48 motor cars

Launched on 16 January 1930, she arrived at Vancouver on 3 May to operate on the Vancouver–Victoria route. In December 1960, she was sold to Epirotiki, Piraeus, becoming *Pegasus* for the Venice–Patras–Corinth Canal–Piraeus service. She was later employed in cruising duties for Epirotiki's Hellenic Mediterranean Cruises & Car Ferry Company. She left Piraeus on 14 February 1973 on charter to Brown & Root Incorporated, Houston, for service as an accommodation ship at Nigg Bay, Cromarty Firth, for North Sea oil workers. She arrived on 3 March and was renamed *Highland Queen*. She was sold to the Highland Shipping Company in 1975, and left the Tees River on 26 March 1976 for Zeebrugge, and was broken up at Bruges.

Princess Joan (1930–60)

1930
5,251grt
3,023n
366 x 52 x 28ft
ID: 5149124
Twin-screw, 2 x 4-cylinder, quadruple-expansion engines by builder
16 knots
b. Fairfield Ship Building & Engineering Company, Glasgow
Yard No. 639
Passengers: 1,000 + 48 motor cars

Launched on 4 March 1930, she was delivered to Vancouver for the Victoria–Vancouver route. She made her final evening sailing on 24 February 1959, and was withdrawn on 27 March and laid up. She was sold to Epirotiki in December 1960, becoming *Hermes*, and then rebuilt and placed on

service with her sister *Pegasus* (*Princess Elizabeth*). In 1970, she was sold to the Government of Nigeria, to be used as a floating hotel, arriving at Lagos on 28 September. Her owners later became L. Dupes & Associates, Cyprus, and in October 1973 she became an accommodation vessel at Nigg Bay, alongside her sister. She was later owned by Loima Shipping Company, Famagusta, and arrived at Inverkeithing on 29 August 1974, and was broken up by Thos W. Ward.

Princess Marguerite (2)[1] (1949–75)

1949
5,911grt
2,379n
359 x 56 x 25ft
IMO: 5284900
Twin-screw, BTH Rugby 2ST-EL 2S by British Thomson-Houston, Rugby
23 knots
b. Fairfield Ship Building & Engineering Company, Glasgow
Yard No. 729
Passengers: 2,000 + 50 vehicles

Launched on 26 May 1948, she sailed from the Clyde to Victoria via the Panama Canal on 6 March 1949. In 1963, she was operating summer services only, and was laid up at Victoria in the winter. In 1971, her ownership was transferred from Canadian Pacific Railway Company to Canadian Pacific Limited, and she was owned by the British Columbia Steam Ship Company (1975) Limited in 1975, operated by the Province of British Columbia Department of Transportation. In July 1988, she was sold to the British Columbia Stena Line and was used as a summer excursion vessel. She was sold to Mykris Hotels plc in 1990 to be used as a hotel and conference ship at Bristol, England. However, she was arrested on behalf of the Canadian Merchant Service Guild, who were in dispute with the

---

1   Pictured in the colour section.

previous owner over severance pay. The arrest order was later lifted and *Princess Marguerite* went to Singapore, where she was sold to Sea Containers Limited. In 1992, she was converted into a Singapore-based gambling ship, and was broken up at Alang in 1997.

Princess Patricia (2)[2] (1949–85)

1949
5,911grt
2,379n
359 x 56 x 25ft
IMO: 5284924
Twin-screw, BTH Rugby 2ST-EL 2S by British Thomson-Houston, Rugby
23 knots
b. Fairfield Ship Building & Engineering Company, Glasgow
Yard No. 730

Launched on 5 October 1948, she arrived at Victoria on 3 June 1949, for the Vancouver–Victoria–Seattle day service. In 1963, she was converted for summer cruising to Alaskan waters. She was chartered to Princess Cruises in 1966 for a Los Angeles–Acapulco service, and was owned by Canadian Pacific Limited in 1971. She was sold to Hampstead Holdings Limited, Vancouver, in 1985, and was chartered to the Great American Cruise Lines in 1987. She was sold in 1989 and left Vancouver on 19 April, towed by *Baltic Rescuer* to Kaohsiung, where she arrived on 8 June and was broken up.

Yukon Princess (1950–58)

1946
1,334grt
761n
224 x 38 x 20ft
ID: 5300144
Single-screw, 3-cylinder, triple-expansion engines by Canadian Allis-Chalmers, Montreal

2   Pictured in the colour section.

10 knots
b. North Van Ship Repairs (Pacific Dry Dock Company), North Vancouver
Yard No. 159

Launched on 28 November 1945 as *Ottawa Parapet* (British Type B Standard), she was sold to the Clarke Steam Ship Company and renamed *Island Connector* in 1947, and to Canadian Pacific in December 1950, becoming *Yukon Princess*. In April 1958, she was purchased by the Westley Shipping Company, and renamed *West Princess*, becoming *Rosita* in 1961. On 21 June 1963, she ran aground on Cape Gracias, Nicaragua, and was declared a constructive total loss. She was sold to Southern Scrap Metals Company, and broken up at New Orleans in 1964.

Veta C (1952–53)

1951
520grt
141 x 33 x 15ft
ID: 6117964
Wood
5-cylinder oil engine by Fairbanks-Morse, Chicago
b. North Western Ship Building Company, Bellingham, Washington
Yard No. 245

Delivered to the Union Steam Ship Company, and chartered to Canadian Pacific on 17 October 1952 to replace *Princess Maquinna*. She reverted back to the Union Steam Ship Company the following year, becoming *Chelan*. On 15 April 1954, she foundered off Cape Decision, Alaska.

Princess Alberni (1953–58)

1945
538grt
142 x 33 x 17ft
ID: 195786
Wood
5-cylinder CSA IS engine by Fairbanks-Morse, Chicago

b. Martinolich Steam Ship Company, San Francisco
Passengers: 30

Delivered as *Pomare* for the United States Army, and sold to Cia Pesquera Ambas Costa, Mexico, in 1947. She was acquired by Canadian Pacific in 1953, and renamed *Princess Alberni*. In July 1958, she was sold to the Northland Navigation Company and renamed *Nootka Prince*, and the following year sold to Great West Towing & Salvage Company. In 1959, she was owned by the Canadian Tugboat Company, becoming *Ocean Crown*, and then *Techno Crown* in 1978 for survey work in the St Lawrence. On 2 February 1985, she foundered and sank.

Princess of Vancouver (1955–82)

1955
5,554grt
2,430n
420 x 65 x 19ft
IMO: 5284998
Twin-screw, oil 4 x 4-cylinder 4s.sa by National Gas & Oil Engine Company, Ashton-under-Lyne. Voith Schneider bow thrust unit
15½ knots
b. Alexander Stephen & Sons, Linthouse
Yard No. 646
Passengers: 1,200, 770 as licensed + 115 vehicles or 28 railcars on recessed rails
Passengers 1963: 170 vehicles (mezzanine deck fitted)

Launched on 7 March 1955 and arrived at Vancouver on 5 June for the 36-mile Vancouver–Nanaimo service. She was designed to carry boxcars and other railway rolling stock on four tracks on the main deck. Four sets of automatic couplers were fitted to bumper posts at the forward end of the rails. Special attention was given to the scantlings of the deep beams and girders to withstand the deck load. To save weight and space, rail heads were specially designed for welding to the deck. The railway rolling stock and other vehicular traffic was loaded over the after end of the main deck, and new piers at Vancouver and Nanaimo were constructed with adjustable loading ramps. Obstructions on the deck were kept to a minimum; the engine casing and stairways to spaces above and below were confined to a narrow house at the centre line, while other items, such as scuttles, vents, pipes and cable trays, were housed within the line of the web frames. Transferred to Canadian Pacific in 1971, and fitted with four General Motors diesels (8,600bhp) in September 1972. She was sold to the Government of Canada (Department of Highways of the Province of British Columbia), Vancouver, in 1982. Transferred to the British Columbia Steamship Company, in 1987 she became *Vancouver Island Princess* and was laid up at Seattle in 1991. Sold to China in 1993, she was renamed *Nan Hai Ming Zhu*, *Pearl of South China Sea* in 2001.

Trailer Princess (1966–86)

1944
1,653grt
4,080dwt
308 x 57ft
IMO: 6701345
Twin-screw, oil 12-cylinder by the General Motors Corporation, Detroit
10½ knots
b. United States Navy Yard, Boston
Delivered as LST 1003 and recommissioned as US *Pomares Coronis*. In July 1966, she was acquired by Canadian Pacific, becoming *Trailer Princess*, operating on the Vancouver–Swartz Bay service. On 30 June 1986, she was sold to Mar-Mac Forest Limited and used as a logging base camp. She was deleted from the register on 23 January 2012.

Greg Yorke (1964–68)

1964
2,443grt
325 x 57 x 13ft
IMO: 6420484
Twin-screw, twin rudders by N.V. Werkspoor, Amsterdam
b. Allied Shipbuilders, Vancouver
Delivered for F.M. Yorke & Sons and chartered to Canadian Pacific on 1 October 1964 for the Vancouver–Nanaimo route. She carried twenty-five railcars on four sets of track. Replaced by *Doris Yorke* on 10 April 1968, she was sold to Aqua Transportation in February 1975, becoming *Seaspan Greg*, on long-term charter to CNR.

Doris Yorke (1968–2012)

1967
2,000grt
325 x 57 x 19ft
IMO: 6801925
4 oil 4SA 8-cylinder by Caterpillar Tractor
9 knots
b. Victoria Machinery Company
Yard No. 145
Delivered to F.M. Yorke & Sons, and chartered to Canadian Pacific on 10 April 1968. She was sold to Aqua Transportation Limited in February 1975 and renamed *Seaspan Doris*, chartered to Canadian Pacific. She was laid up in May 2012.

Haida Transporter (1969–)

1969
2,553grt
3,200dwt
326 x 56 x 13ft
ID: 6816413
2 oil 4SA 6-cylinder by N.V. Werkspoor, Amsterdam
9 knots
b. Allied Shipbuilders, Vancouver
Yard No. 162

Delivered to Kingcome Navigation Company, Vancouver, and leased to Canadian Pacific in July 1969. She was deleted from the register on 1 June 2010.

Carrier Princess (1973–)

1973
4,353grt
3,429dwt
380 x 66 x 24ft
IMO: 7306647
4 Vee 2SA 16-cylinder by General Motors
18 knots
b. Burrard Dry Dock Company, Vancouver
Passengers: 260 + 150 cars or 30 railcars
Launched on 20 February 1973, and delivered for the Vancouver–Swartz Bay service.

TRANSFER BARGES, HANDLING RAIL BOXCARS ON THE BRITISH COLUMBIA COAST

Transfer No. 1 (1905–19)

Transfer No. 2 (1907–30)

Transfer No. 3 (1911–57)

Transfer No. 4 (1913–46)

Transfer No. 6 (1917–27)

Transfer No. 7 (1920–51)

Transfer No. 8 (1921–51)

Transfer No. 4 (2) (1952)

1,593grt
308 x 53ft
Built as a United States landing craft, and acquired by Canadian Pacific in 1952 for the Vancouver–Nanaimo service (thirty-three trucks or twenty-four railcars).

Transfer No. 9 (1929–64)
1,396grt
231 x 43ft
b. Canadian Vickers, Montreal
Built as barge No. 16 for Kootenay Lake and cut in sections in 1941, wheelhouse and steering gear added to carry seventeen railcars, renamed *Transfer No. 9*. Sold to the Island Tug and Barge Company on 1 December 1964.

Prospect Point (1942–51)
1,038grt
b. Star Shipyard, New Westminster
Launched on 2 February 1942 for the Wartime Shipping Board, and leased to Canadian Pacific until 1951.

Island Logger (1951–64)
Leased to Canadian Pacific from June 1951 to March 1964.
   Northland Navigation Limited tugs and barges were leased to Canadian Pacific from 1 January 1978 to 30 January 1980.

Ocean Prince (2) (1978–79)
182grt
Built at Owen Sound as *Manicouagan*.

Northland Fury (1978–79)
118grt
Built at New Westminster as *Pacific Fury*.

Squamish Warrior (1978–79)
15grt
Built at Delta, British Columbia.

Kemano IV (1978–79)
689grt
130ft barge built at Vancouver, British Columbia.

Lakelse (1978–79)
803grt
160ft barge built at North Vancouver.

Northland 101 (1978–79)
2,468grt
Built at North Vancouver.

Northland Transporter (1978–)
2,002grt
Built at North Vancouver.

BRITISH COLUMBIA LAKE AND RIVER STEAMERS

Aberdeen (1893–1919)
1893
554grt
146 x 30 x 7ft
ID: 1100675
Wood sternwheeler
4 rudders, 2-cylinder horizontal trunk, wood burner by British Columbia Ironworks
b. E.G. McKay, Vernon, British Columbia
Passengers: 250 deck, 5 cabins
Launched on 22 May 1893 at Okanagan Landing as Canadian Pacific's first river steamer. She was converted to coal in 1902, and was withdrawn from service in 1916. She was sold to B. Johnson in 1919 and broken up. A section from her became a houseboat.

Denver (1897–1903)
1896
9grt
36 x 9 x 4ft
Wood
Single-screw, 1-cylinder expansion, direct-acting engine
b. New Westminster, assembled at Slocan City
Delivered to W.F. Wardropper, New Denver, as an estuarial and river barge towing tug. Acquired by Canadian Pacific in 1897 to tow barges from Slocan to Rosebery, and was shipped to Shuswap Lake to be a tender for Canadian Pacific houseboat. She was sold in 1903.

Seven steamers and ten barges were purchased from the Columbia & Kootenay Navigation Company on 1 February 1897.

Columbia I (1897–1920)
1896
50grt
77 x 15 x 6ft
Wood screw tug
Single-screw, 1-cylinder, direct-acting engine by builder
Built at Nakusp for the Columbia & Kootenay Steam Navigation Company, and acquired by Canadian Pacific in 1897. She was withdrawn in 1920 and rebuilt to become *Columbia II*. Her machinery was transferred.

Illecillewaet (1897–1902)
1892
98grt
78 x 15 x 4ft
Wood sternwheeler
Engine transferred from Despatch 1-cylinder, horizontal trunk, direct-acting, wood burner
b. A. Watson, Revelstoke
Launched on 30 October 1892 as a cargo-only carrier with iron ore from the Rossland mines to Northport. Also served on the Trout Lake

services, Arrowhead–Beaton. Acquired by Canadian Pacific in 1897, and was dismantled at Kootenay in 1902, and became a barge.

Kokanee (1897–1919)
1896
348grt
143 x 25 x 6ft
Sternwheeler
1-cylinder, horizontal trunk, direct-acting engines by Harlan & Hollingsworth, Wilmington
b. T.J. Bulger, Nelson
Passengers: 200
Launched on 7 April 1896. She was sold to become a fishing lodge at Deanstown in 1923, and her machinery was taken out. She sank in 1930.

Lytton (1897–1903)
1890
452grt
131 x 25 x 5ft
Sternwheeler
1-cylinder, horizontal trunk, direct-acting engine
Wood burner
b. A. Watson, Revelstoke
Delivered in May 1890 for the Revelstoke–Little Dallas, Washington State route, and carried Sir William Van Horne and other Canadian Pacific officials on her maiden voyage on 2 July. She was broken up in 1903.

Nakusp (1897)
1895
1,083grt
171 x 34ft
Wood sternwheeler
2-cylinder, direct horizontal, trunk engines by Iowa Iron Works
b. T.J. Bulger, Nakusp
Passengers: 500 deck + 24 in berths
Launched on 1 July 1895 for the Lake Arrow service, and was the largest vessel on the lake. She was destroyed by fire at Arrowhead on 23 December 1897.

Nelson (1897–1913)
1891
496grt
134 x 27ft
Wood sternwheeler
1-cylinder, direct horizontal, trunk wood burner engines
b. A. Watson, Revelstoke
Launched on 11 June 1891 for the Arrow Lake service. She was withdrawn in 1913, and her engine was removed and she was burnt during a fire display for the public on 16 July 1914.

Trail (1897–1902)
1896
633grt
165 x 31 x 5ft
Wood sternwheeler
1-cylinder, horizontal trunk, direct-acting engines
Wood burner
b. T.J. Bulger, Nakusp
Launched on 9 May 1896 as a cargo version of Nakusp, although deck passengers were carried. She was also able to push barges. She was withdrawn from service in 1900, and destroyed by fire at Robson West in 1902.

Stikine River Steamers were built for a service from Glenora, British Columbia, to Wrangell, Alaska, to cater for gold-rush traffic. The service lasted for one year, and the gold rush ended before the last six came into service.

Constantine (1897–98)
1897
337grt
150 x 30ft
Wood sternwheeler
1-cylinder, horizontal trunk, direct-acting engines
Launched at Port Blakely, and was sold in November 1898 and taken to Alaska. She was lost on 4 July 1899.

Dalton (1897–1901)
1897
337grt
150 x 30ft
Wood sternwheeler
1-cylinder, horizontal trunk, direct-acting engines
Sold to the White Pass & Yukon Railway Company in January 1901, becoming Capital City. She was abandoned and broken up in 1919.

Dawson (1897–99)
1897
779grt
167 x 34 x 4ft
Wood
Paddle, 1-cylinder, expansion, direct-acting engines
b. T.J. Bulger, False Creek, Vancouver
Operated on the Wrangell–Petersburg route, and sold to the British Yukon Navigation Company in 1899. She was altered at Dawson to allow forward cargo handling when the vessel was bow ashore when there was no landing. She was wrecked on Tache Reef, Rink Rapids, Yukon River, in September 1926.

Duchesnay (1898–99)
1898
277grt
120 x 21 x 4ft
Wood paddle steamer
1-cylinder, vertical, direct-acting engines
b. T.J. Bulger, False Creek, Vancouver
She was sold to E.T. Rathbone in 1899, and renamed General Jefferson C. Davis.

Hamlin (1898–1901)
1898
515grt
146 x 31 x 5ft
Wood paddle steamer
2 x 1-cylinder, vertical, direct-acting engines
b. T.J. Bulger, False Creek, Vancouver

She was sold to the British Yukon Navigation Company in 1901, and to William McCallum, Vancouver, in 1903, and was owned by T.J. Kickham in 1904. Sold to E.J. Coyle, Victoria, in 1910, the Hamlin Tug Boat Company in 1911, J.H. Greer in 1913, and the Defiance Packing Company, Vancouver, in 1917. She was lost in the Fraser River.

McConnell (1898–1901)

1898
496grt
142 x 30 x 5ft
Wood paddle steamer
2 x 1–cylinder, vertical, direct-acting engines
b. T.J. Bulger, False Creek, Vancouver
Delivered for the Stikine River service and sold to the British Yukon Navigation Company on 20 March 1901. She was broken up at Skagway, Alaska, where she arrived on 4 September 1901.

Ogilvie (1898–1901)

1898
541grt
147 x 31 x 5ft
Wood paddle steamer
2 x 1–cylinder, vertical, direct-acting engines
b. T.J. Bulger, False Creek, Vancouver
Built for the Stikine River services and sold to the British Yukon Navigation Company on 20 March 1901. She was dismantled at Skagway, where she arrived on 4 September 1901.

Schwatka (1897–1904)

1897
337grt
150 x 30ft
Wood sternwheeler
1-cylinder, horizontal trunk, direct-acting engines
Launched at Port Blakely and delivered for the Glenora–Wrangell service. Sold out of lay up to the White Pass & Yukon Railway Company in August 1904.

Tyrrell (1897–98)

1898
678grt
146 x 31 x 5ft
Wood paddle steamer
2 x 1–cylinder, vertical, direct-acting engines
b. T J Bulger, False Creek, Vancouver
She was sold to the British American Corporation in July 1898, who added deck cabins. Sold to D.W. Davis, Yukon in 1905, and taken over by the British Yukon Navigation Company in 1915. Broken up in 1919.

Walsh (1897–1902)

1897
337grt
150 x 30ft
Wood sternwheeler
1-cylinder, horizontal trunk, direct-acting engines
Built at Port Blakely, Seattle, for the Glenora–Wrangell service, and later on the Stikine River. She was laid up at Lulu Island and was sold in September 1902.

Kootenay (1897–1920)

1897
1,117grt
184 x 33 x 6ft
Wood sternwheeler
1–cylinder, horizontal trunk, direct-acting, 4 steam-powered rudders
b. T.J. Bulger, Nakusp (owned by Canadian Pacific, with J.M. Bulger as manager)
Sailed on her maiden voyage on 19 May 1897, Nakusp–Castlegar–Trail route, and sold to Captain Sanderson in 1919. The following year she became a houseboat at Nakusp, but was destroyed by fire in 1942.

Rossland (1897–1917)

1897
1,117grt
184 x 33 x 6ft
Wood sternwheeler
1–cylinder, horizontal trunk, direct-acting, 4 steam-powered rudders by British Columbia Iron Works, Vancouver
b. T.J. Bulger, Nakusp (owned by Canadian Pacific, with J.M. Bulger as manager)
Launched on 18 November 1897, and operated on the Nelson–Trail service from 2 May 1898. Her hull was rebuilt in 1908, with new superstructure added. She was employed on Arrowhead Lake (Robson–Arrowhead), making one round trip a day. In December 1916, she sank at Nakusp under the weight of snow on her decks and was raised in March 1917. She was sold to Captain Forslund to be a wharf near Needles, Lower Arrow Lake.

Slocan I (1897–1905)

1897
578grt
156 x 25 x 6ft
Wood sternwheeler
1-cylinder, horizontal trunk by British Columbia Iron Works, Vancouver
b. T.J. Bulger, Rosebery
Launched on 22 May 1897 and entered service on the Slocan Lake. She was rebuilt in 1905 with berths for 300 passengers, and engine increased to 2-cylinder trunk, direct-acting to the stern wheel for the Arrowhead–Castlegar service. She was broken up in 1928.

Minto (1898–1954)

1898
829grt
162 x 30 x 6ft
Wooden sternwheeler
2-cylinder, compound, horizontal trunk, double-beam, direct-acting engines

b. Bertram Iron Works, Toronto, and shipped in parts to CPR yard at Nakusp
Passengers: 225, 40 berths

She was packed in over 1,000 crates and taken by rail to Vancouver, and then to Nakusp, where she was reassembled. She was launched on 19 November 1898, and entered service on the Arrowhead–West Robson service. The journey covered 134 miles and took twelve hours to complete. On 23 April 1954, she operated her last round trip and was presented to the Nakusp Chamber of Commerce and used by the Rotary Club. In April 1956, she was sold for $750 for scrap, but was purchased by John Nelson for $800 and towed to Galena Bay, Upper Arrow Lake, where he intended to restore her. However, he died on 26 November 1967, and the ship was burned on 1 August 1968. Her name board is preserved at the Selkirk College, Castlegar.

Moyie (1898–1957)

1898
835grt
162 x 30 x 6ft
Wood sternwheeler
2-cylinder, compound, horizontal-trunk, double-beam, direct-acting engines
b. Bertram Iron Works, Toronto, and shipped in parts to CPR Yard at Nelson
Passengers: 225, 40 berths

She sailed on her maiden voyage on 7 December 1898 from Nelson to Lardo, British Columbia (87 miles in eight hours, including eleven stops). She was withdrawn on 27 April 1957, after which she was preserved by the Kootenay Historical Society. She was the last British Columbia sternwheeler.

Sandon (1898–1927)

1898
97grt
76 x 17 x 6ft
Wood screw tug
Single-screw, 1-cylinder, vertical, direct-acting by builder
8 knots
b. CPR, Rosebery

Delivered for towing barges on Lake Slocan. She was dismantled in 1927.

William Hunter (1897–1903)

1893
51grt
59 x 13 x 3ft
Wood screw tug
b. W. Hunter & A. McKinnon, New Denver

Launched on 7 November 1892, and completed as a private steam launch and towing vessel for the Slocan Trading & Navigation Company. She was acquired by Canadian Pacific in 1897 and was withdrawn in 1903.

Ymir (1899–1928)

1899
90grt
86 x 17 x 6ft
Wood screw tug
Single-screw, 1-cylinder, vertical, direct-acting engine
b. CPR, Nelson

Launched on 27 February 1899 for towing barges on the Nelson–Kootenay Landing route. She was scuttled in Kootenay Lake in 1929.

Procter (1900–17)

1900
43grt
65 x 14 x 5ft
Wood screw tug
Single-screw, 1-cylinder, vertical, direct-acting engine
b. J.M. Bulger, CPR, Nelson.

Delivered for the Kootenay Lake Kalso–Duncan River service, competing with the Great Northern Railway's sternwheeler Argenta. She was transferred to the Nelson–Kootenay Landing route in 1901, and Trout Lake in 1904, based at Gerrard. She operated on this service until 1917, when she was sold to W.A. Foote, Revelstoke, and continued in service until 1921.

Valhalla (1901–31)

1901
153grt
103 x 21 x 9ft
Wood tug
Single-screw, 2-cylinder, compound, inverted engine by the Polson Iron Works, Toronto
10 knots
b. J.M. Bulger, CPR, Nelson.

Tug on Kootenay Lake, based at Nelson. She towed railway flats to the lakeside railheads at Kootenay Landing, Procter, Lardo and Kalso. She later operated on the Fraser River and was sold to R.P. Dill in 1931. She was beached in a bed of concrete at the spring high-water mark and converted into a residential home.

York (1902–32)

1902
134grt
88 x 16 x 5ft
Steel tug
Twin-screw, 2 x 1-cylinder, direct-acting engine by builders
8 knots
b. Bartram Engine Works, Toronto

She was delivered as a smaller version of Valhalla for the Lake Okanagan service but with passenger accommodation below deck aft. Transferred to Skaha Lake in 1921 and dismantled in 1932.

Victoria (1900–04)

1898
107grt
75 x 15 x 4ft
Wood sternwheeler
1-cylinder, horizontal, direct-acting engine

Built at Victoria, Victoria Island, and acquired by Canadian Pacific in 1900 for the Trout Lake City–Gerrard service. In 1904, she was beached and used as a wharf and freight shed on Trout Lake.

Slocan (2) (1905–28)
1905
605grt
158 x 28ft
Wood sternwheeler
b. CPR, Rosebery
In May 1928, she was sold to become a warehouse for a logging camp at the north end of Slocan Lake.

Kushanook (1906–30)
1906
1,008grt
194 x 31 x 7ft
Wood sternwheeler
1-cylinder, horizontal trunk engines by the Polson Iron Works, Toronto
Launched on 5 May 1906 by CPR, Nelson, for the Nelson–Kootenay service. Her maiden voyage was an excursion for 300 passengers. Her final voyage was on 31 December 1930, and she was dismantled the following year and used as a hotel at Nelson.

Okanagan (1907–38)
1907
1,078grt
193 x 32 x 8ft
ID: 1122378
Wood sternwheeler
1-cylinder, horizontal trunk engines by the Polson Iron Works, Toronto
b. J.M. Bulger, CPR, Okanagan Landing
Launched on 16 April 1907 for the Okanagan Landing–Penticton service. She was laid up in 1916 when the Kettle Valley Railway was completed, and used as a cargo-only vessel from 1928. She was laid up again in 1934 at Okanagan

Landing and sold in 1938, hulked, and her machinery was removed and a boiler was installed at a cannery at Kelowna.

Hosmer (1909–34)
1909
154grt
110 x 21 x 8ft
ID: 1126551
Wood
Single-screw, 2-cylinder, compound engine
b. J.M. Bulger, CPR, Nelson
River towage tug based at Vancouver. She was burnt to the waterline and rebuilt in 1925, and withdrawn from service and laid up in 1931. She beached near Nelson in 1934 and converted into a houseboat.

Whatshan (1909–20)
1909
106grt
90 x 19 x 8ft
Wood
Single-screw, 2-cylinder, compound engine by the Polson Iron Works, Owen Sound
b. J.M. Bulger, CPR, Nelson
Built as a barge-towing tug for Lake Kootenay. She was dismantled in 1920, and her engine and boilers were transferred to Kelowna.

Kaleden (1910–20)
1910
180grt
94 x 18 x 4ft
Wood sternwheeler
2-cylinder, compound, direct-acting engine from Victoria
b. J.M. Bulger, CPR, Okanagan
Cargo carrier for the service on Skaha Lake on the Penticton–Kaleden–Okanagan Falls route. As the river was too shallow for her to navigate, she was transferred onto Okanagan Lake, and later

became the workboat for the construction of the Kettle Valley Railway. She was laid up in 1917 and dismantled in 1920.

Bonnington (1911–42)

1911
1,700grt
202 x 39 x 7ft
ID: 1130555
Sternwheeler
2-cylinder, horizontal, direct-acting engine
b. J.M. Bulger, CPR, Nakusp
Launched on 24 April 1911, and operated out of Nakusp, Upper Arrow Lake. She was laid up in 1931 and sold to Mr Sutherland, operating cargo only when required. Purchased by the Government of British Columbia in 1942, and was dismantled and converted into a barge in 1946.

Castlegar (1911–25)
1911
104grt
94 x 19 x 8ft
ID: 1130556
Wood screw tug
Single-screw, 2-cylinder, compound engine by Collingwood Ship Building Company, Vancouver
b. J.M. Bulger, CPR, Okanagan
Launched on 12 April 1911 for work on the Okanagan Lake, towing two eight-car barges. She was broken up in 1925.

Nasookin (1913–32)

1913
1,869grt
200 x 40 x 7ft
ID: 1133885
Steel sternwheeler
2-cylinder, horizontal, direct-acting engine by
builder
b. J.M. Bulger, CPR, Nelson
Passengers: 400

The hull was built in parts by the Western Dry
Dock Company, Port Arthur, and transported
by rail to Nelson, where it was assembled. She
was launched on 30 April 1913 and replaced
Kuskanook. She was the largest sternwheeler
in British Columbian waters. In the 1920s she
was used as a car ferry and operated her final
passenger sailing on 31 December 1930. She was
sold to the Government of British Columbia in
1932, modified forward to carry vehicles, and used
as a ferry across Lake Kootenay. The boiler from
Bonnington was installed in 1942, and she was
withdrawn from service and laid up in 1946. She
was taken over by the Navy League of Canada in
1947, and used as a cadet training and club ship.
In 1948, during floods she broke free, ran aground
and was wrecked.

Naramata (1914–69)

1914
150grt
90 x 19 x 8ft
ID: 1134271
Single-screw, 2-cylinder, compound engine by
Western Dry Dock Company, Port Arthur
b. Western Dry Dock Company, Port Arthur,
assembled by J.M. Bulger, CPR, Okanagan
Landing

Delivered for towing services on Lake Okanagan.
She was withdrawn in 1967 and sold in June 1969
to a Calgary syndicate.

Nelson (2) (1913–20)

1913
25grt
61 x 11 x 4ft
Wood screw tug
Single-screw, engine by builder
b. J.M. Bulger, CPR, Nelson

Delivered to the Kootenay Lake services, towing
railway wagon flats. She was laid up in 1919, and
sold the following year.

Sicamous[1] (1914–49)

1914
1,787grt
201 x 40 x 8ft
ID: 1134276
Steel sternwheeler
2-cylinder, compound, horizontal, direct-acting
engine by builder
17 knots
b. Western Dry Dock Company, Port Arthur,
assembled by J.M. Bulger, CPR, Okanagan
Landing
Passengers: 400

Sister to *Nasookin*. Launched on 26 May 1914
for the Okanagan–Penticton service. She was
rebuilt as a cargo vessel in 1930, and operated
her final voyage on 31 January 1935. She was sold
in June 1949 to the City of Penticton for use as a
museum ship.

Columbia (2) (1920–48)

1920
90grt
72 x 15 x 7ft
Wood screw tug
Engine from *Columbia* (1)
b. CPR, Nakusp

Delivered as a barge tug for the Arrow Lake
service. Sold in 1948 and converted into a
houseboat.

Kelowna (1920–57)

1920
96grt
89 x 19 x 8ft
Wood screw tug
Single-screw, 2-cylinder, compound engine from
Whatshan
b. CPR, Okanagan Landing

Delivered for towing duties on Okanagan Lake.
She was withdrawn in 1956, laid up and sold to
P. Ellergodt, Penticton, in May 1957.

Rosebery (1928–43)

1928
133grt
92 x 20 x 7ft
Wood screw tug
Single-screw, 2-cylinder, compound engine by
Collingwood Ship Building Company, Ontario
b. CPR, Rosebery

Delivered for service on Lake Slocan, and
withdrawn from service in 1943. Machinery
transferred to *Rosebery* (2), who replaced her on
the service.

Grantall (1928–64)

1928
164grt
92 x 24 x 10ft
Steel tug
Single-screw, triple-expansion engine by builder
b. Canadian Vickers, Montreal

Launched on 7 March 1928 at Nelson, and
delivered for the Kootenay Landing–Procter
route. She was laid up in 1957, and sold to
Mardell Limited, Edmonton. Acquired by the
Yellowknife Transportation Company in 1964 for
service at New Westminster, but was declared not
seagoing.

---

1   Pictured in the colour section.

Rosebery (2) (1943–58)

1943
166grt
98 x 20 x 7ft
Tug
Single-screw, 2-cylinder, compound engine by
Collingwood Ship Building Company, Ontario
b. CPR, Montreal
Built in sections at Montreal and transported by rail
to Rosebery, where she was assembled. Designed
for wood burning. She sailed on her maiden voyage
on 5 November 1943 from Rosebery to Slocan. She
was laid up in 1957 and sold to Fowler & Martin on
21 July the following year for scrap. She was beached
at New Denver and burned.

Okanagan (2) (1947–72)

1947
204grt
110 x 24 x 12ft
IMO: 5261491
Tug
Single-screw, oil, 8-cylinder engine by
Washington Engine Works, Seattle
Built at West Coast Shipbuilders, Vancouver,
and transported on railcars to Vernon, British
Columbia, for reassembling.
Delivered for towing duties on Lake Okanagan
from Okanagan Landing–Penticton–Kelowna.
The service ceased on 31 May 1972, and she was
laid up and sold to Fintry Estates. She was sold to
Payco Holdings Limited in 1980.

Columbia (3) (1948–54)

1948
22grt
50 x 11ft
Wood tug
Delivered as Surfco at Vancouver for the Alberni
Canal Company, and acquired by Canadian Pacific
in 1948 to replace Columbia (3). Sold to Ivan Horie
on 24 April 1954, and sank in 1968. She was raised
the following year and shipped to Vancouver.

BAY OF FUNDY SHIPS TAKEN OVER FROM THE DOMINION ATLANTIC RAILWAY IN 1911

Boston (1911–12)

1890
1,694grt
734n
245 x 36 x 21ft
ID: 1098585
Single-screw, triple-expansion engines by builder
15 knots
b. Alex Stephen & Sons, Linthouse
Yard No. 328
Passengers: 1,200, 300 berths
Delivered to the Yarmouth Steam Ship Company
for the Yarmouth, NS–Boston, Mass, service.
The company were taken over by the Dominion
Atlantic Railway Company in June 1901, and were
acquired by Canadian Pacific in 1911, when Boston
was put up for sale. She was sold to the Eastern
Steamship Company on 20 August 1912, and was
laid up at Boston in 1917. She was sold, renamed
Cambridge in 1917, and broken up in 1920.

Prince George (1911–12)

1898
1,990grt
863n
290 x 38 x 16ft
Twin-screw, 2 x triple-expansion engine by
builder
16 knots
b. Earle & Company, Hull
Yard No. 430
Passengers: 700 deck, 200 berths
Delivered to the Dominion Atlantic Railway
Company, Yarmouth, for the Nova Scotia–Boston
service. Acquired by Canadian Pacific in 1911, and
sold to the Eastern Steamship Company, Boston,
on 20 August 1912 (registered as owned by the
Yarmouth Steam Ship Company, Boston). In May
1917, she operated as a cross-Channel hospital
ship, and the lifeboats were increased to seven
each side. She returned to her owners in 1919, and
was sold to the Boston Iron & Metal Company in
1929 and broken up.

Prince Arthur (1911–12)

1899
2,041grt
923n
290 x 38 x 16ft
ID: 1110131
Twin-screw, 2 x triple-expansion engine by
builder
16 knots
b. Earle & Company, Hull
Yard No. 439
Passengers: 700 deck, 200 berths
Sister to Prince George
Taken over by Canadian Pacific in 1911, and sold
to the Eastern Steamship Company, Boston.
In May 1917, she operated as a cross-Channel
hospital ship, and the lifeboats were increased to
seven each side. She returned to her owners in
1919, and was sold to the Boston Iron & Metal
Company in 1929 and broken up.

Prince Albert (1911–27)

1899
112grt
97 x 20 x 8ft
Wood
Single-screw, 2-cylinder, compound engine by
W. & A. Moir, Yarmouth
9 knots
b. J. McGill, Shelburne, Nova Scotia
Passengers: 180 deck
Delivered to S.E. Messenger of Yarmouth as
Messenger for coastal passenger sailings. She was
acquired by the Dominion Atlantic Railway
Company in 1904, renamed Prince Albert
(Kingsport–Parrsboro route). She was taken
over by Canadian Pacific in 1911, and sold to the

Eastern Steamship Company, Boston. In 1927, she was acquired by the Albert Steam Ship Company, and on 5 March 1929, she was lost in pack ice at Mulgrave, Nova Scotia.

Prince Rupert (1911–19)
1894
1,159grt
620n
260 x 32 x 11ft
ID: 1104789
Steel paddlewheeler
3-cylinder, triple-expansion, diagonal engine by builder
18 knots
b. William Denny & Brothers, Dumbarton
Yard No. 496
Passengers: 103 in 59 cabins, 900 deck
Launched on 23 May 1894 for the Dominion Atlantic Railway Company. Acquired by Canadian Pacific in 1911, and sold to United States interests in 1919. She was broken up in the United States in 1924.

Yarmouth (1911–18)
1887
1,452grt
725n
220 x 35 x 13ft
ID: 1093373
Single-screw, triple-expansion engine by W.V. Lidgerwick, Glasgow
12 knots
b. A. McMillan & Sons, Dumbarton
Yard No. 276
Passengers: 300
Delivered to the Yarmouth Steam Ship Company, taken over by the Dominion Atlantic Railway Company in 1901 and Canadian Pacific in 1911. She was sold to the North American Steam Ship Company, Yarmouth, in 1918, and chartered to the Black Star Line. In 1924, she was sold to the Pottstown Steel Company, USA, and broken up.

St George (1913–19)
1906
2,456grt
1,012n
352 x 41 x 16ft
ID: 1123673
Triple-screw, 3 direct-drive steam turbines by builder
20 knots
b. Cammell Laird & Company Limited, Birkenhead
Yard No. 665
Passengers: 1,200
Delivered to the Great Western Railway Company for the Fishguard–Rosslare route. She was sold to Canadian Pacific in 1913 as a replacement for Prince Rupert, and entered service on the Digby–Saint John, New Brunswick, service across the Bay of Fundy. Operated as a cross-Channel hospital ship in 1917, and sold to the Great Eastern Railway Company in 1919 for the Harwich–Hook of Holland service. She was sold in October 1929 to Hughes, Bolckow & Company, and broken up at Blyth.

Empress (1916–34)
1906
1,342grt
612n
235 x 34 x 20ft
Twin-screw, 2 x triple-expansion engine by builder
12 knots
b. Swan, Hunter & Wigham Richardson, Newcastle
Yard No. 754
Passengers: 600
Delivered to the Charlottetown Steamship Company, Prince Edward Island, for the Charlotteville–Pictou service, and acquired by Canadian Pacific in 1916 to replace Yarmouth. In May 1926, she was damaged and flooded during a severe gale, and was replaced by Princess Helene

in 1930. On 22 June 1931, she caught fire at West Saint John, New Brunswick, and her accommodation was gutted. She was sold to the Dominion Coal Company on 2 November 1934, and became a hulk.

Kipawo (1925–41)
1925
200grt
123 x 26 x 9ft
ID: 1150498
Twin-screw, oil, 2 x 4-cylinder engine by Fairbanks, Morse & Company, Beloit, Wisconsin
b. Saint John Dry Dock & Shipbuilding Company
Yard No. 1
Passengers: 127, 8 vehicles
Built to replace Prince Albert on the Kingsport–Parrsboro–Wolfville route. When the service was withdrawn in 1940, she was requisitioned by the Canadian Government and operated as a coastal military supply ship. She was sold to Crosbie & Company on 20 September 1946, and was owned by the Terra Nova Transportation Company in 1952, operating as a car ferry. The following year she was fitted with a Ruston & Hornsby, Lincoln, 6-cylinder oil engine, operating on the St John's–Conception Bay inter-port routes. On 12 November 1974, she was acquired by Fogo Transportation Limited, Fogo, Newfoundland, and Bonavista Bay Boats Limited, Trinity Bay, Newfoundland, on 6 June 1975. In 1982, she became part of a floating theatre complex at Wolfville, Nova Scotia.

Princess Helene (1930–63)
1930
4,505grt
2,022n
320 x 51 x 27ft
ID: 5411515
Twin-screw, 2 x 3-stage, steam turbine by builders
19 knots

b. William Denny & Brothers, Dumbarton
Yard No. 1244
Passengers: 1,000, 45 cars

Launched on 12 May 1930, and arrived at Saint John, New Brunswick, on 22 August for the Saint John–Digby service. She was fitted with an extra Scotch boiler for use when in port. She was sold in May 1963 to the Marvic Navigation Company, Liberia, and left Saint John for the Mediterranean as *Helene*. She was sold to Chandris Line, becoming *Carina II*, and *Carina* when the first vessel of the name was renamed *Fiesta* in 1967. On 7 March 1977, she was sold and broken up by Kyriazis Brothers, Perama.

Princess of Nanaimo/Princess of Acadia/ Princess of Nanaimo/Henry Osborne[1] (1951–73)

1950
6,787grt
3,409n
358 x 62 x 26ft
IMO: 5408063
Twin-screw, 4 steam turbines by builder
20½ knots
b. Fairfield Shipbuilding & Engineering Company, Govan, Glasgow
Yard No. 750
Passengers: 1,500 + 130 vehicles

---

1   Pictured in the colour section.

Launched on 14 September 1950 as *Princess of Nanaimo* for the Vancouver–Nanaimo service. She was laid up in 1962 and transferred to the Saint John–Digby route in 1963, becoming *Princess of Acadia*. On 27 May 1971, she was replaced by *Princess of Acadia* (2), and was laid up, reverting to *Princess of Nanaimo*, owned by Canadian Pacific. In 1972, she lost most of her passenger accommodation and was converted into a car ferry for 225 vehicles, for the Saint John, New Brunswick–Halifax–St John's, Newfoundland, service. On 16 May 1973, she stranded outside Saint John, NB, in fog and was abandoned by the underwriters. She was renamed *Henry Osborne* on 14 November and sold to the Union Pipe & Machinery Company, Montreal. She arrived at Bilbao on 29 January 1974 in tow of *Hansa*, and was broken up.

Princess of Nova/Princess of Acadia (2) (1971–74)

1971
10,051grt
6,199n
480 x 66 x 15ft
IMO: 7039567
Twin-screw, Kamewa controllable, pitch-inward turning oil 'Vee' engines, type 16-645-E5 by the General Motors Corporation, Le Grange, Detroit
Bow thrust propeller
15½ knots
b. Saint John Shipbuilding & Dry Dock Company, Saint John, New Brunswick
Passengers: 650 + 159 cars or 40 trailers

Launched as *Princess of Nova* and renamed *Princess of Acadia* while fitting out for the Saint John–Digby service. On 24 December 1974, she was sold to the Government of Canada, and operated by Canadian Pacific. On 1 September 1976, she was transferred to East Coast Marine & Ferry Service, and to CN Marine Incorporated, Saint John, in 1979. She was owned by Marine Atlantic Incorporated, Canada, in 1987.

GREAT LAKES SHIPS

Athabascka/Athabasca (1883–1946)

1883
2,269grt
1,545n
263 x 38 x 23ft
ID: 1085764
Single-screw, 2-cylinder compound engine by D. Rowan, Glasgow
8 knots
b. Aitken & Mansel, Kelvinhaugh, Glasgow
Yard No. 123
Passengers: 240 and 1,000 deck

Launched on 3 July 1883 as *Athabascka*, on arrival at Montreal she was renamed *Athabasca*, halved and taken to Buffalo. She was rejoined in January 1884 and laid up awaiting the thaw. She entered service on 17 May 1884 on the Owen Sound–Port Arthur (railhead for Winnipeg) route. The railway was completed in 1885 and *Athabasca*, *Alberta* and *Algoma* took up service on the route. On 13 October 1909, she went aground on Flowerpot Island, Owen Sound, and was sent to Collingwood for rebuilding. She was rebuilt at Ontario (299ft/2,784grt/2,349n) and fitted with a new engine by the Western Dry Dock & Shipbuilding Company, Port Arthur. In 1912, Port McNicoll replaced Owen Sound as the embarkment point. In August 1946, she was sold for use as a pallet-loading (via her side doors) fruit carrier in Florida. She was still recorded as owned by Canadian Pacific when she was sold for scrap in 1948.

Alberta (1883–1946)

1883
2,282grt
1,552n
263 x 38 x 23ft
ID: 1085765
Single-screw, 2-cylinder, compound engine by

D. Rowan, Glasgow
8 knots
b. Chas Connell & Company, Glasgow
Yard No. 136
Passengers: 240, and 1,000 deck
Launched on 12 July 1883, she left Montreal in two halves for Buffalo on 10 November, and was rejoined. In 1911, she was rebuilt by the Collingwood Shipbuilding Company (310ft/2,829grt/2,377n). In 1916, she operated a freight service, was sold with her sister for service in Florida, and was broken up in 1948.

Algoma (1883–85)

1883
2,272grt
1,554n
263 x 38 x 23ft
ID: 1085766
Single-screw, 2-cylinder, compound engine by D. Rowan, Glasgow
8 knots
b. Aitken & Mansel, Kelvinhaugh, Glasgow
Yard No. 124
Passengers: 240, and 1,000 deck
Launched on 31 July 1883, she left Montreal for Buffalo on 4 November. She inaugurated the Great Lakes service on 11 May 1884. She was wrecked near Port Arthur on Greenstone Island on 7 November 1885 in a severe gale. She broke in two, forty-eight people lost their lives and fifteen were saved, many by her sister, *Athabasca*. Her engines were salvaged and transferred to *Manitoba*.

Manitoba (1889–1950)

1889
2,616grt
1,699n
303 x 38 x 15ft
Single-screw, 2-cylinder compound engine by D. Rowan, Glasgow. Engine from *Algoma*
b. Polson Iron Works, Owen Sound

Launched on 4 May 1888, and completed to replace *Algoma* on the service. In 1912, she was transferred to the new Port McNicoll–Port Arthur service, and in 1920, the Lakes fleet were given white hulls. On 17 September 1928, *Manitoba* rescued the five crew from the foundered *Manasoo*. She was laid up at Port McNicoll in 1950, and scrapped the following year.

TRAIN FERRIES ON THE WINDSOR–DETROIT SERVICE

Ontario (1890–1924)

1890
1,615grt
1,018n
297 x 41 x 15ft
ID: 1094885
Steel paddle steamer
2-cylinder engine by S.F. Hodge, Detroit
b. Polson Iron Works, Owen Sound, Ontario
Yard No. 25
Maiden voyage on 25 April 1890 for the Detroit River ferry, Owen Sound–Windsor route, registered at Windsor, Ontario. *Michigan* and *Ontario* were acquired by the Newaygo Timber Company in 1924 as wood pulp barges. On 13 October 1927, following an engine failure she foundered in a storm on Lake Ontario, near Outer Island.

Michigan (1890–1924)

1890
1,739grt
1,020n
296 x 41 x 15ft
ID: 1098904
Steel paddle steamer
2-cylinder engine by S.F. Hodge, Detroit
b. F.W. Wheeler, West Bay City, Michigan
Yard No. 76

Launched on 30 October 1890 and delivered for the Windsor–Detroit service. Laid up in 1915 and sold to the Newaygo Timber Company in 1924 and converted into a wood pulp barge. On 14 November 1942, she was wrecked on Lottie Wood Shoal, Georgian Bay, Ontario. All the crew were rescued by the tug *Favorite*, of the Great Lakes Towing Company.

Assiniboia[1] (1908–68)

1907
3,880grt
2,486n
337 x 44 x 15ft
ID: 5027326
Single-screw, 4-cylinder, quadruple-expansion engine by builder
14 knots
b. Fairfield Shipbuilding & Engineering Company, Govan, Glasgow
Yard No. 452
Passengers: 400 (280 in berths)
Launched on 25 June 1907 and divided by the Davie Shipyard and rejoined at the Buffalo Dry Dock. She entered service on 4 July 1908, on the Owen Sound–Fort William service. Her cargo was loaded through side doors in the hull, which was an early form of palletisation. On 9 June 1909, she was involved in an accident in Soo Locks while waiting to be dropped to Lake Huron, when she was joined by *Crescent City*, and the upper locks were not yet closed. *Perry G. Walker* was coming up the river and failed to stop, and rammed the lower gates, releasing the water. *Assiniboia* and *Crescent City* were caught in a torrent of water and the two ships collided with the *Perry G. Walker*. The lock closed and none of the ships were lost, being halted by tugs, and they docked under their own power with some hull damage. In the winter of 1950/51, steel bulkheads were fitted at the Midland Shipyard, and three wooden masts were replaced

---

1   Pictured in the colour section.

by two steel ones. She was converted to oil burning in 1953, and reboilered in 1955. In October 1965, she ceased to carry passengers, was reduced to carry cargo only, and arrived at Port McNicoll on 26 November 1967 and was laid up. On 19 May 1968, she was sold to the JAL Steamship Company, and towed to West Deptford, New Jersey, for use as a restaurant. She was destroyed by fire in November 1968 and broken up.

The Pennsylvania–Ontario Transportation Company was formed on 16 February 1906 as a joint venture between John W. Ellsworth, Canadian Pacific Railway, and the Pennsylvania Railroad Company, to operate the 81 miles from Ashtabula to Port Burwell, Canadian Pacific's main port on Lake Erie. The company was initially named Ellsworth Transportation Company after the Ashtabula coal merchant, who was responsible for the deal. It was dissolved on 29 September 1961.

Keewatin (1908–66)
1907
3,856grt
2,486n
337 x 44 x 15ft
ID: 5184538
Single-screw, 4-cylinder, quadruple-expansion engine by builder
14 knots
b. Fairfield Shipbuilding & Engineering Company, Govan, Glasgow
Yard No. 453
Passengers: 400 (280 in berths)
In 1950–51 she had steel bulkheads and two steel masts fitted, and was converted to burn oil in 1953, when her hull was painted white. An echo sounder and radar were fitted in 1956, and she was withdrawn from passenger service in October 1965. The following year, she was sold to Marine Salvage, Port Colborne, and to River Queen Boat Works, Gary, Indiana, and was opened as a museum at Saugatuck in June 1967.

RAIL FERRY SHIPS

Ashtabula (1906–58)

1906
2,670grt
1,525n
338 x 56 x 17ft
ID: 2203071
Twin-screw, 2 x triple-expansion engine by builder
12 knots
b. Great Lakes Engineering Works, St Claire, Michigan
Yard No. 19
Launched in May 1906 for the Ellsworth Transportation Company, and the company name was changed in August, with Canadian Pacific and the Pennsylvania Railroad Company owning half each. The main traffic was coal from the United States for Canadian Pacific, returning with Canadian wheat or meat. On 12 December 1909, she grounded during a storm off Port Burwell, and on 10 February 1933, she became stuck in ice off Port Burwell, and was brought off by icebreakers the following day. On 18 September 1958, she was in collision with the Ben Moreell in Ashtabula Harbour. She was struck behind the bridge, and the report found

the captain of Ashtabula guilty of crossing the bow of the oncoming vessel and underestimating her speed. Ashtabula's captain, Louis Sabo, committed suicide the evening before the disciplinary court convened. The ship was raised and broken up by the Acme Scrap Metal & Iron Company of Port Burwell. The Ben Moreell was also scrapped.

Maitland No. 1 (1916–35)
1916
2,757grt
338 x 56 x 18ft
b. Great Lakes Engineering Works, Ecorse, Michigan
Canadian Pacific Railways had a 27.1 per cent interest in the Toronto, Hamilton & Buffalo Navigation Company, which owned Maitland 1. She was a sister to Ashtabula and was built in the same yard in 1916. On 21 August 1926, she rescued the crew of the Howard S. Gerken. The service was withdrawn on 28 June 1932, and she was laid up at Ashtabula. In 1935, she was leased to the Nicholson Steamship Company. She was requisitioned by the War Shipping Administration in August 1942. She operated for sixteen years in service, followed by ten years laid up, and ended up as a wood barge.

The Canadian Pacific Car & Passenger Transport Company was acquired by Canadian Pacific on 1 September 1929, and owned jointly with the New York Central Railroad.

Charles Lyon (1929–37)
1908
1,658grt
1,127n
280 x 40 x 20ft
ID: 1125975
Twin-screw, 2 x 2-cylinder, inclined, compound engine by builder
b. Polson Iron Works Company, Toronto
Yard No. 92

Ordered as *Ogdensburg* and launched on
7 December 1907 for Captain D.H. Lyon.
Delivered as a railcar ferry with three tracks and
fourteen wagons, and acquired by Canadian Pacific
Car & Passenger Transfer Company in 1929 to
replace two older vessels. She was sold in 1937 to
J.P. Porter & Sons, Montreal, reduced to a barge,
and broken up at Hamilton, Ontario, in 1941.

Ogdensburg (1930–72)
1930
1,405grt
290 x 45 x 12ft
1 auxiliary power diesel generator
b. American Shipbuilding Company, Lorain,
Ohio
Yard No. 806
Entered service on 2 November 1930, with
Prescotont. Passenger car ferry services were
withdrawn in 1958, and the freight service
withdrawn on 25 September 1970. She was sold
to the Windsor Detroit Barge Line Limited,
Detroit, on 10 January 1972.

Prescotont (1930–72)
1930
302grt
117 x 28 x 12ft
ID: 5283712
Single-screw, diesel-electric by Winton
Engineering Company, Cleveland. 4SA 12
cylinder
11 knots
b. Davie Shipbuilding Company, Lauzon, Quebec
Yard No. 508
Delivered as a strengthened-for-ice fire float tug
for the *Ogdensburg*, which was controlled by the
tug. The rudders of both synchronised from the
bridge of the tug. During the winter she acted as
an icebreaker to keep the channel open between
the two terminals. The passenger car service
was withdrawn in 1958, and the freight service
withdrawn on 25 September 1970. She was sold

to Windsor Detroit Barge Line Limited on
10 January 1972 to tow containers. In 1986, she
was laid up at Detroit following a serious fire.

The Quebec Salvage & Wrecking Company
was formed in 1914 by Canadian Pacific and
George T. Davie for tug and salvage operations
out of Quebec, and was sold to the Foundation
Company of Canada.

GTD (1914–30)
1891
333grt
154n
123 x 30 x 12ft
Wood schooner
b. T.A. Wilson, Bridgewater, Nova Scotia
Delivered as *Tyree*, and purchased by George
T. Davie & Sons, Lauzon, in 1907, and renamed
GTD (George Taylor Davie). Sold to the Quebec
Salvage & Wrecking Company in 1914 as a diver
and wreck equipment store ship, and broken up
in 1930.

Lord Strathcona (1914–19)
1902
495grt
160 x 27 x 13ft
ID: 1099478
Tug
Twin-screw, 2 x triple-expansion engine by
builder
b. J.P. Rennoldson & Sons, South Shields
Yard No. 215
Delivered to G.T. Davie & Sons, Lauzon, and
transferred to the Quebec Salvage & Wrecking
Company in 1914. On 30 September 1944,
she was acquired by the Foundation Maritime
Company, Halifax, and was broken up in 1947.

Traverse (1930–44)
1930
317grt
152n
130 x 26 x 10ft
ID: 5118149
Single-screw, oil 2s.sa engine by Worthington,
Simpson & Company, Newark
b. G. Brown & Company, Glasgow
Yard No. 172
Launched on 12 May 1930, she left Greenock
on 23 June, arriving at Quebec on 14 July. She
was sold to Foundation Maritime Company
on 30 September 1944, and to Lévis Shipping
Company in 1952, becoming *Fort Lévis*. In 1958,
she was owned by R.L. Leclerc, and was sold to
B. Dufour in 1961. On 20 March 1964, she was
crushed by ice off the Magdalen Islands, and was
salvaged and broken up.

MERSEY TOWING COMPANY

Beaver (1903–22)
1898
154grt
13n
106 x 20 x 11ft
Single-screw, 2-cylinder, compound by builder
b. Elliot & Jeffrey, Cardiff
Yard No. 4
Delivered as *Powerful* for J. Elliot, Cardiff,
renamed *Lady Lewis* in 1899, and acquired by
Elder, Dempster & Company for the Mersey
Towing Company, Liverpool, in 1901 and
renamed *Beaver*. She was sold to Canadian Pacific
on 6 April 1903, and to J. Davies & Company,
Cardiff, in 1922. She was broken up by Reese &
Company, Llanelli, in 1938.

Otter (1903–22)

1887
145grt
13n
105 x 20 x 14ft
ID: 1089213
Single-screw, 2-cylinder, compound engine by builder
b. Elliot & Jeffery, Cardiff
Yard No. 2

Delivered as the two-funnelled tug *Sir W.T. Lewis* for J. Elliot & Company, and sold to Mersey Towing in 1901, becoming *African*. She was acquired by Canadian Pacific in 1903, and rebuilt with one funnel in 1906, renamed *Otter*. In 1922, she was purchased by the Liverpool Screw Towing & Lighterage Company, and renamed *Marsh Cock*. On 27 May 1946, she was sold for scrap to Rootledge & Company, Bromborough.

Panther (1903–21)

1884
150grt
19n
105 x 20 x 11ft
ID: 1089188
Single-screw, 2-cylinder, compound engine by builder
b. Elliot & Jeffery, Cardiff
Yard No. 1

Delivered as *Elliot & Jeffery* for J. Elliot, Cardiff, and acquired by the Mersey Towing Company, Liverpool, in 1901, renamed *Panther*. She was taken over by Canadian Pacific in 1903, and the Coulson Tug Company, Newcastle, in 1921. Sold to France, Fenwick Tyne & Wear Company, in 1925, when they took over the Coulson fleet. She was broken up in 1926.

Bison (1906–46)

1906
274grt
37n
125 x 24 x 11ft
ID: 5251290
Single-screw, triple-expansion engine by Crabtree & Company, Great Yarmouth
b. H. & C. Grayson, Garston, Liverpool
Yard No. 57
Passengers: 316

Delivered as a passenger tender and replaced *Otter*. Her passenger licence was increased to 537, plus crew of eleven in 1936. On 4 May 1941, she was sunk by a bomb, raised and repaired. On 9 November 1946, she was sold to John Latsis, Piraeus, and renamed *Niki*, and to N. Lambiris in 1954, re-engined, renamed *Hydra*, and used for day excursion work to the island of Hydra. She was renamed *Nicolas L* in 1957, and *Aghios Georgios* in 1964, owned by Alexiadis & P. Iliadis, Piraeus. She was broken up at Skaramangas in 1966.

Cruizer (1907–13)

1895
380grt
24n
150 x 24 x 13ft
ID: 1104606
Single-screw, triple-expansion engine by Rankin & Blackmore, Greenock
b. William Hamilton & Company, Glasgow
Yard No. 119

Delivered as *Flying Buzzard* to the Clyde Steamship Company, Glasgow, and purchased by the Liverpool Steam Tug Company in 1900, becoming *Cruizer*. She was acquired by Canadian Pacific in 1907, then C. Bristler & Company, Halifax, in 1913, and the Cruizer Shipping Company in 1925. She was broken up by the Dominion Steel Company, Halifax, in 1952.

Gopher (1910–23)

1910
198grt
100 x 23 x 12ft
ID: 1131308
Single-screw, triple-expansion engine by Crabtree & Company, Great Yarmouth
b. H. & C. Grayson, Garston, Liverpool
Yard No. 67

Delivered to the Mersey Towing Company, and requisitioned by the Admiralty in 1914 and then transferred to the Quebec Salvage & Wrecking Company. Worked out of Saint John, New Brunswick. Purchased by the Saint John Dry Dock Company in 1923, renamed *Ocean King* and purchased by Davie Shipbuilding & Repair Company in 1926, becoming *Chateau*. She was sold on 30 October 1961 and broken up.

Musquash (1910–20)

1910
198grt
100 x 23 x 12ft
ID: 1131307
Single-screw, triple-expansion engine by Crabtree & Company, Great Yarmouth
b. H. & C. Grayson, Garston, Liverpool
Yard No. 66

Launched on 20 September 1910 for the Mersey Towing Company, with Canadian Pacific as managers. Requisitioned by the Admiralty in 1914, leaving Liverpool with *Gopher* on 3 June for Quebec and Moville, Ireland, and St John's, Newfoundland. Transferred to the Quebec Salvage & Wrecking Company. In 1920, she was sold to the Atlantic Salvage Company, Halifax, and sank in a collision off Anticosti Island, Quebec, on 4 August 1921.

Moose (1915–46)

1915
208grt
87n
105 x 25 x 13ft
ID: 1137482
Single-screw, triple-expansion engine by Crabtree & Company, Great Yarmouth
b. H. & C. Grayson, Garston, Liverpool
Yard No. 94
Ordered by the Mersey Towing Company and requisitioned by the Admiralty to operate in the Dardanelles, north Russian waters, Murmansk and Archangel. She was returned to Canadian Pacific on 20 October 1919, operating at Liverpool. On 28 July 1945, she sank in the Mersey in collision with *Kawartha Park* of the Park Steam Ship Company. She was refloated on 2 August. Purchased by the Liverpool Screw Towing Company on 1 February 1946, becoming *Prairie Cock*, she was broken up at Passage West, Cork, in 1959.

Elk/Wapiti (1915–45)

1915
208grt
87n
105 x 25 x 13ft
ID: 1137488
Single-screw, triple-expansion engine by Crabtree & Company, Great Yarmouth
b. H. & C. Grayson, Garston, Liverpool
Yard No. 95
Delivered as *Elk* and operated with *Moose* during the First World War. She returned to Canadian Pacific on 12 June 1919, becoming *Wapiti*. Sold to the Liverpool Screw Towing Company in 1945, and renamed *Weather Cock*. On 16 August 1958, she arrived at Barrow in tow of *Rosegarth*, and was broken up.

WORKING BOATS GREAT LAKES

Champion (2) (1883–85)

1877
323grt
131 x 23 x 11ft
Sidewheeler
b. G.T. Davie, Lévis, Quebec
Delivered in 1877, and acquired by Canadian Pacific in 1883. She was sold in 1885, and rebuilt in 1887 at Owen Sound.

Dolphin

Emily

Sold by Canadian Pacific on 16 July 1885 to J. Whelan.

Georgian (1884–88)

1864
377grt
130 x 22 x 11ft
Single-screw, 1-cylinder by builder
b. J. Potter, Georgian Bay, Ontario
Delivered to J.C. Graham, and acquired by Canadian Pacific on 1 April 1884. On 9 May 1888, she sank in Owen Sound, Ontario.

Juliette (1878)

b. Burlington, Ontario
Sank on 21 November 1883 at Pine Tree Harbour, Ontario.

Magdalena (1875)

Launched at Buffalo, New York.

Siskiwit (1883–94)

1879
61grt
67 x 16 x 8ft
Launched at Buffalo, New York, and acquired by Canadian Pacific in 1883 for towing duties on the Kaministikwia River. She was sold to C. Drinkwater of Montreal in 1894.

BRITISH COLUMBIA

Skuzzy (2) (1885–90)

1885
297grt
133ft
Machinery was taken from *Skuzzy* (1)
b. Savona British Columbia
She was delivered to operate on the Thompson and Shuswap rivers, and was sold in 1890.

CPR No. 1 (1923–52)

26ft wooden motor launch
14 knots

CPR No. 2 (1923–52)

30ft wooden launch
10 knots

Nipigonian (1923–52)

34ft wooden launch
16 knots

Misty Maid (1954)

26ft cabin cruiser
17 knots
b. Turner Boat Works, Vancouver
Built in 1954. On 17 May 1954, she exploded and caught fire.

Misty Maid (1953–56)

25ft wooden motor launch
Replaced CPR Nos 1 & 2. Exploded at Kenora Dock in 1956.

Canadiana (1954–61)
26ft cabin cruiser
b. Richardson Boat Works, Meaford, Ontario
Sold in 1961.

VANCOUVER HARBOUR

Green Jade (1924–52)
26ft motor boat
Built in north Vancouver in 1924.

Green Jade (2) (1952)
17ft motor boat
b. S. Madil, Nanaimo, British Columbia

The Canadian-Australasian Line was formed jointly by the Union Steam Ship Company of New Zealand and Canadian Pacific in 1931. The Union Steam Ship Company remained as managers for the service operating between Sydney and British Columbia. The service ceased in 1941 and recommenced from 1948 until May 1953, when the company was wound up.

Niagara (1913–40)
1913
13,415grt
7,582n
525 x 66 x 35ft
ID: 1135193
Triple-screw, 2 x 4-cylinder, triple-expansion engines by builder
17 knots
b. John Brown & Company Limited, Clydebank
Yard No. 415
Launched on 17 August 1912 for the Union Steam Ship Company of New Zealand to operate on the Canadian–Australasian service. She sailed on her maiden voyage in April 1913 and was the first passenger vessel to be given a Board of Trade certificate to burn oil fuel. She was transferred, with *Aorangi*, on charter to the newly formed Canadian-Australasian Line in July 1931. She collided with King Line's *King Egbert* in the Juan de Fuca Strait off Victoria in July 1935. On 18 June 1940, she left Auckland with a cargo that included rifle ammunition and £2.5 million in gold ingots. The following day at 00.30, she struck a mine while entering the Hauraki Gulf and by 05.30 she sank. It was assumed that the mines had been laid by the German raider *Orion*. *Niagara* sank in 439ft of water. The previous record attempt to retrieve gold was made at 396ft from the P&O vessel *Egypt*. An attempt to recover the gold from *Niagara* was made by the coaster *Claymore*, which was equipped with a remotely controlled grab and a diving bell. The wreck was located on 2 February 1941, and the divers gained access to the strong room. It was a difficult salvage operation as the work could only be carried out at slack water. The first gold ingots were brought ashore in October, and 277 out of 295 boxes were recovered by the beginning of December. It was decided that the rest of the gold had to be left because the hull had settled. Claymore returned to Whangarei to find that the Japanese had attacked Pearl Harbor and the salvage operation was abandoned. In August 1953, another attempt was made by *Foremost 17*, and thirty bars were recovered from the wreck.

Aotearoa (1915–17)
1915
13,415grt
7,582n
525 x 66 x 35ft
ID: 6104629
Triple-screw, 2 x 4-cylinder, triple expansion engines by builder
17 knots
b. John Brown & Company Limited, Clydebank
Yard No. 499
She was launched on 30 June 1915 as a sister to *Niagara* and was requisitioned by the Admiralty and completed as the auxiliary cruiser HMS *Avenger*. On 14 June 1917, she was torpedoed and sunk by the German submarine *U-69*, and one person lost their life.

Aorangi (1925–53)
1925
17,491grt
10,773n
580 x 72 x 43ft
ID: 1148515
Quadruple-screw, oil, 4 x 6–cylinder, 2s.sa Sulzer diesel by builder
17 knots
b. Fairfield Ship Building & Engineering Company, Glasgow
Yard No. 603
She was the first motor ship on the Pacific and was designed with four sets of machinery and four shafts. She was launched on 17 June 1924 for the Union Steam Ship Company of New Zealand. She sailed from Southampton to Vancouver on her maiden voyage on 3 January 1925, and was placed on the Sydney–Vancouver route. She was transferred to the Canadian-Australasian Line in 1931 and refitted at Sydney in 1938 (to accommodate 248 first-, 266 cabin- and 125 third-class passengers). In February 1940, she was requisitioned as a troop ship and assisted in the evacuation of Singapore in 1941. She became the mothership for 150 tugs that were used to tow caissons during the Normandy invasion in 1944. The following year she was converted into the flagship for the Pacific Squadron of the Royal Fleet Auxiliary, and was returned to her owners in 1946. Her first commercial sailing took place on 19 August 1948, when she sailed from Sydney to Auckland, Fiji and Vancouver, and she was painted with a white hull and thin green band for two round voyages (with 212 first-, 170 cabin- and 104 third-class passengers). On 8 June 1953, she arrived at Sydney on her final voyage and was sold for scrap, arriving at W.H. Arnott Young at Dalmuir on 27 July.

Canadian Pacific took over the St Lawrence & Ottawa Railway Company in 1881, which operated from Saint John, New Brunswick, and Boston and Brockville, Ontario, and Morristown, New York, with the ferry *William Armstrong*, under the name Car Ferry Company. The Canada Central Railway became part of Canadian Pacific in 1885, and in 1888 the service was renamed the Canadian Pacific Car & Passenger Transfer Company. Canadian Pacific did not own the company but provided the railway cars. The service between Brockville and Morristown was discontinued in 1896 and the *Charles Lyon* entered service in 1908. On 1 September 1929, Canadian Pacific took control of the company, and the following year, the New York Central Railroad acquired an interest, and *Prescotont* and *Ogdensburg* replaced *Charles Lyon*. In 1970, a bridge was built to connect Prescott with Ogdensburg and the passenger service on that route was closed. However, the freight service continued but when the Ogdensburg terminal was destroyed by fire in 1972, this was also closed.

Transit (1886–1901)

1874
141grt
108 x 21 x 6ft
Wood
Twin-screw, 2 single-cylinder engines by John King, Oswego, New York
b. Clayton Ship Building Company, New York
Built for Isaac D. Purkis and taken over by Canadian Pacific Car & Passenger Transfer Company in 1886. She was sold and broken up in 1901.

William Armstrong (1881–1910)

1876
181grt
100 x 30 x 6ft
Wood
Single-screw, 2-cylinder, compound, 2 single

boilers by John King, Oswego, New York
b. A. & J. W. Wood, Ogdensburg
Launched on 23 November 1876 for David H. Lyons for the Brockville route. On 20 June 1889, she left Morristown with three loaded coal wagons. The river began to flood into the engine room and she sank, with the loss of one passenger. She was raised and returned to service. In 1910, she was sold to Robert Weddell of Ontario and became the drilling barge *Mons Meg*. She was broken up in 1938.

City of Belleville (1881–1908)

1878
101grt
69n
90 x 15 x 7ft
Wood
Single-screw, 1-cylinder engine
Built for Isaac D. Purkis for towing a three-railcar barge named *Jumbo* on the Prescott–Ogdensburg crossing. In 1881, she was acquired by the South Eastern Railway Company for use on the Brockville–Morristown service. In 1886, she was operated by the Car Ferry Company, and was owned by Canadian Pacific Car & Passenger Transfer Company in 1888. She was transferred to the Prescott–Ogdensburg route in 1896, and replaced by *Charles Lyon* in 1908.

International (1881–1910)

1881
395grt
269n
182 x 30 x 10ft
ID: 1080690
Wood
Twin-screw, 2 x 2-cylinder compound engine by E. Gilbert & Sons, Montreal
b. A. Cantin, Montreal
Completed as *South Eastern* for Longueuil Navigation Company, Montreal, and was sold to the Richelieu & Ontario Navigation Company

in 1886. On 14 April 1890, she was acquired by Canadian Pacific Car & Passenger Transfer Company and was replaced by *Charles Lyon* in 1909. The following year she was sold to Sincennes-McNaughton and converted into a sand barge. She was acquired by Touzin Sand Company, Montreal, in 1912, and scrapped two years later.

The Pennsylvania–Ontario Transportation Company was founded on 16 February 1906 as a joint venture between J.W. Ellsworth, Canadian Pacific, and the Pennsylvania Railroad Company to provide a service from Ashtabula to Port Burwell. The organisation was originally named the Ellsworth Transportation Company after the Ashtabula coal merchant. It survived until 29 September 1961, when it was wound up.

Canadian Pacific also held a 27.1 per cent interest in the Toronto, Hamilton & Buffalo Navigation Company, which owned *Maitland 1*, which was a sister of *Ashtabula*.

Incat Marine Limited was formed in 1973, with Canadian Pacific holding a 40 per cent share, and Inchcape (Canada) Limited having a 60 per cent share. Incat Ships Limited was also formed, with Canadian Pacific holding 43 per cent and Inchcape 57 per cent. A route was established from the Canadian Pacific railhead at McKellar Island, Thunder Bay, Ontario, across Lake Superior to Superior, Winconsin. The round trip took thirty-six hours. Newsprint and wood pulp were carried from the Great Lakes Paper Company at Thunder Bay, and the service was operated by two ships.

Incan Superior (1974–)

1974
3,838grt
1,733n
382 x 66 x 24ft
IMO: 7343669
Twin-screw, oil, 2 x 12–cylinder, 2s.sa engines by
General Motors, La Grange, Illinois
14 knots
b. Burrard Dry Dock Company, Vancouver
Yard No. 211

Launched, unnamed on 28 February 1974 and
delivered and named at Vancouver on 3 May.
She was renamed *Princess Superior* in 1993.

Incan St Laurent (1976)

1976
3,838grt
1,733n
382 x 66 x 24ft
IMO: 7401021
Twin-screw, oil, 2 x 12–cylinder, 2s.sa engines by
General Motors, La Grange, Illinois
b. Burrard Dry Dock Company, Vancouver
Yard No. 212

She was built for a proposed service from Quebec
City–Baie-Commeau but this failed to operate.
She was chartered to the Alaska Trainship
Corporation for service between Whittier, Alaska
and New Westminster. However, when it was
decided that this route was not viable, she was
laid up at Vancouver. On 4 January 1977, she was
sold to CN Marine, Canadian National Railway
Company, Montreal, and renamed *Georges
Alexandre Lebel* for the service between Matane
on the Gaspé Peninsular and Baie-Commeau.

OZMILLION SHIPPING CORPORATION

Repap Enterprise (1972)

1972
10,999grt
6,806n
533 x 64 x 24ft
IMO: 7208209
Twin-screw, variable pitch, 2 x 8–cylinder, 4s.sa
Pielstick engine by builder
15 knots
b. O/Y Wärtsilä, Turku, Finland
Yard No. 1,197

Delivered as *Mont Royal* for A/B Svenska
Amerika Linien, Gothenburg, and lengthened
and converted to a ro-ro vessel in 1978. Her
name was changed to *Mount Royal*. She became
Atlantic Premier in 1984, and *Incotrans Premier*
the following year. She then reverted back to
Atlantic Premier briefly before a new charter,
when her name was changed to *Atlantic Star*.
She was acquired by Bore Line (Singapore) Pte
in 1985 and renamed *Canada Maritime*. In 1986,
she was purchased by Canadian Pacific and was
converted into a china clay and paper carrier
at Boele's yard at Dordrecht, becoming *Repap
Enterprise*, owned by the Ozmillion Shipping
Corporation, Monrovia. In 1991, she became the
last ship owned by Canadian Pacific. In 1992, she
was renamed *New Enterprise* and *Neptune Princess*,
and *Marmara Princess* in 1995. Broken up in India
2004.

SHIPS MANAGED BY CANADIAN PACIFIC DURING THE SECOND WORLD WAR

Empire Cutlass (1946)

1943
7,117grt
4,923n
418 x 60 x 35ft
ID: 5139947
Single-screw, 2 x double-reduction geared steam
turbines
14 knots
b. Consolidated Steel Corporation, Wilmington,
California
Yard No. 346

Launched on 27 July 1943 as *Cape Compass*, a
United States standard type CI-S-AY1 (Landing
Ship Infantry), and completed as *Empire Cutlass*
on lease to the Ministry of War Transport. In
1944, she was transferred to the Royal Navy,
becoming HMS *Sansovino* (F162). In June 1946,
she reverted to *Empire Cutlass*, with Canadian
Pacific as managers, making three voyages for
the company repatriating troops. The following
year she was returned to the United States
Maritime Commission, reverting back to *Cape
Compass*, and in 1948 she was sold to the National
Republic of China as *Empire Cutlass*, but the
transfer was postponed because of lack of finance.
She was then owned by the United States
Department of Commerce and laid up in the
James River, Virginia. In 1960, she was renamed
Hai Ou, operated by the China Merchants Steam
Navigation Company, Keelung, Taiwan. She was
broken up in 1970 at Kaohsiung.

Empire Lance (1946–49)

1943
7,117grt
4,923n
418 x 60 x 35ft
ID: 5061748
Single-screw, 2 double-reduction, geared steam turbines
14 knots
b. Consolidated Steel Corporation, Wilmington, California
Yard No. 349

Launched on 28 August 1943 as *Cape Pine*, and completed as *Empire Lance*. Following the D-Day invasion in 1944, she was used as a troop transport from Southampton–Le Havre, completing forty voyages. On 9 May 1945, the Channel Islands were retaken by the British and she was used to take supplies to the islands. In July that year, she was transferred to the Royal Navy and renamed *Sir Hugo*, taking troops from Hull to Cuxhaven, Germany, with a Royal Navy Volunteer Reserve crew, under the Blue Ensign. In 1945, she was returned to the Ministry of War Transport as *Empire Lance*, with Canadian Pacific as managers, making thirty-three voyages on the Hull–Cuxhaven route in 1946. She reverted to *Cape Pine* in 1949, owned by the United States Department of Commerce, and was broken up in 1966 at Baltimore, as *Imperial Lance*.

Empire Kitchener see Beaverford (2)

Empire Magpie (1941–48)

1919
6,211grt
3,837n
396 x 55 x 31ft
ID: 2218988
Single-screw, 2 double-reduction, geared steam turbines by Mid-West Engine Company, Indianapolis, Indiana
12 knots

b. Federal Ship Building Company, Kearny, New Jersey
Yard No. 30

Completed in October 1919 as *Bellemina* for the United States Shipping Board and transferred to the Ministry of War Transport in 1941, as *Empire Magpie*, with Canadian Pacific as managers. Operated by Williamson & Company, Hong Kong, in 1946. She was renamed *Jui Hsin* in 1948 when purchased by the Zui Kong Steam Ship Company, Shanghai, with Chinese Maritime Trust Limited as managers. In 1950, she became *Oriental Dragon*, owned by the Pacific Union Marine Corporation of Panama, and *Atlantic Unity* in 1955, when she was operated by Atlantic Bulk Carriers Incorporated. She was broken up in 1959 at Hirao, Japan.

Empire Mouflon (1944)

1921
3,234grt
1,976n
321 x 46 x 24ft
ID: 2221043
Single-screw, triple-expansion engines by the Allis-Chalmers Manufacturing Company, Milwaukee
10 knots
b. Hanlon Dry Dock & Ship Building Company, Oakland, California
Yard No. 88

Completed as *Memnon* for the United States Shipping Board, San Francisco, in February 1921 and sold to Fred Barker in 1926, operating for the Columbia River Packers Association Incorporated, Astoria. In 1940, she became *Empire Mouflon* operated by the Ministry of War Transport, with Sir R. Ropner & Company as managers. She was reboilered in 1943 after putting back to various ports with boiler troubles. In 1944, she made seven voyages for Canadian Pacific before she was returned to Ropner's. In 1946, she was purchased by the Preston Shipping Company (Sir R. Ropner

& Company as managers) and renamed *Preston*. She was purchased by Avance Cia Maritima S.A., Panama, in 1951, becoming *Avance*, and *Avlis* in 1957, owned by Avlis Shipping Company, S.A., Greece. In June 1962, she was broken up by Elbes Limited, Ambelaki, Greece.

Empire Sailor (1940–42)

1926
6,140grt
3,691n
430 x 56 x 28ft
ID: 1168024
Single-screw, oil, 6-cylinder, 2s.sa direct-acting engines by Fiat, Turin
12½ knots
b. Stabilimento Tecnico, Trieste
Yard No. 746

Launched as *Cellina* on 29 April 1926 for Naviera Libera Triestino, Trieste, for the Italy–Vancouver service, and transferred to the Italia Line with ten other vessels in the fleet on 17 December 1936. She was re-engined at Monfalcone in 1937 (Fiat 6,000 bhp, 13½ knots). On 10 June 1940, she was captured off Gibraltar on the day that Italy entered the war. She was renamed *Empire Sailor*, managed by Canadian Pacific. In convoy ON 145 she was torpedoed off Cape Race by *U-518* on 21 November 1942. It was reported that she was carrying a cargo of phosgene and mustard gas. The submarine also sank *British Renown* and *British Promise* in the same action.

Empire Union (1941–42)

1924
5,952grt
4,068n
391 x 54 x 29ft
ID: 1171328
Single-screw, triple-expansion engine by builder
12½ knots
b. Stabilimento Tecnico, Trieste
Yard No. 734

Launched as *Salvore* and delivered as *Sistiana* to Navigazione Libera Triestina, as one of five cargo sister ships and transferred to Lloyd Triestino with eighteen other sisters on 17 December 1936. She was seized at Cape Town on 10 June 1940, when Italy entered the war, and renamed *Myrica* by the South African Government. In 1941, she was transferred to the Ministry of War Transport, becoming Empire Union, managed by Canadian Pacific, and was torpedoed by *U-356* in convoy ONS 154 on 26 December 1942 off south-west Ireland.

Empire Woodlark (1942–46)

1913
7,793grt
4,448n
424 x 55 x 18ft
ID: 2211442
Twin-screw, 2 x 3-cylinder, triple-expansion engines by builder
12 knots
b. New York Ship Building Company, Camden, New Jersey
Yard No. 135
500 passengers
Delivered as *Congress* for the Pacific Coast Company Incorporated, New York, for Pacific coast passenger services for the Seattle, San Francisco, Los Angeles and San Diego route. On 14 September 1916, she caught fire off Crescent City, California, in the after hold, the blaze spreading to the cargo and superstructure. As it was found that the machinery was undamaged, she was rebuilt at Seattle, becoming *Nanking*, for the China Mail Steamship Company of New York. In 1922, the company were in financial difficulties and she was seized and auctioned, becoming *Emma Alexander* in 1923, owned by H.F. Alexander's Pacific Steamship Company, Seattle. In 1934, she was laid up at Oakland following the final passenger sailing from Seattle to San Francisco. She was

acquired by the British Government in 1940, and arrived at Liverpool in December 1941. The following year she was renamed *Empire Woodlark*, with Canadian Pacific as managers, and operated as a troopship. However, following machinery problems she was limited to short voyages and was later used as an accommodation ship. On 2 November 1946, she was scuttled in the Atlantic, north of the Hebrides, with a cargo of gas bombs and chemical weapons.

Empire Yukon (1942–46)

1921
7,651grt
4,464n
451 x 57 x 32ft
ID: 1168993
Single-screw, triple-expansion engines by builder
11½ knots
b. Stabilimento Tecnico, Trieste
Yard No. 566
Laid down as *Zrmanja*, but construction was held up during the war and she was launched on 11 October 1919 as *Duchessa d'Aosta* for Navigazione Libera Triestina, Trieste, for the Trieste–New York service. In 1923, she was chartered to Lloyd Triestino for two years on the Far East routes, and again in 1929 for the Trieste–Kobe services. She was modernised in 1930 (7,872grt, oil burning, 48 cabin-class and 12 third-class passengers). She was given

an extra deck and refrigeration was fitted. She was laid up in 1932 and used as an air force transport to Eritrea during the Abyssinian War in 1935. She was transferred to Lloyd Triestino on 17 December 1936, and was at Santa Isabel, Fernando Po, when Italy entered the war in June 1940. On 14 January 1942, she was captured at sea by Free French naval forces and taken to Calabar, Nigeria, by the Royal Navy. She caught fire on 13 July during discharge at Greenock, and all holds were extensively damaged; the vessel was flooded and settled on the bottom of the dock. She was refloated on 22 July and repaired. She was renamed *Empire Yukon* by the Ministry of War Transport in 1943, who appointed Canadian Pacific as managers. Her upper passenger deck was removed and she was designated to carry cargo only. In 1945, Canadian Pacific declined an offer from the Ministry of Transport to purchase her, and she was sold to the Petrinovic Steamship Company of London in 1947, becoming *Petconnie*. In 1951, she was sold to the Italian operator COSCA SA, renamed *Liu O*, and was broken up in Italy the following year.

MANAGED FOR ONE VOYAGE

Empire Allenby 1945 (1945)
9,904grt
J.L. Thompson, Sunderland

Empire Balfour 1944 (1944)
7,201grt
Lithgows, Glasgow

Empire Buffalo 1919 (1942)
6,404grt
Skinner & Eddy, Seattle

Empire Camp 1943 (1944)

7,046grt
Short Brothers, Sunderland

Empire Cromer 1944 (1944)
7,058grt
Short Brothers, Sunderland

Empire Dabchick 1919 (1942)
6.089grt
Atlantic Corporation, Portsmouth, New
Hampshire

Empire Doredo 1920 (1941)
5,595grt
Atlantic Corporation, Portsmouth, New
Hampshire

Empire Flame 1941 (1943)

7,069grt
Cammell Laird & Company, Birkenhead

Empire Gannet 1941 (1941)
5,673grt
J. Duthie, Seattle

Empire Gazelle 1920 (1945)
4,828grt
Todd Consolidated Corporation, Tacoma,
Washington

Empire Grange 1943 (1943)
6,981grt
Harland & Wolff Limited, Belfast

Empire Lady 1944 (1944)
7,046grt
Shipbuilding Corporation, Newcastle

Empire Mist 1941 (1945)
7,241grt
W. Doxford & Company Limited, Sunderland

Empire Moulmein 1944 (1944–45)
7,047grt
Readhead & Sons Limited, South Shields

Empire Ploughman 1943 (1944)
7,045grt
W. Gray & Company, West Hartlepool

Empire Prowess 1943 (1944)
7,058grt
W. Gray & Company, West Hartlepool

Empire Rosalind 1943 (1945)
7,290grt
Burntisland Ship Building Company, Burntisland,
Fife

Empire Tamar 1907 (1943)
6,604grt
Workman, Clark, Belfast

MANAGED FOR TWO VOYAGES

Empire Bittern 1902 (1943–44)
8,546grt
Harland & Wolff Limited, Belfast

Empire Thrush 1919 (1940–42)
6,213grt
Federal Shipbuilding Corporation, Kearny,
New Jersey

MANAGED FOR THREE VOYAGES

Empire Glen 1941 (1944–45)
6,327grt
C. Connell & Company, Glasgow

Empire Mariner 1922 (1943–44)
4,957grt
Deutsche Werke, Hamburg

MANAGED FOR FOUR VOYAGES

Empire Reindeer 1919 (1940–42)
7,058grt
Federal Shipbuilding Corporation, Kearny,
New Jersey

PARK STEAMSHIP COMPANY LIMITED

The Park Steamship Company Limited was formed by the Canadian Government on 8 April 1942 and operated 176 standard ships. Of these, 114 were 'Park' ships, which were around 10,000 tons, but tankers and smaller cargo vessels were also operated. Park ships and Fort ships were the Canadian equivalent of the American Liberty ships. Fort ships were built with triple-expansion machinery and a single screw, and were transferred to the British, and the Park ships were employed by the Canadian Government. Both were of a similar design. The Park ships were named after local and national parks of Canada. However, some Park ships were launched as 'Camp ships', named after Canadian military camps, but were later named after Parks. *Jasper Park* was the first Park ship lost to enemy action, sinking in the Indian Ocean after a torpedo attack from *U-177*, south of Durban. Two of the Park ships were lost to natural hazards and four to enemy action. *Avondale Park* was one of the two Allied ships destroyed by enemy action in the North Sea in the last hours of the war in Europe on 7 May 1945. Canada had only four operational shipyards with nine berths in 1940. By 1943, there were an additional six shipyards and a total of thirty-eight berths. By 1945, there were 57,000 men and women employed in building or repairing merchant ships in Canada, and several thousand more employed in building ships for the Royal Canadian Navy. Canadian Pacific managed twenty-two of the fleet, and some of these were for single voyages to Europe. At the end of hostilities, the company sold all of the vessels and none were purchased by Canadian Pacific.

CANADA MARITIME SERVICES LIMITED

Canmar Ambassador see CP *Ambassador* 1971

Canmar Conquest 1979
15,584grt
18,643dwt
177 x 27m
IMO: 7718632
b. *Seatrain Yorktown*; 1981 *Seapac Yorktown*; 1981 *Dart Continent*; 1987 *Continent*; 1990 CMB *Mallet*; 1991 *Sea Pride*; 1994 *Canmar Conquest*; 2002 *Elisa B*; 2011 *Scorpius*. Arrived at Alang on 16 August 2011.

Canmar Europe 1970
30,491grt
29,204dwt
232 x 31m
IMO: 7027540
b. *Dart Europe*; 1984 CMB *Europe*; 1985 *Canmar Europe*; 1996 *Folly*; 1996 *Zim Colombo*. Arrived at Alang on 8 October 1998.

Canmar Force 1977
28,176grt
23,058dwt
204 x 31m
IMO: 7435292
b. *Caraibe* 2000.

CANMAR FORCE 2001

MSC *Denisse*
Arrived at Alang on 3 September 2009 and broken up.

Canmar Glory see Fleet List A

Canmar Triumph see Fleet List A

Canmar Venture * 1971 see CP *Discoverer* 1971

Canmar Victory see Fleet List A

San Lorenzo * see CP *Trader* 1971

---

* Owned or managed by Jadroplov, Croatia.

Canmar Enterprise 1972
28,592grt
31,830dwt
243 x 32m
IMO: 7205843
b. *Asiafreighter*; 1980 re-engined 2D-20; 1981 *Seapac Concord*; 1981 *Oriental Diplomat*; 1987 *Dart Atlantic*; 1988 OOCL *Atlantic*; 1990 *Atlantic Senator*; 1990 OOCL *Dynasty*; 1991 *Ville De Tucana*; 1995 *Canmar Enterprise*; 1996 *Med Naples*. Arrived at Alang on 2 February 1999.

Canmar Fortune 1995
33,735grt
34,330dwt
216 x 32m
IMO: 9108128
2003 *Cast Prospect*; 2005 CP *Prospect*; 2006 *Lisbon Express*.

Canmar Pride 1985
22,677grt
33,857dwt
188 x 28m
b. *World Success*; 1985 *Alameda*; 1986 *Modern Trader*;
1987 *Scandutch Honshu*; 1988 *Bremen Senator*; 1992
Hellas Senator; 1992 *Sea Macedonia*; 1994 *Canmar
Pride*; 1995 *Canmar Fortune*; 1996 *Hellas Macedonia*;
1999 MSC *Caracas*; 2000 P&O *Nedlloyd Peru*; 2001
MSC *Recife*; 2002 *Hellas Macedonia*; 2002 MSC
Africa; 2003 *Hellas Macedonia*; 2004 *Nautic*; 2007
MSC *Accra*. Arrived at Alang on 17 September 2013.

CAST MARINE HOLDINGS LIMITED

Cast Bear[1]* 1987
23,761grt
34,380dwt
202 x 28m
IMO: 8619053
b. *Norasia Al Muntazah*; 1994 *Cast Bear*; 1999
Bear; 2000 *Cielo Di Livorno*; 2001 P&O *Nedlloyd
Falcon*; 2002 MSC *Peru*; 2011 *Marina South*.
Arrived at Chittagong on 2 April 2012.

Cast Beaver[x] 1984
40,260grt
71,229dwt
236 x 32m
IMO: 8023656
b. *Konavle*; 1989 *Cast Beaver*; 1995 *Atlant 2*; 1996
Atlant II; 1997 *Miho Pracat*; 2007 *Theotokos*.
Arrived at Alang on 24 February 2012.

Cast Elk[+] 1989
23,761grt
33,561dwt
202 x 28m
IMO: 8716095
b. *Norasia Sun*; 1994 *Cast Elk*; 1999 HSH *Ubin*;

2000 *Kota Sahabat*; 2001 HSH *Ubin*; 2005
Thorsriver; 2007 *Eurus Ottowa*; 2010 *Hong
Leopard*. Arrived at Alang on 11 April 2017.

Cast Lynx[2]* 1987
23,761grt
34,380dwt
202 x 28m
IMO: 8619065
b. *Norasia Mubarak*; 1994 *Cast Lynx*; 1999 *Lynx*;
2000 *Cielo Di Valencia*; 2002 MSC *Parana*; 2008
Eurus Ohio; 2008 MSC *Parana*; 2010 *Marina
Bay*. Arrived at Chittagong on 23 June 2012 and
broken up.

Cast Wolf[3+] 1989
23,761grt
34,380dwt
202 x 28m
IMO: 8716083
b. *Norasia Singa*; 1994 *Cast Wolf*; 1999 HSH *Kusu*;
2005 *Thorstream*; 2007 *Eurus Oslo*; 2010 *Hong
Tiger*. Arrived at Alang on 19 December 2016 and
broken up.

* Owned by Jaya TDS Shipping Limited, Singapore, and
  managed by A/S Thor Dahl Shipping.
+ Owned by Norasia Schiffahrts GmbH, Switzerland,
  managed by O.W. Ship Management Limited, Singapore
  (Wallenius Rederierna).
x Owned by Croatia Line (Atlantska Plovidba), Croatia.

LYKES BROTHERS STEAMSHIP COMPANY INCORPORATED

Charles Lykes[+] 1978
18,792grt
22,500dwt
173 x 27m
IMO: 7704461

b. *Nedlloyd Bahrain*; 1993 *Charles Lykes*; 1998
Lykes Pathfinder; 2000 *Pathfinder*; 2001 *Delmas
Jacaranda*; 2004 *Bosco Jumbo*; 2006 BSLE *Empress*.
Arrived at Alang on 22 April 2010 and broken up.

Doctor Lykes[+] 1979
18,792grt
22,500dwt
173 x 27m
IMO: 7708900
b. *Nedlloyd Barcelona*; 1992 *Doctor Lykes*; 1998
Lykes Commander; 2000 *Commander*; 2001
Commander Express; 2004 BSLE *Express*. Arrived
at Alang on 25 November 2009 and broken up.

Howell Lykes[*] 1973
21,467grt
23,212dwt
204 x 27m
IMO: 7232420
b. *President Madison*; 1992 *Howell Lykes*. Arrived
at Tuxpan on 15 December 1999 and broken up.

Jean Lykes[*] 1973
21,475grt
23,212dwt
204 x 27m
IMO: 7320409
b. *President Pierce*; 1992 *Jean Lykes*. Arrived at
Tuxpan on 26 November 1999 and broken up.

Lykes Discoverer see Fleet List A

Lykes Enterprise 1960
11,037grt
14,747dwt
151 x 21m
IMO: 5359717
b. *Thompson Lykes*; 1971 lengthened 181m/
11,891grt/14,515dwt; 1994 barge *Lykes Enterprise*.
Reported to have been broken up in 1996.

1   Pictured in the colour section.
2   Pictured in the colour section.
3   Pictured in the colour section.

Lykes Explorer see Fleet List A

Lykes Liberator see Fleet List A

Lykes Navigator see Fleet List A

*Lykes Osprey** 1993
16,233grt
21,648dwt
181 x 25m
IMO: 9064035
b. *La Paloma*; 1994 *Red Sea Expert*; 1995 *Expert*;
1996 *La Paloma*; 1998 *Niver Med*; 1999 *Lykes
Osprey*; 2001 *La Paloma*, 2005 CMA CGM
Capricorne; 2008 *La Paloma*, 2011 *Rike*. Broken up
in 2012.

* On charter from Kiepe-Schepers KG Schiffahrt.

*Thompson Lykes** 1974
21,475grt
23,520dwt
204 x 27m
IMO: 7328621
b. *President Johnson*; 1992 *Thompson Lykes*. Arrived
at Tuxpan on 7 December 1999 and broken up.

Tillie Lykes 1985
31,920grt
36,004dwt
206 x 32m
IMO: 8200711
b. *American Georgia*; 1987 *Chesapeake Bay*; 1990
Tillie Lykes; 1999 *Chesapeake Bay*; 2006 *Maersk
Nebraska*. Arrived at Jiangyin on 15 February 2009
and broken up.

Tillie Lykes see *Lykes Liberator*,
Fleet List A

Tyson Lykes 1985
31,920grt
36,004dwt
206 x 32m
IMO: 8200709
b. *American Ohio*; 1986 *Delaware Bay*; 1990 *Tyson
Lykes*; 1999 *Delaware Bay*; 2005 *Maersk Nevada*.
Arrived at Jiangyin on 20 February 2009 and
broken up by the Changjiang Shipbreaking
Company.

* Owned by American President Lines limited.
+ Owned by Alfred C. Toepfer Schiff GmbH, Germany.

CONTSHIP HOLDINGS NV

CONTSHIP CONTAINERLINES LIMITED

Contship Action+ 1996
38,400grt
31,207dwt
210 x 32m
IMO: 9122215
b. *Tegesos*; 1996 *Contship Action*; 2003 *Tegesos*;
2004 *Norasia Tegesos*; 2009 *Tegesos*; 2012 *Tag 81*.
Arrived at Alang on 8 October 2012 and broken
up by Shirdi Steel Traders.

*Contship Ambition*X 1996
38,400grt
31,207dwt
210 x 32m
IMO: 9122203
b. *Telamon*; 1996 *Contship Ambition*; 2002
Telamon; 2004 *Norasia Telamon*; 2007 *Nautic*; 2010
Tara; 2010 *Piste*; 2015 *Isti*. Arrived at Alang on 16
March 2015 and broken up by the Navyug Ship
Breaking Company.

Contship America 1985
33,860grt
22,667dwt
188 x 28m
IMO: 8408856
b. *World Peace*; 1985 *Arosia*; 1986 *Andra 1*; 1987
Scandutch Luzon; 1988 *New York Senator*; 1993
Arabian Sea; 1994 *Canmar Intrepid*; 1995 *Contship
America*; 1996 *Buxsea*; 1996 *Contship America*;
1998 MSC *Paraguay*; 2004 *Mediterranean Express*;
2007 MSC *Zanzibar*. Arrived at Alang on 21
December 2009 and broken up.

Contship Argentina 1990
26,288grt
18,037dwt
177 x 28m
IMO: 8900218
b. CGM *Provence*; 1992 *Ville De Provence*;
1993 *Hansa Clipper*; 1994 CMBT *Africa*; 1995
Hansa Clipper; 1996 *Contship Argentina*; 1997
D.G. Harmony. On 9 November 1998 on a voyage
from the United States to South America she
suffered a serious explosion and fire. She was
salvaged and broken up at Tampico, where she
arrived on 4 May 1999.

Contship Asia 1993
16,282grt
23,596dwt
163 x 28m
IMO: 9053244
1998 *Conti Asia* 2012 *Asia*. Arrived at Alang on
1.10.12 and broken up.

Contship Champion+ 1997
38,400grt
31,207dwt
210 x 32m
IMO: 9137909
Launched as *Telendos*; 2002 *Champion*; 2003
Indamex Delaware; 2004 CMA CGM *Dardanelles*;
2008 *Champion*; 2010 *Nanjing Dragon*; 2012

Champion; 2012 *Champion 1*. Arrived at Alang on 13 October 2012 and broken up.

Contship Europe[*] 1994
19,500grt
23,600dwt
163 x 28m
IMO: 9106144
1998 *Maersk Shimizu*; 2002 *Buxsund*; 2004 *Shanghai Star 1*; 2004 *Marcompetition*; 2011 *Ren Jian ER*.

Contship France[*] 1993
23,596grt
16,236dwt
163 x 28m
IMO: 9053232
1998 *Conti France*; 1998 *Maersk Jakarta*; 2000 *Conti France*; 2003 MSC *France*; 2004 YM *Xingang 1*; 2009 *Mastro Nicos*; 2009 YM *Port Kelang*; 2011 *Marinos*. Arrived at Chittagong on 23 November 2015 and broken up by Ocean Ispat.

Contship Germany[*] 1992
23,596grt
16,236dwt
164 x 28m
IMO: 9051222
1998 MSC *Victoria*; 2001 *Conti Germany*; 2010 *Da Xin Hua Lian Yun Gang*; 2014 *Xin Bin Jiang*. Arrived at Xinhua on 2 July 2019 and broken up.

Contship Innovator 1997
31,207grt
38,400
210 x 32m
IMO: 9137894
Launched as *Timarchos*; 1997 *Contship Harmony*; 1999 *Contship Innovator*; 2002 *Conti Harmony*; 2010 *San Pedro Bay Dragon*; 2010 *Conti Harmony*. Arrived at Alang on 25 July 2014 and broken up.

Contship Italy[*] 1994
23,425grt
16,270dwt
163 x 28m
IMO: 9109029
1998 *Kota Perwira*; 2000 *Indamex New Delhi*; 2003 YM *Surabaya*; 2004 *Buxlagoon*. Arrived at Chittagong on 21 July 2013 and broken up.

Contship Lavagna[*] 1995
23,425grt
16,270dwt
163 x 28m
IMO: 9109017
1998 *Maersk Osaka*; 2001 *Buxmoon*; 2003 YM *Kwang Yang*; 2004 *Melbourne Star 1*; 2006 *Buxmoon*; 2009 *St John Grace*; 2009 *Buxmoon*; 2010 YM *Kwang Yang*; 2012 *Buxmoon*. Arrived at Chittagong on 21 July 2013 and broken up.

Contship Mexico 1999
22,817grt
35,466dwt
171 x 31m
IMO: 9131278
b. CCNI *Antofagasta*; 1999 *Contship Mexico*; 2001 CCNI *Antofagasta*; 2001 CSAV *Barcelona*; 2002 CCNI *Antofagasta*; 2002 CSAV *Barcelona*; 2002 CCNI *Antofagasta*; 2005 CCNI *Aviles*; 2008 *Sophie Rickmers*; 2010 *Sophie*. Arrived at Alang on 21 November 2014 and broken up.

Contship New Zealand 1994
19,500grt
23,600dwt
163 x 28m
IMO: 9070034
1997 *Rejane Delmas*; 2004 *Lina*; 2006 *Marcampania*; 2007 *Niledutch Shanghai*; 2009 *Marcampania*; 2012 *Ania*; 2013 *Marc*. Arrived at Alang on 2 January 2016 and broken up by the Kiran Shipbreaking Company.

Contship Nobility[*] 1997
34,894grt
31,730dwt
216 x 32m
IMO: 9128192
b. *Conti Brisbane*; 1997 *Contship Nobility*; 2003 *Conti Brisbane*; 2003 P&O *Nedlloyd Newark*; 2005 YM *Ibiza*; 2010 *Conti Brisbane*; 2014 OEL *Dubai*. Arrived at Alang on 25 February 2017 and broken up by the Harikrishna Steel Corporation.

Contship Optimism[*] 1997
35,200grt
34,790dwt
216 x 32m
IMO: 9128207
Launched as *Conti Albany*; 2002 *Conti Albany*; 2003 ANL *Albany*; 2003 *Conti Albany*; 2006 *Emirates Spring*; 2009 *Conti Albany*; 2010 MSC *Fuji*; 2014 *Fuji*. Arrived at Alang 7 June 2014 and broken up by Saumil Impex.

Contship Romance[*] 1996
34,927grt
31,730dwt
193 x 32m
IMO: 9124500
Launched as *Conti Esperance*; 2003 *Conti Esperance*; 2010 MSC *Kirari*; 2011 *Conti Esperance*; 2014 *Rance*. Arrived at Alang on 30 May 2014 and broken up.

Contship Singapore[*] 1994
19,500grt
23,600dwt
163 x 28m
IMO: 9070046
1998 *Maersk Bangkok*; 2000 *Conti Singapore*; 2004 *Pride of Delhi*; 2005 *Marcatania*; 2010 *St Nikolaos*. Arrived at Alang on 2 July 2013 and broken up.

Contship Spirit 1997
33,870grt
25,361dwt
207 x 30m
IMO: 9153381
Michaela S; 1997 Contship Spirit; 2003 Michaela S;
2004 Maersk Nantes; 2007 MSC Cristobal; 2009
Michaela S; 2016 Ela S. Arrived at Alang on 24
November 2016 and broken up.

Contship Tahiti 1994
14,300grt
20,200dwt
163 x 28m
IMO: 9057135
b. Bernhard Schulte; 1994 Contship Tahiti; 1995
Calapedra; 1996 TMM Tuxpan; 1997 Maersk
Paita; 1998 Bernhard Schulte; 1999 Tema Star II;
2000 Bernhard Schulte; 2004 CMA CGM
Papagayo; 2008 MSC Prospect. Arrived at Aliaga
on 25 June 2012 and broken up by Sok Denizcilik

Contship Ticino* 1995
23,456grt
16,282dwt
164 x 28m
IMO: 9111565
1998 Buxhill; 2002 Indamex Malabar; 2003
Buxhill; 2003 CSAV Santos; 2004 Buxhill; 2014 Jin
Sheng He.

Contship Vision* 1997
34,731get
31,370dwt
216 x 32m
IMO: 9128180
Launched as Conti Wellington; 2003 Conti
Wellington; 2003 Indamex Alabama; 2004 CMA
CGM Alabama; 2014 Conti Wellington. Arrived at
Gadani Beach on 6 April 2014 and broken up.

Contship Sydney see Canmar Dynasty, Fleet List A

* Owned or managed by NSB Niederelbe Schiffahrts GmbH & Company.
\+ Managed by Interorient Navigation, Hamburg GmbH.
x Managed by Interorient Navigation Company Limited, Cyprus.

A/S IVARANS REDERI IN 1998

Americana 1988
19,203grt
19,830dwt
177 x 26m
IMO: 8608119
2004 Golden Trade. Arrived at Jiangyin in
February 2010 and broken up.

San Antonio 1994
16,043grt
20,194dwt
167 x 28m
IMO: 9046241
1999 Jolly Avorio; 2000 San Antonio; 2000 Indamex
New York; 2003 Delmas Charcot; 2004 Asia Star.
Arrived at Alang on 15 April 2014 and was broken
up by the Alang Ship Breaking Corporation.

Santa Rosa 1992
21,053grt
30,078dwt
182 x 28m
IMO: 9006514
1995 Nedlloyd Van Rees; 1996 Santa Rosa; 1997
Panatlantic; 1997 Santa Rosa; 1999 P&O Nedlloyd
Tema; 2000 P&O Nedlloyd Pinta; 2002 Libra
Brasil; 2003 Cap Vilano; 2004 Caribia Express;
2006 Santa Rosa; 2007 CMA CGM Oubangui;
2008 Santa Rosa. On a voyage from Jebel Ali
to Karachi she was lost on 16 September 2014,
salvaged and broken up at Alang, where she
arrived on 5 March 2015.

Santos 1985
12,569grt
17,261dwt
151 x 25m
IMO: 8411205
b. Torenia; 1985 Ville D'Aurore; 1987 Torenia;
1987 Maersk Bella; 1987 Belgium Senator; 1988
Torenia; 1988 Far Eagle; 1989 Contship Italy; 1990
Santos; 2001 Kota Makmur; 2002 Santos; 2006
Eax Rafiki; 2008 Santos; 2010 Baruna Mega.
She was wrecked on a reef near Berhala Island,
Singkep, Sumatra, while travelling at full speed on
9 October 2010.

TRANPORTACION MARITIMA MEXICANA SA DE CV IN 1999

Aguascalientes 1978
6,309grt
2,589dwt
106 x 17m
IMO: 7805825
b. Prince Maru No. 8; 1986 Prince Owl; 1987
Aguascalientes; 2001 Sea Ali; 2003 Cetam Nicea;
2004 Sea Ali; 2006 Seatran Venture; 2008 Ky
Luna; 2010 N Venture. Arrived at Chittagong on
13 May 2010 and broken up.

Anahuac 1986
18,960grt
33,186dwt
178 x 28m
IMO: 8420189
b. Oriental Friendship; 1989 OOCL Friendship;
1996 Eagle Anahuac; 1997 Anahuac; 1998 OOCL
Friendship. Broken up in 2009.

Aya II 1978
38,266grt
13,833dwt
176 x 32m
IMO: 7801659
b. *Pioneer Ace*; 1989 *Aya II*; 2001 *Sea Ahmed*. Arrived at Chittagong on 5 March 2010 and broken up.

Blue Symphony 1993
52,499grt
95,636dwt
247 x 42m
IMO: 9052874
b. *Salida*; 1995 *Arce*; 1995 *Blue Symphony*; 1999 *Nord Symphony*; 2001 *Ocean Concord*. 2018 *Star Concord*. Broken up at Chittagong 2018.

*Guanajuato** 1977
30,256grt
10,703dwt
180 x 28m
IMO: 7631391
b. *President*; 1986 *Guanajuato*; 2001 *Veracruz*; 2002 *Veracruz 1*. Arrived at Alang on 15 February 2009 and broken up.

Mitla 1985
29,660grt
46,650dwt
196 x 32m
IMO: 8310803
1999 *Maria*; 2003 *York Castle*; 2009 *King Edward*. Arrived at Alang on 19 May 2015 and broken up by KPG Enterprise.

Monte Alban 1986
23,127grt
37,583dwt
175 x 30m
IMO: 8312344
b. *Atlantic Concord*; 1990 *Al Salam*; 1994 *Monte Alban*; 2008 *Hua Sheng*; 2010 converted to bulk carrier (24,126grt). Arrived at Chittagong on 9 January 2017 and broken up.

Nuevo Leon 1994
30,971grt
36,887dwt
202 x 32m
IMO: 9051478
2000 TMM *Nuevo Leon*; 2003 *Nuevo Leon*; 2005 MSC *Jemima*.

Pacific Falcon 1986
37,817grt
60,960dwt
217 x 32m
IMO: 8406872
b. *Sweetbrier*; 1990 *President*; 1998 *Pacific Falcon*; 2005 *Taxiarchis 1*. Beached at Gadani Beach on 6 November 2009 and broken up.

Palenque 1987
23,127grt
37,574dwt
175 x 30m
IMO: 8312356
b. *Atlantic Conquest*; 1990 *Al Soor*; 1994 *Palenque*. Arrived at Gadani Beach on 16 September 2009 and broken up.

TMM *Mexico* see *Lykes Commander*, Fleet List A

TMM *Oaxaca* 1988
31,430grt
41,828dwt
199 x 32m
IMO: 8420907
b. *Oaxaca*; 1996 *Contship Houston*; 1997 TMM *Oaxaca*; 2000 MSC *Jasmine*. Converted to a containership in 2004.

Toluca 1988
31,340grt
41,771dwt
199 x 32m
IMO: 8509375

1998 MSC *Nicole*; 1999 *Toluca*; 1999 MSC *Orinoco*; 1999 MSC *Alexandra*; 2010 MSC *Denisse*.

Uxmal 1991
5,675grt
9,549dwt
129 x 18m
b. *Asean Princess*; 1992 *Uxmal*; 2000 *Tradewind Explorer*; 2008 *AOG Explorer*. Arrived at Aliaga on 20 September 2016 and broken up by Aliaga Denizcilik GS.

Yucatan 1994
30,971grt
36,887dwt
202 x 32m
IMO: 9051492
2000 TMM *Yucatan*; 2001 *Contship Inspiration*; 2002 P&O *Nedlloyd Pinta*; 2005 MSC *Nilgun*.

*   Managed by Cardiff Ship Management & Services Limited.

ITALIA DI NAVIGAZIONE SPA FLEET IN 2002

Cristoforo Colombo 1989
32,630grt
33,310dwt
206 x 32m
IMO: 8618449
1999 *Zim Antwerp*; 2001 *Cristoforo Colombo*; 2004 CMA CGM *Energy*; 2006 ANL *Energy*; 2006 *Energy*; 2008 MSC *Hanne*. Arrived at Alang on 12 April 2012 and broken up by Diamond Industries.

Amerigo Vespucci 1989
32,630grt
33,310dwt
206 x 32m
IMO: 8618451

1999 *Zim Hamburg*; 2001 *Amerigo Vespucci*; 2004 CMA CGM *Force*; 2006 *Sci Tej*; 2007 MSC Oslo. Arrived at Alang on 8 March 2012 and broken up.

Cielo di San Francisco see Fleet List A

Cielo del Canada see Fleet List A

Cielo d'America see Fleet List A

Cielo d'Europa see Fleet List A

S Caboto 1991
15,783grt
14,764dwt
167 x 26m
2005 *Horizon*. Arrived at Alang on 18 September 2012 and broken up by the Patel Ship Breaking Company.

California 1989
17,123grt
23,724dwt
174 x 27m
IMO: 8901743
b. *WH 201*; 1990 *Wan Hai 201*; 1992 *California*; 2003 MSC *Lebanon*; 2003 *Magna Vision*; 2006 S*inar Lombok*; 2008 *Far Singapore*; 2011 *Tiger Cloud*; 2011 *Tiger*. Arrived at Chittagong on 12 July 2012 and broken up.

Cielo del Caribe 2000
13,066grt
20,140dwt
153 x 24m
IMO: 9202053
b. *Trina Oldendorff*; 2000 *Cielo Del Caribe*; 2003 *Trina Oldendorff*; 2004 MSC *Toulouse*; 2007 *Trina Oldendorff*; 2007 *Niledutch Kuito*; 2010 *Marchicora*.

Cielo del Cile 1994
15,778grt
20,300dwt

166 x 28m
IMO: 9046253
b. *San Clemente*; 1999 *Columbus Bahia*; 2001 *San Clemente*; 2001 *Cielo Del Cile*; 2003 *San Clemente*; 2004 *Canmar Fortune*; 2005 *San Clemente*; 2012 *Sawasdee Laemchabang*. Arrived at Alang on 29 January 2020 and broken up.

Dollart Trader 1997
16,165grt
22,024dwt
168 x 27m
IMO: 9162356
Launched as *Dollart Trader*; delivered as *Repubblica De La Boca*; 1999 *Libra Genoa*; 2000 *Dollart Trader*; 2004 *Cap Serrat*; 2005 *Maruba Trader*; 2006 *Dollart Trader*; 2006 MOL *Achievement*; 2009 *Dollart Trader*. Arrived at Aliaga on 30 September 2012 and broken up.

CHRISTIAN CANADIAN AFRICAN LINES (CCAL) IN 2000

BNC *Thor*[*] 1978
15,290grt
20,075dwt
165 x 23m
IMO: 7619123
b. *Thor 1*; 2000 BNC *Thor*; 2000 *Jaya Sun*; 2000 *Safinaz*. Beached at Gadani Beach on 4 December 2008 and broken up.

Thorscape[*] 1977
15,290grt
20,321dwt
165 x 23m
IMO: 7619111
2000 *Jaya Star*; 2001 *Sara Star*. Arrived at Alang on 19 June 2003 and broken up.

Lynx see *Cast Lynx*

Bear see *Cast Bear*

[*]   Owned by A/S Thor Dahl Shipping, Norway.

FLEET LIST A

SHIPS OWNED AND CHARTERED BY CP SHIPS ON 1 JANUARY 2004

Canmar Honour
US/Canada via Montreal–North Europe
Owned
22 knots
1998
39,174grt
40,879dwt
245 x 32m
IMO: 9165360
2005 CP *Honour*; 2006 *Ottowa Express*.

Canmar Pride
US/Canada via Montreal–North Europe
Owned
22 knots
1998
39,174grt
40,881dwt
245 x 32m
IMO: 9165358
2005 CP *Pride*; 2006 *Mississauga Express*.

Cast Prominence
US/Canada via Montreal–North Europe
Owned
20 knots
1996
33,735grt
34,330dwt
216 x 32m
IMO: 9108130

b. *Canmar Courage*; 2003 *Cast Prominence*; 2005 *Lykes Performer*, 2005 CP *Performer*; 2006 *Valencia Express*.

Cast Premier
US/Canada via Montreal–North Europe
Owned
21 knots
1995
33,663grt
33,659dwt
216 x 32m
IMO: 9112296
b. OOCL *Canada*; 2003 *Cast Premier*; 2005 *Cielo Di Los Angeles*; 2005 CP *Los Angeles*; 2006 *Milan Express*.

Cast Prospect
US/Canada via Montreal–North Europe
Owned
21 knots
1995
33,735grt
34,330dwt
216 x32m
IMO: 9108128
b. *Canmar Fortune*; 2003 *Cast Prospect*; 2005 CP *Prospect*; 2006 *Lisbon Express*.

Canmar Spirit
US/Canada via Montreal–North Europe
Owned
23 knots
2003
55,994grt
47,828dwt
294 x 32m
IMO: 9253741
b. *Canmar Spirit*; 2005 CP *Spirit*; 2006 *Montreal Express*.

Canmar Venture
US/Canada via Montreal–North Europe
Owned
23 knots
2003
55,994grt
47,840dwt
294 x 32m
IMO: 9253727
2005 CP *Venture*; 2006 *Toronto Express*.

Canmar Endurance
US/Canada via Montreal–Mediterranean
Owned
20 knots
1983
32,152grt
32,312dwt
222 x 32m
IMO: 8204626
b. *Tokyo Maru*; 1990 *Alligator Joy*; 1995 *Canmar Endeavour*; 1998 *Contship Endeavour*; 1999 *Cast Performance*; 2003 *Canmar Endurance*; 2005 CP *Endurance*; 2006 *Endurance*; 2012 *Endura*. Arrived at Alang on 21 June 2012, and broken up.

Canmar Valour

US/Canada via Montreal–Mediterranean
Owned
19 knots
1979
15,584grt
18,643dwt
177 x 27m
IMO: 7718644
b. *Seatrain Oriskany*; 1981 *Seapac Oriskany*; 1981 *Dart Britain*; 1987 *Taiwan Senator*; 1990 OOCL *Assurance*; 1997 *Canmar Valour*; 2005 CP *Valour*. Wrecked Praia da Faja on 9 December 2005 and sank in tow on 20 September 2006.

Canmar Glory

US/Canada via Montreal–Mediterranean
Owned
19 knots
1979
15,826grt
18,964dwt
177 x 27m
IMO: 7816824
b. *Seatrain Saratoga*; 1980 TFL *Jefferson*; 1986 *Jefferson*; 1988 *Asian Senator*; 1990 CMB *Monarch*; 1991 *Sea Falcon*; 1994 *Canmar Glory*; 2005 CP *Glory*; 2006 *Glory*; 2009 OIA. Arrived at Alang on 21 August 2009 and broken up.

Canmar Triumph

US/Canada via Montreal–Mediterranean
Owned
19 knots
1978
15,826grt
18,964dwt
177 x 27m
IMO: 7718620
b. *Seatrain Independence*; 1980 *Seapac Independence*; 1981 *Dart America*; 1987 *American Senator*; 1989 CMB *Marque*; 1990 *Canmar Triumph*; 2005 CP *Triumph*; 2006 *Triumph*; 2009 *Mica*. Arrived at Alang on 2 September 2009 and broken up.

Canmar Victory

US/Canada via Montreal–Mediterranean
Owned
19 knots
1979
15,584grt
18,381dwt
177 x 27m
IMO: 7718656
b. *Seatrain Chesapeake*; 1981 *Seapac Chesapeake*; 1981 *Dart Atlantica*; 1987 *Singapore Senator*; 1989 *American Senator*; 1990 *Canmar Victory*; 2005 CP *Victory*; 2006 *Victory*; 2009 *ELA*. Broken up in 2009.

Canmar Bravery

US/Canada via Montreal–Mediterranean
Owned
19 knots
1978
26,096grt
33,869dwt
219 x 31m
IMO: 7529122
b. *Dart America*; 1981 *Canadian Explorer*; 1990 OOCL *Bravery*; 1998 *Canmar Bravery*; 1999 *Cast Privilege*; 2001 *Canmar Bravery*; 2005 CP *Bravery*; 2006 *Bravery*; 2006 *SIU*. Arrived at Chittagong on 25 December 2006 and broken up.

Lykes Hero

US East Coast–North Europe
Owned
21 knots
1986
40,762grt
40,009dwt
242 x 32m
IMO: 8609254
b. *Astro Prosperity*; 1996 *Alligator Reliance*; 2001 *Cast Progress*; 2003 *Lykes Hero*; 2005 CP *Hero*; 2006 *Hero*; 2011 *Heron*. Arrived at Alang on 6 March 2011 and broken up.

TMM *Jalisco*

Gulf–North Europe
Owned
21 knots
1988
40,435grt
40,845dwt
270 x 32m
IMO: 8501452
b. *Ming Progress*; 2001 TMM *Jalisco*; 2005 CP *Jalisco*; 2006 *Genoa Express*; 2013 *NOA*. Arrived at Alang on 29 December 2013 and broken up.

Lykes Discoverer

Gulf–North Europe
Owned
19 knots
1987
39,132grt
44,969dwt
259 x 32m
IMO: 8413239
Launched as *James Lykes*; delivered as *President Harding*; 1996 *Margaret Lykes*; 1998 *Lykes Discoverer*; 2005 CP *Discoverer*; 2006 *Helsinki Express*; 2009 *Lilly 2*. Arrived at Alang, beached on 17 December 2009 and broken up.

Lykes Explorer

Gulf–North Europe
Owned
19 knots
1987
39,132grt
44,966dwt
259 x 32m
IMO: 8413277
Launched as *Doctor Lykes*; delivered as *President Arthur*; 1996 *Genevieve Lykes*; 1998 *Lykes Explorer*; 2005 CP *Explore*; 2006 *Copenhagen Express*; 2010 *Lilly 4*. Arrived at Alang on 7 May 2010 and broken up.

Lykes Liberator
Gulf–North Europe
Owned
19 knots
1987
39,132grt
44,966dwt
259 x 32m
IMO: 8415952
Launched as *Tillie Lykes*; delivered as *President Garfield*; 1996 *Stella Lykes*; 1997 *Lykes Liberator*; 2005 CP *Liberator*; 2006 *Gothenburg Express*; 2010 *Express*. Arrived at Alang on 30 April 2010 and broken up.

Lykes Navigator
Gulf–North Europe
Owned
19 knots
1987
39,132grt
44,966dwt
259 x 32m
IMO: 8413289
Launched as *Almeria Lykes*; delivered as *President Buchanan*; 1998 *Lykes Navigator*, 2005 CP *Navigator*; 2007 *Oslo Express*; 2010 *Lilly 3*. Arrived at Alang on 15 April 2010 and broken up.

Lykes Motivator
Gulf–North Europe
Owned
22 knots
1991
37,235grt
43,714dwt
242 x 32m
IMO: 8905969
b. CGM *Pascal*; 1995 *Nedlloyd Pascal*; 1998 CGM *Pascal*; 2000 *Ville de Jupiter*; 2000 *Jupiter*; 2000 *Lykes Motivator*; 2006 *Livorno Express*. Arrived at Aliaga on 27 April 2015 and broken up.

TMM Campeche
Gulf–North Europe
Owned
21 knots
1989
35,958grt
42,794dwt
240 x 32m
IMO: 8714229
b. *Choyang Park*; 2001 TMM *Campeche*; 2005 CP *Campeche*; 2006 *New Orleans Express*. Arrived at Jiangyin on 30 June 2014 and broken up.

TMM Yucatan
Gulf–North Europe
Owned
22 knots
2003
40,146grt
40,478dwt
243 x 32m
IMO: 9243203
2005 CP *Yosemite*; 2006 *Philadelphia Express*.

Lykes Ambassador
Gulf–Mediterranean
Owned
21 knots
1987
40,439grt
40,845dwt
270 x 32m
IMO: 8501426
b. *Ming Plenty*; 2001 *Lykes Ambassador*; 2005 CP *Ambassador*; 2006 *Altamira Express*; 2013 *Altamira*. Arrived at Alang on 17 September 2013 and broken up.

TMM Sinaloa
Gulf–Mediterranean
Owned
21 knots
1987
40,439grt
40,870dwt
270 x 32m
IMO: 8406286
b. *Ming Promotion*; 2001 TMM *Sinaloa* CP *Sinaloa*; 2006 *Barcelona Express*; 2013 *Elona*. Arrived at Alang on 2 December 2013 and was broken up.

TMM Hermosillo
Gulf–Mediterranean
Owned
21 knots
1986
40,447grt
40,744dwt
270 x 32m
IMO: 8406262
b. *Ming Propitious*; 2001 TMM *Hermosillo*; 2005 *Hermosillo*; 2006 *Madrid Express*; 2013 *Madrid*. Arrived at Alang on 26 September 2013 and was broken up.

Lykes Achiever
Gulf–Mediterranean
Owned
21 knots
1987
40,439grt
40,870dwt
270 x 32m
IMO: 8406298
b. *Ming Pleasure*; 2001 *Lykes Achiever*; 2005 CP *Achiever*; 2006 *Veracruz Express*; 2013 *Vera*. Arrived at Alang on 10 July 2013 and broken up.

Lykes Challenger
Gulf–Mediterranean
Owned
21 knots
1986
40,439grt
40,744dwt
270 x 32m
IMO: 8406274
b. *Ming Peace*; 2001 *Lykes Challenger*; 2005 CP *Challenger*; 2006 *Rome Express*; 2013 *EXP*. Arrived at Alang on 27 December 2013 and broken up.

TMM *Sonora*
West Coast North America–Mediterranean
MTC
20 knots
1994
30,971grt
36,887dwt
202 x 32m
IMO: 9051480
b. *Sonora*; 1999 *Houston Express*; 2000 TMM *Sonora*; 2004 MSC *Elena*. Arrived at Alang on 16 November 2014 and broken up.

Lykes Commander
West Coast North America–Mediterranean
MTC
20 knots
1994
30,971grt
36,200dwt
202 x 32m
IMO: 9051507
b. *Mexico*; 1994 *Sea Guardian*; 1996 TMM *Mexico*; 2001 *Lykes Commander*; 2004 MSC *Krittika*.

Cielo di San Francisco
West Coast North America–Mediterranean
MTC
21 knots
1998
25,359grt
33,964dwt
195 x 30m
IMO: 9153408
b. *Ute Oltmann*; 1999 *Cielo Di San Francisco*; 2005 *Contship Rangitoto*; 2005 CP *Rangitoto*; 2006 *Ute Oltmann*; 2016 *Mann*. Arrived at Chittagong on 23 December 2016 and broken up.

Cielo del Canada
West Coast North America–Mediterranean
MTC
21 knots
1998
25,361grt
33,919dwt
207 x 30m
IMO: 9138290
b. *Juist Trader*; 1999 *Cielo Del Canada*; 2005 CP *Canada*; 2006 *Juist Trader*; 2007 *Maruba Orion*; 2010 *Juist Trader*. Arrived at Alang on 30 May 2017 and broken up.

Cielo d'America
West Coast North America–Mediterranean
MTC
21 knots
2002
25,580grt
34,038dwt
202 x 30m
IMO: 9239733

Cielo d'Europa
West Coast North America–Mediterranean
MTC
21 knots
2002
25,580grt
34,038dwt
202 x 30m
IMO: 9236664
2009 RR *Europa*; 2017 *Euro*. Broken up at Alang 2017.

Contship Rome
Europe and US East Coast–Australasia
MTC
21 knots
1998
26,131grt
30,781dwt
196 x 30m
IMO: 9152753
Launched as *Annie Rickmers*; 2005 CP *Rome*; 2006 *Aenne Rickmers*; 2016 *Aenne*. Arrived at Alang on 25 April 2016 and broken up.

Contship London
Europe and US East Coast–Australasia
MTC
21 knots
1997
26,131grt
30,781dwt
195 x 30m
IMO: 9152739
b. *Alexandra Rickmers*; 1997 *Contship London*; 2005 CP *London*; 2006 *Alexandra Rickmers*; 2017 *Alexandra Rickmers I*. Arrived at Gadani Beach on 12 September 2017 and broken up.

Contship Aurora
Europe and US East Coast–Australasia
Owned
25 knots
2002
46,009grt
54,155dwt
270 x 32m
IMO: 9232565
2005 CP *Aurora*; 2006 *Maersk Dexter*; 2007 *Liverpool Express*.

Contship Australis
Europe and US East Coast–Australasia
Owned
25 knots
2002
46,009grt
54,157dwt
281 x 32m
IMO: 9232577
2005 CP *Australia*; 2006 *Maersk Dale*; 2007 *Dublin Express*.

Contship Borealis
Europe and US East Coast–Australasia
Owned
25 knots
2002
46,009grt
54,155dwt
281 x 32m
IMO: 9232589
2005 CP *Borealis*; 2006 *Maersk Dayton*; 2007 *Glasgow Express*.

Contship Auckland
Europe and US East Coast–Australasia
STC
21 knots
1998
26,131grt
30,781dwt

196 x 30m
IMO: 9160396
Launched as *Patricia Rickmers*; entered service as *Contship Auckland*; 2005 *Patricia Rickmers*; 2006 CMA CGM *Buenos Aires*; 2013 *Patricia Rickmers*. Arrived at Alang on 21 July 2016 and broken up.

Contship Asia* 1988
13,315grt
16,768dwt
159 x 23m
IMO: 8609589
b. *Columbus Ohio*; 1996 *Jurong Express*; 1996 *Tiger Wave*; 1998 *Contship Asia*; 2002 NDS *Benguela*; 2002 *Contship Asia*; 2003 *Promoter N*; 2004 MSC *Annick*. Arrived at Alang on 25 May 2013 and broken up.

* Owned by Pacific & Atlantic Corporation.

Direct Kea
US West Coast–Australasia
MTC
21 knots
1998
26,131grt
30,726dwt
196 x 30m
IMO: 9152765
Launched as *Alice Rickmers*; 2000 CMA CGM *Cezanne*; 2001 *Direct Kea*; 2004 *Alice Rickmers*; 2010 *Kota Maju*; 2015 *Ali*. Arrived at Alang on 27 December 2015 and broken up.

Direct Tui
US West Coast–Australasia
MTC
21 knots
1998
26,131grt
30,721dwt
196 x 30m
IMO: 9152741

Launched as *Albert Rickmers*; 2002 *Direct Tui*; 2005 CP *Tui*; 2006 *Albert Rickmers*; 2010 *Kota Manis*; 2012 *Albert Rickmers*. Arrived at Alang on 13 February 2016 and broken up.

Direct Condor
US West Coast–Australasia
STC
20 knots
2000
18,335grt
23,579dwt
175 x 27m
IMO: 9155365
b. *Hansa Flensburg*; 2000 *Direct Condor*; 2005 CP *Condor*; 2006 *Melbourne Express*; 2006 *Hansa Flensburg*.

Direct Jabiru
US West Coast–Australasia
STC
20 knots
2000
23,579grt
18,037dwt
175 x 27m
IMO: 9155377
b. *Hansa Rendsburg*; 2001 *Direct Jabiru*; 2005 CP *Jabiru*; 2006 *Hansa Rendsburg*.

Direct Kestrel
US West Coast–Australasia
STC
18 knots
2000
18,335grt
23,579dwt
175 x 27m
IMO: 9155389
b. *Hansa Sonderburg*; 2001 *Direct Kestrel*; 2005 CP *Kestrel*; 2006 *Hansa Sonderburg*; 2010 *Anthea*; 2011 YM *Dalian*; 2012 *Anthea*; 2016 MTT *Pasir Gudang*.

Direct Eagle
US West Coast–Australasia
STC
20 knots
2000
17,167grt
21,152dwt
169 x 27m
IMO: 9202479
b. *Spica*; 2000 *Direct Eagle*; 2004 *Maersk Vienns*; 2007 *Maruba Confidence*; 2009 *Frida Schulte*; 2014 *Neopolis*; 2020 *Neapoli*. Arrived at Alang on 27 February 2020 and broken up.

Direct Falcon*
1999
16,803grt
23,075dwt
185 x 26m
IMO: 9150406
Laid down as ER *Durban*; delivered as *Griffin Clio*; 1999 *Direct Falcon*; 2003 ER *Durban*; 2004 *Maersk Verona*; 2006 ER *Durban*; 2013 *Smiley Lady*.

* On charter from Nordcapital, Germany (E.R. Schiffahrt GmbH & Cie).

Direct Kookaburra+
1993
16,233grt
21,540dwt
182 x 25m
IMO: 9056284
Built as *Ilse*; 1993 *Contship Rotterdam*; 1994 *Ilse Wulff*; 1995 TSL *Unity*; 1998 *Maersk Piraeus*; 1998 *Maersk Pretoria*; 1999 *Ilse Wulff*; 1999 *Direct Kookaburra*; 2001 *Ilse Wulff*; 2001 *Nigeria Star*; 2003 *Ilse Wulff*; 2006 *Kollmar*. Arrived at Alang on 26 February 2016 and broken up.

+ On charter from Reederei Hermann Wulff, Germany.

Rotoiti
Trans-Tasman
Owned
16 knots
Ro-ro
1977
23,971grt
20,270dwt
203 x 26m
IMO: 7366233
b. *Union Rotoiti*; 1988 re-engined (2DE-19); 1999 *Rotoiti*; 2005 CP *Rotoiti*; 2006 *Rotoiti*; 2006 *Gulf Strait*; 2006 ULF. Arrived at Chittagong on 25 December 2006 and broken up.

Rotorua
Trans-Tasman
STC
16 knots
Ro-ro
1993
16,075grt
17,420dwt
174 x 23m
IMO: 8902280
b. *Georgiy Tovstonogov*; 1996 *Global Falcon*; 1998 *Bremer Falcon*; 1999 *Seaboard Peru*; 2002 *Nordana Surveyor*; 2003 *Nord I*; 2003 *Rotorua*; 2008 *Atlantic Impala*. Arrived at Chittagong on 3 December 2014 and broken up.

Lykes Envoy
North Europe–East Coast South America
MTC
23 knots
2003
25,407grt
33,701dwt
207 x 30m
IMO: 9241463
b. *Nordpacific*; 2003 *Lykes Envoy*; 2005 *Libra Corcovado*; 2011 *Corcovado*.

Altonia
North Europe–East Coast South America
STC
20 knots
2000
16,803grt
22,968dwt
184 x 25m
IMO: 9217553
Launched as *Antonia*; delivered as CSAV *Marsella*; 2000 *Maersk Felixstowe*; 2001 *Safmarine Buffalo*; 2003 *Altonia*; 2004 *Safmarine Mgeni*; 2006 *German Senator*; 2008 MOL *Ultimate*; 2012 *Altonia*. Broken up at Alang 2020.

Lykes Flyer
Gulf–East Coast South America
Owned
22 knots
2002
40,146grt
40,478dwt
243 x 32m
IMO: 9243198
2005 CP *Denali*; 2006 *Washington Express*; 2021 *Sounion Trader*.

Lykes Ranger
Gulf–East Coast South America
Owned
22 knots
2002
40,146grt
40,478dwt
243 x 32m
IMO: 9243162
2005 CP *Everglades*; 2007 *Charleston Express*.

TMM *Colima*
Gulf–East Coast South America
Owned
22 knots
2002
40,146grt

40,478dwt
243 x 32m
IMO: 9243174
b. *Contship Tenacity*; 2002 TMM *Colima*; 2002
Contship Tenacity; 2005 CP *Shenandoah*; 2007
Yorktown Express.

TMM *Guanajuato*
Gulf–East Coast South America
Owned
22 knots
2002
40,146grt
35,200dwt
243 x 32m
IMO: 9243186
2005 CP *Yellowstone*; 2006 *St Louis Express*.

TMM *Chiapas*
Gulf–Caribbean
STC
21 knots
2001
15,988grt
20,700dwt
170 x 25m
IMO: 9221059
b. *Hansa Arendal*; 2002 TMM *Chiapas*; 2005
Hansa Arendal; 2016 *Easline Qingdao*.

Colombia
Gulf–Caribbean
STC
20 knots
1996
19,147grt
24,074dwt
171 x 28m
IMO: 9114191
b. *Dorikos*; 1996 *Nedlloyd Seoul*; 1998 *Nedlloyd
Bahrain*; 1999 *Dorikos*; 1999 MSC *Africa*; 2001
Colombia; 2004 *Dorikos*; 2004 CMA CGM
Quetzal; 2012 *Dorikos*. Arrived at Alang on 5
January 2016 and broken up.

Puerto Limon
Gulf–Caribbean
STC
20 knots
1996
15,859grt
20,058dwt
166 x 28m
IMO: 9119660
b. *San Felipe*; 1998 *Ivaran Eagle*; 1999 *Lykes Eagle*;
2000 *Columbus Mexico*; 2001 *San Felipe*; 2002
Puerto Limon; 2004 *San Felipe*; 2013 *Suwasdee Hong
Kong*.

TMM *Tabasco*
Asia–Americas
Owned
22 knots
2000
23,828grt
30,700dwt
188 x 30m
IMO: 9224051
b. *Silvia*; 2005 CP *Tabasco*; 2006 *Wellington
Express*; 2016 MSC *Rhiannon*.

Lykes Voyager
Asia–Americas
Owned
21 knots
1995
23,540grt
30,645dwt
187 x 30m
IMO: 9062996
b. *Pax*; 1995 *Contship Melbourne*; 1997 CMBT
Melbourne; 1997 *Pax*; 1998 P&O *Nedlloyd Yafo*;
1999 P&O *Nedlloyd Bander Abbas*; 2001 *Lykes
Voyager*; 2005 CP *Voyager*; 2006 *Fremantle Express*;
2015 MSC *Mila 3*.

Lykes Deliverer
Asia–Americas
Owned
25 knots
2003
39,941grt
50,813dwt
260 x 32m
IMO: 9233832
2005 CP *Deliverer*; 2006 *Westfalia Express*; 2010
Qingdao Tower.

Lykes Provider
Asia–Americas
Owned
25 knots
2003
39,941grt
50,500dwt
260 x 32m
IMO: 9233856
2005 CP *Provider*; 2006 *Holsatia Express*; 2012
Holsatia.

TMM *Monterrey*
Asia–Americas
Owned
25 knots
2003
39,941grt
50,813dwt
260 x 32m
IMO: 9233844
2005 CP *Mont*; 2006 *Saxonia Express*; 2011
Nagoya Tower.

Canmar Dynasty
Asia–Americas
Owned
21 knots
1994
23,540grt
30,621dwt
187 x 30m

IMO: 9062984
b. *Coral Seatel*; 1994 *Contship Sydney*; 1998 P&O *Nedlloyd Melbourne*; 2001 TMM *Guadalajara*; 2003 *Canmar Dynasty*; 2005 CP *Dynasty*; 2006 *Sydney Express*; 2015 MSC *Hina*.

Dorian
Asia–Americas
STC
20 knots
1994
16,191grt
22,426dwt
179 x 25m
IMO: 9060546
1994 TSL *Bold*; 1996 *Maersk Charleston*; 1997 *Sea Bold*; 1997 *Dorian*; 1998 *Sea Bold*; 1998 *Dorian*; 1999 *Karawa*; 2000 P&O *Nedlloyd Karawa*; 2000 *Karawa*; 2000 *Dorian*; 2001 *Dal Karoo*; 2002 *Dorian*; 2007 *Kota Manis*; 2009 *Dorian*; 2013 *Dor.* Arrived at Chittagong on 25 February 2013 and broken up.

TMM *Aguascalientes*
Asia–Americas
Owned
25 knots
2003
39,941grt
50,760dwt
260 x 32m
IMO: 9238777
2005 CP *Aguascalientes*; 2006 *Hammonia Express*; 2011 *Osaka Tower*.

TMM *Hidalgo*
Asia–Americas
STC
20 knots
1997
16,799grt
22,900dwt
185 x 25m

IMO: 9123221
b. *Jan Ritscher*; 1997 *Adrian*; 1997 *Santa Paula*; 1998 *Adrian*; 2000 CSAV *Barcelona*; 2001 *Adrian*; 2001 TMM *Manzanillo*; 2001 *Ivory Star*; 2002 *Adrian*; 2002 *Delmas Tourville*; 2003 TMM *Hidalgo*; 2006 *Adrian*; 2016 MSC *Elsa 3*.

Canmar Promise
Asia–Americas
STC
20 knots
1997
21,531grt
30,188dwt
182 x 30m
IMO: 9141792
Launched as *Santa Giorgina*; delivered as P&O *Nedlloyd Rio Grande*; 2002 *Santa Georgina*; 2003 *Canmar Promise*; 2006 CMA CGM *Lagos*; 2009 *Santa Giorgina*; 2015 *Cielo Di Rabat*.

Lykes Eagle
Asia–Americas
Owned
22 knots
2000
23,828grt
30,700dwt
188 x 30m
IMO: 9224049
b. *Clivia*; 2000 *Lykes Eagle*; 2005 CP *Eagle*; 2006 *Canberra Express*; 2015 MSC *Shirley*.

Indamex Mumbai
US East Coast–India
STC
22 knots
1996
30,280grt
35,980dwt
201 x 32m
IMO: 9124354
b. *Hanjin Dalian*; 2000 *Donau*; 2002 ER

Canberra; 2003 *Indamex Mumbai*; 2004 CMA CGM *Virginia*; 2004 CMA CGM *Power*; 2009 ER *Canberra*; 2013 *Canberra*. Arrived at Alang on 27 May 2013 and broken up.

Contship Champion
Europe–India/Pakistan
STC
23 knots
1994
35,595grt
42,085dwt
240 x 32m
IMO: 9064865
b. *Ville De Vela*; 2002 *Northern Reliance*; 2002 *Contship Champion*; 2004 *Indamex New York*; 2005 *Northern Reliance*; 2010 *Kalani*; 2011 *Northern Reliance*. Arrived at Alang on 25 January 2013 and broken up.

Contship Innovator
Europe–India/Pakistan
STC
23 knots
1994
35,595grt
42,673dwt
240 x 32m
IMO: 9064877
Launched as *Northern Faith*; delivered as *Ville De Libra*; 2002 *Northern Faith*; 2002 *Contship Innovator*; 2004 *Indamex Mumbai*; 2005 *Northern Faith*; 2012 *Faith*. Arrived at Chittagong on 6 December 2012 and broken up.

Lykes Energizer
North America–South Africa
MTC
17 knots
1992
16,075grt
18,731dwt
173 x 23m

IMO: 8902292
b. *Kovrov*; 1997 *Thorsriver*; 2000 *Lykes Energizer*;
2004 *Atlantic Navigator*; 2007 *Elan Vital*. Arrived
at Chittagong on 5 January 2017 and broken up.

Lykes Raider

North America–South Africa
MTC
17 knots
1990
16,075grt
17,565dwt
174 x 23m
IMO: 8811704
b. *Kislovodsk*; 1996 *Barbara L*; 1997 *Bremer Voyager*;
1998 *Nordana Successor*; 1999 *Seaboard Venezuela*;
2000 *Nota Libre*; 2000 *Global Brazil*; 2001 *Lykes
Raider*; 2005 *Shahrazade Dream*; 2009 *Yong An
Men*. Arrived at Alang on 27 June 2012 and
broken up.

Lykes Inspirer

North America–South Africa
MTC
17 knots
Ro-ro
1990
16,075grt
17,450dwt
173 x 23m
IMO: 8811716
b. *Krasnodon*; 1996 *Elena K*; 1998 *Res Cogitans*;
1999 *Thorslake*; 2000 *Lykes Inspirer*; 2004 *Res
Cogitans*; 2004 OBL *Mariner*; 2005 *Sinbad
Dream*; 2009 *Atlantic Eland*. Arrived at Alang on
31 January 2015 and broken up.

Lykes Osprey

19 knots
1984
16,517grt

22,233dwt
166 x 27m
IMO: 8303147
b. *Heicon*; 1988 *Euro Texas*; 1989 *Belgian Senator*;
1990 *Red Sea Energy*; 1991 *Calapadria*; 1993 CGM
Icuacu; 1994 *Heicon*; 1994 CSAV *Rubens*; 1995
Heicon; 1995 CSAV *Rauten*; 1996 *Heicon*; 1997 *Sea
Victory*; 1997 *Heicon*; 1999 MSC *Patagonia*; 2001
Heicon; 2001 MSC *Patagonia*; 2004 *Lykes Osprey*;
2006 *Pacific Osprey*. Broken up in 2009.

Lykes Winner

North America–South Africa
MTC
17 knots
1990
16,075grt
17,565dwt
174 x 23m
IMO: 8811699
b. *Yevgeniy Mravinskiy*; 1996 *Marcela R*; 1996
Alioth Star; 1997 *Global Hawk*; 1998 *Nordana
Kampala*; 1999 *Cobra*; 1999 *Thorshope*; 2000 *Lykes
Winner*; 2004 OBL *Winner*; 2005 *Aladdin Dream*;
2009 *Atlantic Nyala*. Arrived at Chittagong on
29 June 2015 and broken up.

Lykes Runner

North America–South Africa
MTC
17 knots
1992
16,075grt
18,731dwt
174 x 24m
IMO: 8902307
Launched as *Krasnograd* and delivered as
Beloostrov; 1998 *Nordana Kigoma*; 1999 *Nordana
Surveyor*; 2001 *Lykes Runner*; 2004 *Atlantic
Runner*. Arrived at Alang on 18 April 2017 and
broken up.

National Pride

Break-bulk
16 knots
1981
13,886grt
19,097dwt
173 x 23m
IMO: 7915254
b. *Galleon Emerald*; 1983 *Galleon Pride*; 1984
National Pride; 2006 *Hong Prosperity*. Arrived at
Alang on 3 August 2011 and broken up.

Montreal Senator

Sub-charter
Owned
20 knots
1983
31,854grt
32,207dwt
223 x 32m
IMO: 8103406
b. *America Maru*; 1990 *Alligator Excellence*; 1995
Canmar Success; 1999 *Cast Power*; 2003 *Montreal
Senator*; 2005 CP *Power*; 2006 *Power*; 2012 *Tower*.
Arrived at Alang on 17 June 2012 and broken up.

APL *Honduras*

Sub-charter
Owned
25 knots
2002
39,941grt
50,790dwt
260 x 32m
IMO 9238765
Launched as *Lykes Adventurer*; 2004 *Contship
Tamarind*; 2005 CP *Tamarind*; 2006 *Thuringia
Express*; 2012 *Thuringia*.

APL *Panama*

Sub-charter
Owned
25 knots
2002
39,941grt
50,900dwt
260 x 32m
IMO: 9238753
Launched as APL *Panama*; delivered as TMM *Chihuahua*; 2004 *Contship Ingigo*; 2005 CP *Indigo*; 2006 *Bavaria Express*; 2012 *Bavaria*; 2014 *Niledutch Giraffe*; 2015 *Bavaria*; 2019 *Florida Bay*; 2021 CMA CGM *Algeciras*.

STC
Short-term charter of one year or less.

MTC
Medium-term charter of more than one year but less than three.

Lake Manitoba.

BIBLIOGRAPHY

Bowen, Frank C., *Ships For All* (Melbourne: Ward, Lock & Co. Ltd, 1923).

Cary, Alan L., *Famous Liners and their Stories* (London: Sampson, Low Marston & Co. Ltd), 1937.

Hardy, A.C., *British Ships Illustrated* (London: A&C Black Limited, 1933).

Haws, Duncan, *Merchant Ships in Profile 3: Canadian Pacific* (Cambridge: Patrick Stephens, 1979).

Mitchell, W.H., *Canadian Pacific and Southampton* (Windsor: World Ship Society, 1991).

Musk, George, *Canadian Pacific* (Newton Abbot: David & Charles, 1989).

Musk, George, *Canadian Pacific 1891–1956* (Windsor: World Ship Society, 1956).

Turner, Robert D., *The Pacific Princesses* (Victoria, British Columbia: Sono Nis Press, 1977).

Vernon Gibbs, Commander C.R., *Passenger Liners of the Western Ocean* (London: Staples Press Ltd, 1957).

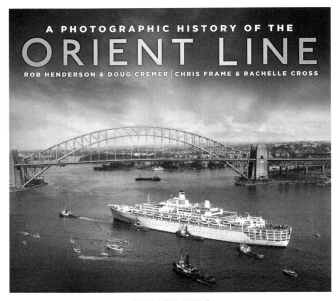

978 0 7509 6992 5

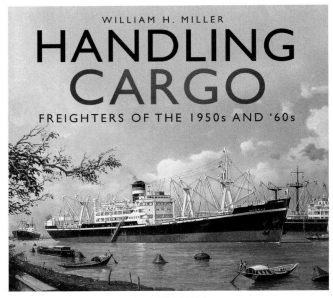

978 0 7509 8434 8

The Orient Line's beginnings can be traced back to 1797. Created for the purpose of operating a fleet of steamships between London and the Australian colonies, it was a venture into the unknown, its success testament to the acumen of its founders, two of London's oldest shipping firms, Anderson, Anderson & Co., and F. Green & Co. They had extensive shipping interests from the West Indies to South America and the Pacific Coast, and owned and operated a fleet of famous clipper ships on the Australian wool trade, when their fleet would bring out immigrants to the colony and sail back laden with prime fleece. Cruise ships today owe a great legacy to the pioneering work done by the Orient Line when it developed and perfected seasonal cruising in 1889 from British ports.

Freighters of the 1950s and '60s – with masts, booms and hatches – were the last of their generation. It was the end of an era, just before the massive transition to faster, more efficient containerised shipping on larger and larger vessels. These were 'working ships', but many would be retired prematurely and finish up under flags of convenience, for virtually unknown owners, before going off to the scrappers in the 1970s and '80s. For some ships, their life's work was cut short and their decommissioning was quick. In *Handling Cargo*, William H. Miller remembers the likes of Cunard, Holland America and United States Lines on the North Atlantic, Moore McCormack Lines to South America, Farrell Lines to Africa and P&O out East.

The destination for history
www.thehistorypress.co.uk